Creating Effective Community Partnerships for School Improvement

Creating Effective Community Partnerships for School Improvement places the school within the community which is composed of a number of key players, including school leaders, classroom teachers, private foundations, higher education institutions, business and community-based organizations, and government agencies. This book encourages leaders to embrace this broader community of stakeholders and to focus on the often overlooked and underutilized college and university partnerships. Grounded in case study analysis of innovative programs and practices, this book explores research-based strategies for educational leaders to implement in order to develop and sustain effective partnerships. *Creating Effective Community Partnerships for School Improvement* is an important text for aspiring and practicing administrators interested in creating effective partnerships for school improvement.

Special Features:

- Reflective exercises and portfolio building activities help aspiring and practicing leaders make on-the-ground connections.
- Learning objectives, key terms, and additional resources further engage readers with the chapter content.
- Extensive appendices with sample activities, evaluation plans, meeting agendas, promotional materials, and budgets provide additional support to leaders.
- Alignment to the Educational Leadership Constituent Council (ELCC) Standards.

Hazel M. Carter is Assistant Professor and Program Director of Educational Leadership at the City College of New York, USA.

Creating Effective Community Partnerships for School Improvement

A Guide for School Leaders

Hazel M. Carter

Routledge
Taylor & Francis Group

NEW YORK AND LONDON

First published 2013
by Routledge
711 Third Avenue, New York, NY 10017

Simultaneously published in the UK
by Routledge
2 Park Square, Milton Park, Abingdon, Oxon OX14 4RN

Routledge is an imprint of the Taylor & Francis Group, an informa business

Library of Congress Cataloging in Publication Data
Carter, Hazel M.
    Creating effective community partnerships for school improvement:
a guide for school leaders/by Hazel M. Carter.
    pages cm
    Includes bibliographical references and index.
    1. School improvement programs.   2. Community and school.
    3. Educational leadership.   I. Title.
    LB2822.8.C37 2013
    371.2'07—dc23
    2012037600

ISBN: 978-0-415-52895-5 (hbk)
ISBN: 978-0-415-52896-2 (pbk)
ISBN: 978-0-203-11813-9 (ebk)

Typeset in Aldine 401 and Helvetica Neue
by Florence Production Ltd, Stoodleigh, Devon, UK

Printed and bound in the United States of America
by Edwards Brothers, Inc.

This book is dedicated to my late father, Walter W. Millington, and to my mother, Joyce Millington, who both inspired me to not only be an educator but opened my eyes to the importance of the community in strengthening schools.

Contents

Detailed Contents

Preface

PURPOSE OF THE BOOK

One common denominator that transcends all cultures and continents is that success in college means ample preparation in the lower grades. Since a college degree seems to be the major entrance to profitable employment, it is my belief that each child should have the necessary tools to complete high school and to enter college academically prepared. But minorities, particularly blacks and Hispanics, lag behind their white counterparts in college degree attainment. While I am aware that not everyone may achieve a college education, it will not hurt if each child is given the opportunity to be prepared to succeed in school and enter college well prepared. The issue of retention has usually been viewed as a first-year college student problem and remains a problem that embraces the entire education system as success in college completion is directly related to success in the earlier grades. More emphasis needs to be placed on the failure of school students to articulate with the necessary skills needed for high school completion. Together with the demands of the economy for a college-educated workforce, shouldn't higher education institutions ensure that their classrooms are filled?

Building school community is often interpreted as teachers working together on a project or creating a culture in the school building for improved student learning or school staff working with schools involving parents in the learning experiences of their students. It may also be seen as two separate entities, schools and communities, working together to meet their mutual goals. In other words, the community exists apart from schools. The author uses the African proverb "it takes a village to raise a child" to broaden the definition of community to include all major stakeholders in a child's education (higher education institutions, school systems, community-based organizations, parents, and business and government agencies) and to underscore the importance of all sectors working together.

Utilizing the values, emerging issues and trends, conditions, and dynamics impacting the school community and educational programs, this book provides best practices in creating effective school partnerships. The book focuses on an important, yet often ignored, constituent in the community: the higher education institutions. Many educators have carved out a limited role for colleges and universities as grantors of degrees or transmitters of pedagogy. While schools alone cannot equip at-risk students for success in work or postsecondary education, colleges should add to their purview the role of broker. In fact, higher educational institutions of the future should serve as a community-wide educational clearinghouse bringing members of the community together to address many problems facing students. LaGuardia Community College has admirably performed this role, particularly with the inception of several school–college collaborative programs such as Middle College High School, the Queens Urban Partnership, and Gaining Early Awareness and Readiness of Undergraduate Programs (GEAR UP). This book features the three programs listed above, which were created as grant-funded programs, and stresses the importance of external funding to support the work of school leaders. Unlike several school-based collaborative programs, the ones in this book were all created by college personnel who value the power of community partnering in attaining programmatic success.

THE AUDIENCE

The intended audience includes students, scholars, and professionals. Those who are interested in education reform efforts, specifically collaborative programs, will find this book useful in its pragmatic and innovative approach to addressing the dropout problem and college access. Similarly, professionals from the school system, higher education, policymakers, and the wider community can use this book as a guide to develop effective collaborative programs. This book is relevant to students in all colleges and universities who have registered educational leadership programs (graduate level). These programs are governed by the Standards for Advanced Programs in Educational Leadership for Principals, Superintendents, Curriculum Directors, and Supervisors established by the National Policy Board for Educational Administration. Additionally, teacher candidates pursuing master's degrees and advanced certificates in Childhood Education, Special Education, and Bilingual Childhood Education who are required to take the Building Community courses will find this book useful.

ORGANIZATION OF THE TEXT

The main topics covered in the book pertain most closely to the key elements in designing and implementing a school–college collaborative program initiated by external funding. The creators of the three programs highlighted in this book firmly believed that education reform initiatives that address the total child seem to be the best solution to solving student retention and high school completion. As such, the author takes the reader through various opportunities to address the key issue of retention while drawing off the experiences of program planners. Each chapter begins with the learning objectives and the appropriate Educational Leadership Constituent Council (ELCC) Standards.

Central to effective partnership is the education leader who must install an organizational structure to facilitate partnership building. These general topic areas and the chapter in which they appear, include the following:

- An overview of the issues facing educators (Chapter 1).
- The voice of students in identifying what they think they need (Chapter 1).
- The case studies described in the text draw upon the experiences of the author and highlight the process of creating, implementing, and maintaining effective partnership programs (Chapter 1).
- What is an effective partnership? (Chapter 2).
- Creating a vision for change (Chapter 2).
- Identifying key partners to build collaborative programs and understanding the governance structures that each partner brings to the table (Chapter 2).
- Discussing the various types of organizational structures to implement collaborative programs (Chapter 3).
- Exploring the issues students and teachers face as students transition from middle school to high school (Chapter 4), and from high school to college (Chapter 5).
- Highlighting various strategies and important personnel used to articulate students through the key transition points (Chapters 4 and 5).
- Preparing parents for their children's entry to college (Chapter 6).
- Enlisting teachers and support staff for change (Chapter 7).
- Expanding the traditional role of classroom teacher to facilitate collaboration (Chapter 7).
- The leader's role in building a collaborative culture in the school (Chapter 9).
- Developing relationships with the college partner (Chapter 9).
- Creating community engagement through preparation programs (Chapter 9).
- Customizing services to students on track and those not on track through collaborative efforts (Chapter 10).
- Building community through professional development (Chapter 11).
- Sustaining the collaboration (Chapter 12).

The book is arranged in this manner because it presents the process of designing and implementing a collaborative program. It begins with the exploration of topics around gaps in student achievement, then moves to the selection of a targeted problem, convenes key institutions and personnel to address these concerns, develops a plan of action, creates an organizational structure to implement and sustain a collaborative program. It shows the reader how to leverage resources and learn from successes and failures. The grant writing activity (Chapter 7) is an important tool for school leaders who are seeking to address the needs of students through building partnerships with external agencies. Moreover, it is a crucial skill that effective educational leaders should possess.

USING CASE STUDIES TO EXPLAIN COLLABORATIVE PROGRAMS

Middle College High School, Queens Urban Partnership, and LaGCC/QUP GEAR UP exemplify some of the best practices involved between the school system and a higher education institution. These models are best explained through case study analysis, as this method is often used for analytical generalization (Merriam, 1998). Creswell (1998) defines a case study as an "exploration of a bounded system or a case (or multiple cases) over time through detailed in-depth data collection involving multiple sources of information rich in context." The descriptive case study is useful in studying innovative programs and practices in the field of education. This method allows for a detailed account of the phenomena under study (Merriam, 1998), giving the researcher the opportunity to use a "thick" complete literal description of the programs used in this book. A case study uses multiple sources of information including interviews, observations, audio-visual materials, and documents and reports (Creswell, 1998), all of which are provided to the reader to gain a deeper insight into the workings and understanding of the collaborative programs described in this book.

PEDAGOGICAL FEATURES AND BENEFITS TO READERS

This book attempts to challenge readers to re-think traditional thinking and make meaning about what is needed to improve schools and student success. While this book will explore current innovative programs, it allows the reader to create partnerships that are best suited to his/her experiences.

- Each chapter is framed in case study methodology often relating to the readers' knowledge, experiences, and understandings. Case study methodology resonates with the readers' perspectives, as it is tangible and allows the reader to scaffold and apply the findings to a similar context (Gay, Mills, & Airasian, 2009). Rather than creating different case studies for each chapter, the writer explores the three collaborative programs listed so that the reader can draw upon the various stages in the development and implementation of these programs. Since each program was initiated by the same higher education institution, LaGuardia Community College, the book shows the importance of institutionalized collaborative culture and leadership in creating effective partnerships. Focusing on the same institution also highlights the expansive nature of having several collaborative programs operating at the same time. It also shows one of the key features of collaborative grants: bringing institutional leaders together can result in the acquisition of other grants. For example, several leaders of the Queens Urban Partnership came together to form the LaGCC/QUP GEAR UP, which bears the name of both LaGuardia Community College and the Queens Urban Partnership. While school leaders may benefit from the best practices showcased in this book, leaders at the college and the wider community can benefit by learning about the effective methods of working with the school system as shown in the selected case studies.
- In addition to a literature review on the topic, each chapter provides the reader with reflective exercises, portfolio building activities, artifacts, and exemplars of collaborative techniques used in the case studies. These activities can be used in group format style, individual free writing exercises or reflections, and for general classroom discussion. The end result is not only for the reader to gain insight as to the working of case studies, but to be provided with sufficient support to write a grant, explore an issue, and implement a collaborative program.
- Additional support on effective practices is given in the appendix with sample activities, evaluation plans, meeting agendas, promotional materials, and budgets.

- Special sections entitled "Meeting to Develop a Community Partnership Proposal" and "Sample Community Partnership Proposal" are included in Chapter 7. These sections provide actual meeting notes and proposal developed by the author.
- Each chapter includes the learning objectives for the specific theme(s) covered.
- Each chapter includes standards for educational leadership preparation programs set by the National Policy Board for Educational Administrators.

BUILDING A COURSE SYLLABUS

Course instructors, as well as students, are often concerned about covering expansive content in a single semester. This is particularly the case when the author offers a grant proposal as an activity, particularly for students who may have never written a grant. The same issue exists for attempting to understand how to develop a collaborative program. For a typical 15-week academic term, I might suggest the following plan.

Week	Content	Activity
1	**Course Overview** Requirements and Expectations	
2	**Chapter 1: Overview of Issues Facing Educators**	Discussion of issues identified in chapter and other problems experienced by class participants Other activities as listed in chapter
3	**Chapter 1: Continued** **Chapter 2: Building a Partnership Team**	Introduction to the three case studies/ collaborative programs highlighted in book Identifying key constituents Understanding different governance systems Other activities as listed in chapter
4	**Chapter 2: Neighborhood Walking Tour**	Student presentations
5	**Chapter 3: Creating Structures for Community Involvement**	Exploring different structures used by the collaborative programs/case studies Other activities as listed in chapter
6	**Chapter 4: Transitioning from Middle School to High School**	Exploring various problems of students at transition points; selecting a high school Innovative transition programs Other activities as listed in chapter
7	**Chapter 5: Bridging the Gaps between Higher Education Institutions and the School System**	A brief history of school–college collaboration in the United States Principles of effective collaborative projects Benefits to students and faculty involved in collaborative programs: a case study of Middle College High School Other activities as listed in chapter

continued . . .

Week	Content	Activity
8	**Chapter 6: Involving Parents in Collaborative Efforts**	Getting parents ready for their children going to college Creating a parent involvement program for a school Other activities as listed in chapter
9	**Chapter 7: Private Foundations in School/Community Partnerships**	Selecting a foundation, developing an idea, writing a proposal, building a budget, exploring sample proposals Other activities as listed in chapter
10	**Chapter 7: Continued**	Discussion on the School Community Partnership Grant Proposal Students placed into groups representing each educational sector
11	**Chapter 8: The Importance of the Classroom Teacher and Support Staff in Collaborative Programs**	The role of the caring adult in student engagement Teacher-counselor role and Middle College Enlisting counselors and social workers for change: GEAR UP Teachers and student transition Other activities as listed in chapter Discussion of grant proposal activity
12	**Chapter 9: The Collaborative Leader**	Building a collaborative culture in the school Nurturing connections with college partners Creating new pathways to leadership preparation Other activities as listed in chapter Discussion of grant proposal activity
13	**Chapter 10: Customizing Services for Students**	Working with the hold-over student; working with students who are on track to graduate in time Other activities as listed in chapter Discussion of grant proposal activity
14	**Chapter 11: Professional Development and Portfolio Building** **Chapter 12: Lessons Learned**	Exploring various professional development opportunities; creating a professional portfolio for school staff Sustaining best practices Discussion of grant proposal activity
15	**School/Community Partnership Grant Proposal**	Group presentations

A FINAL NOTE FOR EDUCATORS ENGAGING IN COLLABORATION

The reader should not leave feeling that this book is a quick fix to filling the gaps in student achievement. The book attempts to deconstruct the key elements of effective partnership and allows the reader to understand and reflect on the community stakeholders or potential partners, and to assess the benefits and drawbacks of partnering with them. Creating effective partnerships is not seen as a list of activities but a process of improving student performance. In other words, educators should change the way they currently operate and think of the community as a logical partner in bringing about success for students, their families, and school staff.

Acknowledgments

I owe a debt of gratitude to the many educators with whom I have worked and from whom I have learned so much about the importance of community partnerships to education reform. Without them, this book, which is based on work I did as the beneficiary of several grants at LaGuardia Community College, my experience as a schoolteacher, and as an assistant professor in educational leadership at The City College of New York (CCNY), would never have been possible.

In 1993, I was hired by Janet Lieberman as Project Director of the Queens Urban Partnership at LaGuardia Community College. Janet introduced me to her creation: Middle College High School at LaGuardia. Our friendship over 20 years has been shaped by conversations and joint efforts on projects that were aimed at improving the opportunities for at-risk students. Janet always says, "Never underestimate the power of an idea," a mantra I constantly pass along to my own students in the Educational Leadership program at CCNY, who are on their way to becoming education leaders in their own right. I can only hope that I inspire these students to infuse collaboration into their work in the same way that Janet has inspired me.

My work with the Queens Urban Partnership brought me into contact with many school and college administrators and faculty, and community organizers from Community School District 25, the Queens High School Office, Queens College, St. John's University, Bank Street College of Education, and LaGuardia Community College. The discussions and decision making processes of leaders at these institutions, who were members of the Executive Committee of the Queens Urban Partnership, provided me with numerous lessons on the role of leaders in creating, implementing, and sustaining partnerships.

Middle College High School has been a source of much of my research on effective practices for dealing with at-risk students. Thanks to past principals Arthur Greenberg and Cecelia Cunningham and to current principal Linda Seigmund for giving me their time and access to staff and students in this, the greatest gem I know of in the public school system.

Also instrumental to my work was the opportunity to manage the LaGuardia Community College/Queens Urban Partnership/GEAR UP, a large school–college collaborative grant, which brought me into the everyday world of school principals, teachers, guidance counselors, students, and parents at Newtown High School, Flushing High School, John Bowne High School, IS 145, IS 61, and JHS 189, all in Queens, New York. I am forever indebted to the Queens High School Superintendent, John Lee, and the staff and students at the above schools for allowing me to explore the elements of pragmatic school reform initiatives. My work with GEAR UP would not have been possible, too, without the program staff. Special thanks to Solange Pereira, Patricia Burke, Carol Bisci, Sean Galvin, M'Shell Patterson, and the late Arlene Kahn, GEAR UP's fearless leader, who motivated those involved with this grant to constantly look for ways to ensure that all students succeed.

Capital Assessments, Inc. (acquired by Measurement Incorporated Evaluation Services) and its evaluator, Nina Gottlieb, were the external evaluators of the GEAR UP program and provided much of the participant data used in this book. Nina and the GEAR UP leaders were engaged in many discussions about the progress of the program initiatives, illustrating the importance of linking assessment to program planning. Many thanks go to them as well.

I have also been fortunate to be able to "pick the brains" of Joyce Coppin, who worked with me at the Educational Leadership Program at CCNY. Our countless discussions about school improvement, school collaborations, and leadership strategies have all centered around one common theme: the importance of partnership building to school success. Joyce has long embodied this ideal in her own career at the New York City Department of Education.

Beverly Falk, Sylvia Roberts, and Hope Hartman, my colleagues at City College, and my friend Jacqueline Glasthal, have all supported me with my writing, which has been helped along by our long conversations about effective school reform.

And last, but certainly not least, I reserve the end of the acknowledgments for my family and friends with an expression of gratitude to my dear husband Albert L. Johnson Jr., whose support throughout this process was infinite, my son Jerome Carter, my mother Joyce Millington, my sister Alsuna Millington, my aunt Marilyn Thomas, my late father Walter Millington, my dear friends Marcia Skyers-James, Nesta George, Patricia Hamlet, Patricia Garrett, Lena Mullings, Sharon Savary, Joy DeLancy, Terri Ann Brathwaite, and the many others who are an integral part of my support system. To all of you I offer my most heartfelt thanks.

Hazel M. Carter
January, 2013

CHAPTER 1

Issues Facing Educators

LEARNING OBJECTIVES

After reading this chapter you will be able to:

1. Identify and assess the gaps in student achievement
2. Evaluate the dropout crisis and its impact on society
3. Conduct a needs assessment of your school
4. Analyze your school's report card

INTRODUCTION

It is critical to explore some of the factors leading to the high dropout rates among our nation's youth, including gaps in services and infrastructure in schools, inadequate counseling and lack of sustained and continuous interaction between the various educational sectors. The book explores partnership building and how schools can benefit from collaborative programs. The reader will be asked to participate in reflective exercises addressing the high school dropout problem, and begin to develop a portfolio of activities that can be used by educators seeking to work with the community. Also, the twenty-first-century school leader is required to work with the community in addressing the needs of students, their parents, and teachers. School leaders may find this book helpful as it provides strategies for building and sustaining collaborative programs.

Educational Leadership Constituent Council Standards (ELCC)

This chapter meets the needs of advanced academic programs in preparation for educational leadership:

> Standard 6.0: Candidates who complete the program are educational leaders who have the knowledge and ability to promote the success of all students by understanding, responding to, and influencing the larger political, social, economic, legal, and cultural context.
>
> (National Policy Board for Education Administration, 2002)

★ ★ ★

The United States faces severe challenges in preparing high school students for college, work, and citizenship. An estimated 1.23 million students, or almost 30 percent of the class of 2008, did not graduate with their peers (Education Week, 2011). Only 53 percent enter college directly from high school (Barton, 2005) and of those, only 35 percent earn a college degree (Adelman, 2006). Coupled with this daunting picture is the realization that the value of a high school diploma has changed greatly over the last five decades. In the mid-twentieth century the diploma was an advantage in the workplace while in the 1970s, it was an entrée to various promising careers. With advances in technology, the labor force has to be highly skilled making a high school diploma a minimum requirement for entry into the labor market. Sadly, large numbers of minority youth, particularly blacks and Hispanics, are excluded from productive employment. This is catastrophic to society. This "minority-majority" population is growing at a rapid rate and is ever present in our schools. It is in the interest of society that the minority population receives the type of education that will allow them to succeed economically.

THE DROPOUT CRISIS

Since high school completion has become a requirement for entry into postsecondary education, the labor force or training, the economic consequences of leaving high school without a diploma are severe (Kaufman & Alt, 2001). Dropping out poses a serious

---

REFLECTIVE EXERCISE 1.1

A Collaborative Approach to Studying the Dropout Problem

The persistent dropout problem usually referred to as a "high school problem" extends to other educational sectors and wider society. Schools, on their own, cannot keep at-risk students in school or equip them for success in work or postsecondary education.

Write a response to the above statement.

problem to the social and economic health of the country and has negative consequences for the individual dropout. One consequence of dropping out is limited employment opportunities, as today's economy requires the labor force to have increased literacy, more education, enhanced technological skills, and lifelong learning. Income differences between dropouts and other citizens can be expected to widen as the economy evolves. Dropouts earn on average $10,000 less a year than high school graduates. Each class of high school dropouts damages the economy. The social costs of the dropout problem include an under skilled labor force, lower productivity, lost taxes, and increased public assistance and crime.

The rude awakening is that many high school students lack basic reading and writing skills. This is coupled with the fact that many immigrant students, who speak English as a second language, are dropping out of high school at alarming rates. Another critical issue in the dropout problem today is the rate at which ninth graders in public high school reach regular high school graduate status. Perhaps we can blame the standards movement in K–12 education for causing an acceleration of declining high school graduation rates. The attempt to make the high school curriculum more rigorous has resulted in a growing share of high school students lost before graduation through attrition. More striking is that the proportion of students with high risk behaviors are likely candidates for dropping out and are growing in large numbers signaling increasing dropout rates in the future. Youth from non-English speaking backgrounds are one and a half times more likely to leave high school than those from English-speaking backgrounds (Cardenas et al., 1992). Hispanic dropout rates have increased dramatically. According to the Census Bureau, in 1992 roughly 50 percent of Hispanics ages 16 to 24 dropped out of high school, up from 30 percent in 1990 (Government Accounting Office, 1994). The Final Report of the Hispanic Dropout Project, *No More Excuses*, further notes that while Hispanics account for just 56 percent of all U.S. immigrants, they account for nearly 90 percent of all immigrant dropouts. The report claims that for Hispanics, as with other students, the likelihood of school completion rises with gains in factors such as family income and parent education. However, gaps remain in school completion rates between Hispanic and non-Hispanic students after controlling for social class, language proficiency and immigrant status.

These statistics show a greater crisis in the dropout problem as there is a rapid population growth rate of minority populations (Justiz, Wilson, & Bjork, 1994). This growth is a cause of concern since high dropout and low graduation rates in school and college, and illiteracy are particularly significant for Native American, African American, Hispanic, and Asian American populations. Renowned demographer Harold Hodgkinson projected that by 2010 the Hispanic population would outnumber African Americans for the first time (Hodgkinson, 1994). They will, particularly in large cities like Los Angeles, become the "majority-minority" population (Justiz, Wilson, & Bjork, 1994). While the nation is experiencing growth in public school attendance, the question of educational attainment remains critical: one out of five 18 year olds is functionally illiterate. Additionally, school statistics indicate that 43 percent of Hispanic students and 26 percent of African American students drop out of high school, and those that do graduate, are not prepared for higher education (Justiz, Wilson, & Bjork, 1994). In addition, the large differences between the groups remain while public investments in postsecondary education have declined.

It may well be that access to postsecondary education will be curtailed in years to come due to the dual pressures of tight public budgets and of the increasing admission requirements. If so, we could see college-going rates and college-completion rates stabilize or even decrease.

(National Task Force on Minority Achievement, 1999)

However, the dropout problem cannot be viewed in isolation, as issues affecting the total social and economic structure should be considered: poverty, unemployment, discrimination, family roles, social values, the welfare cycle, child abuse, and drug abuse. Also, poor academic performance is the single strongest school-related predictor of dropping out. One possibility for low high school graduation and low college entry rates for many minority students is that they are often exposed to various ineffective and harmful practices in schools (Cotton, 1991). These include academic tracking, retention in grade without accompanying support, excessive use of pullout programs, and indiscriminate assignments to special education programs. The barriers experienced by African American and other minority students in moving across institutional boundaries signal the problems these students experience in order to effectively participate in school and in wider society. When borders are neutral, movement between worlds occurs with relative ease. When they are obstructive or stressful, movement is difficult. Many students learn to navigate these borders without proper intervention. For others, crossing these borders can be inhibitive and degenerative often resulting in low achievement in school and college. For minority children and youths, these barriers, including less access to social capital and institutional support, can instill feelings that may be disruptive to their ability to carry out school-related tasks, e.g. anxiety, fear, and depression. These feelings also make it difficult for minorities to establish supportive relationships with teachers and peers.

REFLECTIVE EXERCISE 1.2

What factors lead to higher dropout rates among Hispanic students than other ethnic groups?

The Hispanic Dropout Report states: "Regardless of your position in society, if you are an Hispanic student, you are more likely to drop out of school and not earn a diploma than if you are a non-Hispanic American in a similar position" (Hispanic Dropout Project, 1998).

GAPS IN SERVICES AND INFRASTRUCTURE IN SCHOOLS

Perhaps the most important educational challenge for America is eliminating the gap between racial and ethnic groups (Vernes & Krop, 1999). While a college degree seems to be the only gateway to profitable employment, it is our belief that each child should be armed with the necessary tools to complete high school and to enter college academically prepared. However, minorities lag behind their white counterparts in college degree attainment. While we are aware that not everyone may achieve a college education, will it hurt if each child is given the opportunity to be prepared to succeed in school and enter college well prepared? While the issue of retention has usually been viewed as a first-year college student problem, it remains one that embraces the entire education system.

Although much attention is currently being paid to the problem of remediation in the public colleges, greater emphasis needs to be placed on the failure of school students to articulate with the necessary skills needed for high school completion. These problems are attributed to the following gaps in services or opportunities for students in urban public schools.

1. Inadequate Counseling

Most intermediate or junior high schools have one counselor per grade level. It is obvious that one counselor cannot interact and give personal service to so many students. This means that often the counselor's role devolves to one of providing information either in writing or to groups. With a high student to counselor ratio, less individual academic and social counseling is given to students, and those student experiencing learning difficulties or behavioral problems are not easily identified for early interventions. Too often, the result is that students get lost, "fall between the cracks," and drop out. Adequate counseling is needed to ensure that students make correct curricular choices required for college admission. This book discusses strategies educators can use to assist students in making decisions on college.

2. Lack of Sustained and Continuous Interaction between the Various Educational Sectors

Students and their parents are unable to make adequate choices about high school and college due to a lack of sustained and continuous interaction between intermediate, high school, and college personnel. What is needed is a seamless web that maximizes opportunities for middle school students to visit high schools and colleges, and enables students to interact with high school and college students and faculty, allowing them to be better prepared for the high school choice/admission process and later on, the college admissions process.

3. Integrating After-School and Summer Programs with In-School Curriculum

More opportunities are needed for after-school and summer programming that can reinforce and extend instruction provided during the academic year. Summer programs are designated for students performing below the first quartile on standardized examinations. They do not improve skills for youngsters with deficits and engage youth in education through enrichment activities.

4. Communication Gaps at the Point of Transition

A great communication gap, however, exists at the point of transition and articulation between intermediate/junior high school and high school. Across academic disciplines, faculty do not regularly exchange information about the individual needs of their students, their curricula, high school graduation requirements, the standards and state examinations; they have not had systematic opportunities to study curricular sequence, to ask how well academic instruction in the grades seven and eight prepares students for performance at grade nine and, at the high school/college level, how well instruction, grades nine through twelve, prepares students for college entrance examinations and Freshman year academic performance at college. Establishing a forum for this communication would create a context not only for useful appraisal but also for the development of new activities and initiatives.

5. Bridging the Gap: What Students Say They Need

The voice of the student is of critical importance in addressing the gaps in their academic achievement. The Minority Student Achievement Network (MSAN) is a consortium of 25 school districts aimed at raising the achievement of African American and Latino students in U.S. schools. The Consortium looks at issues of closing the achievement gap and understanding why some of these minority students are high academic achievers and why others from well-educated, middle class families underachieve relative to their white counterparts. At a 2004 conference, the consortium raised recommendations that can be applied to all minorities regardless of income. The following is a synthesis of some of the policies the students suggested:

1. Develop more peer and mentoring programs (e.g., peer leadership, big brothers and big sisters, college mentors) geared toward encouraging minority students to succeed.
2. Increase teacher training on the needs of minority students.
3. Develop programs for parents so that they can learn about the situations that affect children's lives at school and become more involved.
4. Create programs for students on diversity, multiculturalism, and stereotypes to "get the word out" about the achievement gap.
5. Push students to strive for higher levels of success.
6. Establish more skill-building programs (e.g., test-taking skills, tutoring, leadership development, time management).
7. Teach students good study habits early, instead of waiting until high school.

(Kidder, 2005)

DEVELOPING LITERACY SKILLS BEYOND THE ELEMENTARY SCHOOL

Educators need to focus on developing the reading skills of students beyond their elementary school years. Historically, there has been more focus at the state, federal, and local levels on beginner readers; the reason being that if students can read by age nine, they can read for life (Rothman, 2004). However, evidence from international and national assessments suggest that beginning reading is not enough. In a 2000 study of the reading literacy of fifteen year-olds from 27 countries, only half of U.S. students performed above the international average. Additionally, results from the National

Assessment of Educational Progress (NAEP) show that while the reading performance of elementary students is improving, that of high school students is declining. Only about a third of twelfth graders performed at the proficient level in reading in 2002, compared with 40 percent in 1992 (NAEP, 2005).

One factor that has prevented educators from focusing more on the literacy needs of adolescents is the lack of understanding of what those needs are. One problem is that most high school educators are trained in their subject-area disciplines, but are not trained to understand and to teach reading. The result is that many teachers misdiagnose the problems struggling readers face and do not address them (Lee, 2004). The nature of materials students read changes in the upper grades just as the direct reading instruction they have received begins to taper off. From the fourth grade, the balance of textbooks shift from narrative fiction to expository text, e.g., the type used in science and social studies. Middle and high school students need to draw more on background knowledge and vocabulary they attained in elementary school in order to negotiate these genre shifts (Rothman, 2004). While this requirement can challenge all students, those who lack the "cultural capital" to pick up such knowledge in their social environments are at a disadvantage.

REFLECTIVE EXERCISE 1.3

Leaving Too Many Children Behind

1. Read the article *Leaving Too Many Children Behind* by Harold Hodgkinson.
2. Summarize Hodgkinson's findings.
3. How is this information helpful to education leaders and to policymakers?
4. How can schools be prepared for the children entering elementary schools in 2015?
5. The United States, according to Hodgkinson, gets a grade "F" for its care of children (health care, educations, child care, etc). How can this grade be improved? Explain.

There are various strategies for addressing the adolescent literacy problem. A recent publication by the Alliance for Excellent Education has launched a campaign to raise awareness on this issue, and notes that effective literacy programs should address the following:

- Student motivation
- Reading fluency
- Vocabulary development
- Comprehension
- Phonics and phonemic awareness
- Writing development, and
- Assessment.

(Alliance for Excellent Education, 2004)

Additionally, schools need to develop professional learning communities among teachers allowing them to share successes and problems. Researchers Susan De La Paz and Steve Graham (2002) looked at the question "Do young writers merely need to learn from their own mistakes over time, or can specific rewriting and writing strategies be taught effectively?" They found that the direct teaching of one method had a dramatic effect on the work of seventh and eighth grade students. These researchers looked at the effects of the Self-Regulated Strategy Development (SRSD) model for teaching writing. SRSD techniques include analyzing the demands of a writing prompt, setting writing goals, and generating and organizing ideas.

PORTFOLIO BUILDING 1.1

Creating a School Needs Assessment Profile

Education in the United States, particularly urban public education, faces major challenges, including declining student achievement. Great emphasis needs to be paid to the failure of school students to articulate with the necessary skills needed for high school and college completion. Create a School Needs Assessment Profile that provides a picture of the needs of your school as it pertains to students, parents, and teachers. You can draw upon data provided in your school's Annual Report Card, Comprehensive Education Plan or other relevant reports, and from your experiences at your school. This should include, but not be limited to:

- size of student population
- teacher : student ratio
- admission criteria
- ELL population
- attendance rates
- graduation rates
- extra-curricular activities
- special education services
- math and English standardized test scores

- parent involvement
- eligibility for free lunch
- neighborhood/location
- community partnerships
- professional development opportunities for teachers
- activities to involve parents
- other

GAPS IN TEACHING

Gaps in student achievement also point to gaps in teaching. Teacher expertise is an important factor in determining student achievement. However, students in the greatest need of the best teaching are the least likely to get it (Darling-Hammond, 1990). Because the qualifications and abilities of American teachers are considerably unequal, not all students receive the same level of instruction. The distribution of teacher quality is tilted toward those students who attend wealthy, well-endowed schools, leaving poor and minority students at a disadvantage as they are often taught by teachers with less training and experience. Several studies have concluded that teacher expertise is the most important factor in determining student achievement. Much of the variation in student achievement is explained by teacher qualifications next to the level of parents' education and other background factors such as poverty and home. In a study in New York, 90 percent of the difference in student achievement was attributed to teacher qualifications (Armour-Thomas et al., 1989). Content knowledge, understanding of the learning process and child development, and pedagogical skills contribute to teacher effectiveness. Not surprisingly, a 1985 study found that students performed better in classes taught by teachers who had solid preparation in math methods, curriculum, and teaching than those taught by teachers out of their license or certification area or who were uncertified or unlicensed (Hawk, Coble, & Swanson, 1985). Another study found that science teachers' effectiveness depends on the amount of discipline-specific training included in the pre-employment preparation programs and on the quality of the staff development opportunities they experienced later in careers (Druva & Anderson, 1983).

MORE CONNECTION WITH FAMILIES AND SCHOOLS

In a report from the National Center for Family and Community Connections with Schools at the Southwest Educational Development Laboratory, the authors state that students perform better in school, stay in school longer, and like school more when schools, families, and communities work together to support learning. They also found that when students are involved with parents, regardless of income or background, they were more likely to succeed in school, attend school regularly, earn higher grades, graduate, and proceed on to postsecondary education (Henderson & Mapp, 2002). However, working with parents still proves to be challenging for school leaders. Chapter 6 will discuss some strategies educators can use to work with families.

GAPS IN AFTER-SCHOOL EDUCATION

Good after-school programming makes a difference in the lives of children. Studies in child development and education suggest that attendance at after-school is associated with better grades, peer relations, emotional adjustment, and conflict resolution skills (Noam, 2004). Children who attend programs spend more time on learning opportunities and academic enrichment activities than their peers. On the other hand, children who are unsupervised after school are associated with involvement in violence, substance abuse, and other risk-taking behaviors. According to a survey released in September 2001 by the National Association of Elementary School Principals, 67 percent of principals now offer optional after-school programs. However, few of these school leaders have received any training in how to organize after-school time in their buildings. And despite the importance of after-school programming and full-service and community school initiatives, few colleges and universities include after-school training in teacher education preparation programs.

CASE STUDIES

The case studies used in this book highlight the process of creating effective partnerships, and serve as models of exemplary practice in community partnership building. They also underscore the importance of external funding of innovative educational initiatives. The cases represent three collaborative programs that were all created by educators from LaGuardia Community College whose commitment to collaborative education has been long-term, innovative, and distinguished. LaGuardia was established by the City University of New York to accommodate students benefiting from the new open admission policy. The college was founded to develop sophisticated new educational techniques, and it enjoyed wide structural freedom from the City University. Experiential learning was the keystone of its strategy. The author served as director of two of these initiatives, the Queens Urban Partnership and the GEAR UP program, and studied the Middle College High School as part of her doctoral studies.

CONCLUSION

Today's economy requires a labor force that is literate, well educated, and technologically advanced. The income difference between dropouts and high school graduates is expected to widen as the economy evolves. Clearly, urban schools are not educating all of their students to the high levels of achievement that are possible. Schools cannot solve these problems alone, making partnership programs the key factor in student success.

KEY TERMS

- Transition points
- Persistence
- Social capital
- Counseling services

CHAPTER 2

Identifying Key Constituents as Partners

LEARNING OBJECTIVES

After reading this chapter you will be able to:

1. Create a vision for school reform
2. Develop a shared vision statement for your ideal school
3. Identify and select the appropriate stakeholders to form a partnership
4. Assemble a team of leaders to create an educational partnership

---

INTRODUCTION

Limited parental and community involvement is all too common in our public schools. The challenge for educational leaders is to leverage public interest in education to bring about citizen action in support of schools. The chapter focuses on the strategies used by the Queens Urban Partnership to form a partnership and go to a foundation for funding. Readers will learn how schools can carefully choose community partners who can make substantive collaborative contributions to a comprehensive program that will enable low-income students to stay in school and progress on to college. These community partners may include degree-granting institutions of higher education, community-based organizations, businesses, faith-based organizations, college student organizations, state agencies, family organizations, and parent groups. The chapter also defines collaboration and effective partnerships.

Educational Leadership Constituent Council Standards (ELCC)

This chapter meets the needs of advanced academic programs in preparation for educational leadership:

Standard 1.0: Candidates who complete the program are educational leaders who have the knowledge and ability to promote the success of all students by facilitating the development, articulation, implementation, and stewardship of a school or district vision of learning supported by the school community.

Standard 4.0: Candidates who complete the program are educational leaders who have the knowledge and ability to promote the success of all students by collaborating with families and other community members, responding to diverse community interests and needs, and mobilizing community resources.

Standard 6.0: Candidates who complete the program are educational leaders who have the knowledge and ability to promote the success of all students by understanding, responding to, and influencing the larger political, social, economic, legal, and cultural context.

(National Policy Board for Education Administration, 2002)

★   ★   ★

COLLABORATION AND PARTNERSHIP

The term partnership is often used to describe a means for leveraging resources, coordinating work, and increasing collaboration among various stakeholders in various policy arenas (Waschak & Kingsley, 2006). Frey et al. (2006) outline five levels of collaboration (see Table 2.1), beginning with the lowest level of networking to the highest level, collaboration. Collaboration is the result of the joint interaction by one or more parties of the partnership who come together to address a specific issue. The programs described in this book relate to the practice of collaboration used by a partnership of constituents, the implementation of the program activities, and the impact of that collaboration on the schools involved.

WHAT IS AN EFFECTIVE PARTNERSHIP?

Effective educational partnerships are formal associations between institutions and agencies that impact directly and indirectly on the education of children. They should be organized to administer a process for systemic change rather than to develop and implement a special program. Effective partnerships are long-term, designed long enough to implement the necessary changes. Also important, is a demonstrated commitment by the member institutions and agencies of the partnership and the individuals representing them to collaboratively identify and address the problems that interfere with effective education (National Center for Educational Alliances, n.d.). There is no perfect formula to developing partnerships. Partnerships respond and set

Table 2.1 Levels of Collaboration Scale

Five Levels of Collaboration and Their Characteristics

1 Networking	2 Cooperation	3 Coordination	4 Coalition	5 Collaboration
Relationship Characteristics				
• Aware of organization	• Provide information to each other	• Share information and resources	• Share ideas • Share resources	• Members belong to one organization or partnership
• Loosely defined roles	• Somewhat defined roles	• Defined roles		
• Little communication	• Formal communication	• Frequent communication	• Frequent and prioritized communication	• Frequent communication is characterized by mutual trust
• All decisions are made independently	• All decisions are made independently	• Some shared decision making	• All members have a vote in decision making	• Consensus is reached on all decisions

Adapted from Frey, B.B., Lohmeier, J.H., Lee, S.W., & Tollefson, N. (2006). Measuring collaboration among grant partners. *American Journal of Evaluation, 27*, 3, 383–392.

an agenda to local needs and build upon available resources. However, successful partnerships are usually comprised of:

- a clearly stated mission
- a commitment to shared goals
- honesty and candor among all partners that leads to a high level of trust
- a visible and consistent presence within the community
- an ongoing search to identify additional resources
- an ongoing evaluation process that uses data for continuous planning and shares progress and problems with constituent groups
- opportunities for collaborative planning
- a clear structure that defines roles and relationships between individuals and between institutions shared responsibility and leadership
- designation of a person responsible for moving the partnerships agenda forward
- a plan for leadership succession
- facilitated retreats to help the partnership work through issues as the work advances.

(National Center for Educational Alliances, n.d., p. 1)

Effective partnerships are knowledge-based unions in which partners teach each other, learn from each other and together. Effective partnerships can bring about systemic change by:

- addressing issues that affect school climate and identify best practices that address these issues
- providing opportunities for ongoing professional development that demonstrate tangible support for faculty, staff, and administrators
- publicizing the work of the partnership within the participating institutions and attracting formal and informal expressions of support from institutional leaders
- expanding the institution's reward system to encourage meaningful partnership work
- carefully integrating new services into a broader plan for systemic change
- analyzing courses and curricula to respond to state and national expectations and standards of learning working closely with parents and the community.

(National Center for Educational Alliances, n.d., p. 1)

CREATING A VISION FOR CHANGE

Placing a "band-aid" on troubled schools with failing students will not work. Too often, educators and policymakers place resources on fixing troubled schools ignoring the root cause of the problems. For those educators who attempt to change or improve the system, they need to feel that reform is feasible and that they can be change agents. This begins with knowing the community in which the participating institutions are created. Portfolio Building 2.1 provides a useful exercise for educators.

PORTFOLIO BUILDING 2.1

Walking Tour of Your School's Community

As we look at our role as educators, it is imperative that we become more in-tuned with the changing demographics of New York City and the impact on education institutions. The community is not static; it comes into the classroom whether we like it or not.

The purpose of this activity is to enable you to become acquainted with the community in which your school is located. Through a walking tour of the neighborhood, students can make observations and speak with community residents about locations of interests. Through photographs or PowerPoint, share with your colleagues your interpretation of this community. The following "clues" can be used as a guide, but do not limit yourself to:

- families—number of children under school age
- feeder schools
- religious organizations
- local businesses
- parks
- houses and apartment buildings
- transportation
- entertainment
- other

The next step is having a vision for improving schools and student academic progress:

The district—including the school board, the superintendent, key staff and influential stakeholders in the community—must have the capacity to develop and articulate both a vision and a set of practices that send a clear message of what schools are to be about. This is a message not only for educators, but for the community at large. This message creates public understanding of what the school system is trying to do to prepare more middle grade students for challenging high school work and to graduate more students from high school prepared for the next step.

(Southern Regional Education Board, 2010, p. iii)

How this vision is manifested is important. Leaders at the district, school, and community level must provide the conditions for change to occur.

REFLECTIVE EXERCISE 2.1

Creating a Vision for Your School

With your team, develop a vision for a school that respects learning for all. Document the process the team uses to develop the vision statement. Each team member is to complete the exercise below. Use the strategies stated below to guide the vision building process.

1. Individually, identify your core beliefs about schooling by completing the following statements:

    I believe that

    schools should teach _____

    a good school is one that _____

    a successful student is able to _____

    a quality instructional program includes _____

    an effective school faculty is one that _____

2. Individually, complete the exercise below for building a shared vision:

    Describe your ideal school. If you were watching the activities in your ideal school, what would you see? Using phrases or bullets describe what you see students doing, teachers doing, administrators doing, and parents doing.

3. Develop team consensus about your core beliefs about schooling. In order to achieve consensus:

    *   Determine the process the team will use to reach consensus.
    *   Share the individual lists of core beliefs.
    *   Reach consensus on core beliefs.

4. Develop a shared vision statement for the team's ideal school.

    *   Modify and fine-tune the individual vision phrases by relating them to the shared core belief.
    *   Using the core beliefs and shared vision phrases, write a shared vision statement for the team's ideal school.

5. As a team, evaluate and reflect on your vision statement and on the process used to develop the statement.

    *   Is the statement consistent with what we know from research and practice?
    *   Does the statement give clear purpose and direction to the school?

- Could the students, school leaders, faculty, staff, parents, and school community members use the vision statement to direct to their actions?

6. Prepare a team report which contains:

- the core beliefs that undergird the school vision
- the vision statement for the team's ideal school
- a description of the process used to develop the vision statement
- strategies the team recommends for improving the process
- the group reflection on the process (what did the group learn during the process?).

A MODEL FOR IDENTIFYING KEY CONSTITUENTS: THE STORY OF THE QUEENS URBAN PARTNERSHIP

While a clearly articulated and accepted statement of mutual self-interest and common goals is a necessary starting point for building a successful collaborative (Gomez et al., 1990), choosing the right partners is a key factor to effective collaboration. The Queens Urban Partnership (QUP), a collaborative program, was part of a national initiative funded by the Ford Foundation, which supported partnerships with top leaders from schools, colleges, government, and community-based organizations. In 1992, the foundation selected 16 cities across the United States to develop and implement comprehensive plans that would involve educational institutions offering programs from pre-kindergarten through senior college. The Queens Urban Partnership was one of the 16 projects that received funding for an unprecedented ten-year period. Although over 20 years has passed since this project started, its impact on the institutions involved has been lasting with several other collaborative programs emerging as a result of the QUP, most notably the LaGuardia Community College/QUP GEAR UP, the Robert F. Kennedy Collaborative School, and the College Bound program. It remains a model of school–college–community partnerships as large urban communities can benefit from lessons learned.

The goal of the QUP was to provide programs and services to advance academic achievement and facilitate the acquisition of a Baccalaureate degree for students. In pursuit of this goal, the QUP fostered systemic integration and focused the attention on the K-16 educational spectrum, and more specifically on the numerous transitions on educational levels. QUP understood that preparing students to handle the numerous transitions from school to college was paramount to attaining the goal of the Partnership. Recognizing and fulfilling that ideal meant involving higher education institutions into the structure.

The 30,364 students who were directly affected by QUP initiatives at 13 Kindergarten-grade 12 schools and their counterparts at LaGuardia Community College and St. John's University were culturally, ethnically, and racially diverse. The majority of students were first and second generation Americans whose linguistic needs have always been at the center of QUP's efforts to provide services for a limited English population.

The project was based in the borough of Queens, New York, known as the most ethnically diverse urban area in the world with a population of over 2.2 million, 46 percent of whom are foreign-born, representing over 100 different nations and speaking over 138 different languages (NYC.gov, 2011). The borough exhibits the largest increases of immigration in New York City. Stressing attention to the "whole child" through whole-language interventions and ancillary programs in health and pupil personnel services, QUP affiliated schools reflected significant improvements in numerous benchmark indicators, including daily attendance (+1 percent), persistence rates (+7 percent), and SAT verbal mean scores (+86 percent) (QUP Report, 1998).

The QUP collaboration fostered programs and initiatives that have resulted in liaisons between educational levels, faculty development programs, and expanded community involvement. One of these initiatives was the Queens School to Work program, joint effort between LaGuardia Community College and the Queens High Schools Division. Perhaps the culminating achievement in academic reform was a combined middle and high school, Robert F. Kennedy Community Middle/High School, which featured cross-sectoral collaboration in curriculum, faculty, administration, and mentoring. A unique public institution for its time, the school embodied all the desired reforms that united different levels of schooling. Recognizing that academic success could be derailed if students were not healthy, the QUP developed a Comprehensive Health Initiative. Its goals were to:

- Work to improve the overall health of students through infusing teaching with basic knowledge of health issues.
- Create community partnerships among students, their families, teachers, and local community health care practitioners.

This collaborative program brought the QUP into partnership with ten health organizations in educating over 29,724 students and their families about health issues (Community School District 25, 1997).

STRATEGIES FOR IDENTIFYING KEY CONSTITUENTS

Often, schools seek outside partners but they do not know how to work with them. QUP's process of building an educational collaborative team to facilitate the progress of disadvantaged and minority students is an example of a community's effort in developing a partnership. The following strategies were used by the QUP:

1. **Create a vision.** Before the Ford Foundation established the Urban Partnership Program, work had begun in New York in 1991 to bring together different sectors of the public educational community. Janet Lieberman, founder of Middle College (a unique public school on the LaGuardia Community College campus) and Special Assistant to the President of LaGuardia, was responsible for bringing together a group of educators from the public school and LaGuardia to talk about ways to develop closer ties between these institutions.

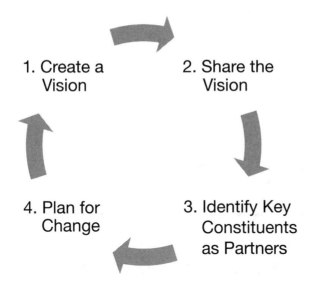

Figure 2.1 Processes for Partnership Building

2. **Collect data and conduct a review of exemplary practices.** The planning team conducted a literature review and collected data on Queens' school districts. Other collaborative programs outside New York were examined.
3. **The vision was shared with possible partners.** Once the data was collected, the team met with area high school principals to discuss the implications of the data and investigate their recommendations for building a team to address these problems. The team also met with the Queens' elementary/middle school superintendents and the high school superintendent to elicit their suggestions for a process that would achieve the goal. After the issues were explored in individual groups, the participants requested a joint meeting of the same superintendents, high school principals, and LaGuardia Community College President to discuss mutual concerns.
4. **The key constituents were identified and became committed to the vision.** The team placed attention on finding common areas of concern that brought together diverse players to formulate collaborative strategies to fix the problems raised. During that time, LaGuardia Community College offered its facilities for the Partnership office in response to a request by members of the group.
5. **The constituents or partners planned for change by preparing and offering a proposal for funding of the partnership.** The Partnership was successful in receiving a Stage I planning Grant for membership in the National Center for Urban Partnerships, a new project funded by the Ford Foundation. A sub-group met with a business sector representative who underscored the perspective of the business community: they want a well-trained prospective workforce. Another sub-group was formed, led by an expert in Whole Language from LaGuardia Community College, to locate other experts in the field.
6. **A program evaluator was also identified.** The Partnership evaluator met with the evaluation team from the National Center for Urban Partnerships, which was commissioned by the Ford Foundation to begin designing an evaluation plan for the QUP.

7. **A retreat was used to bring interested parties together.** A retreat was held for interested faculty and administrators from LaGuardia, Queens College, School District 25, and Queens High School District and community organizations to develop implementation strategies for all phases of the project.

8. **Roles and responsibilities of each partner were identified.** The members of the Partnership discussed the possible input of each segment of the partnership.

9. **A governance system was created.** The Partnership created a governance structure, set up a committee to draft a mission statement, and planned budget allocations.

10. **The QUP received seed funding of $130,000 per year for ten years from the Ford Foundation.**

PORTFOLIO BUILDING 2.2

Building a Key Constituency Chart for Partnership Development

Each partner should be carefully chosen for its potential to make substantive collaborative contributions to a comprehensive program that will enable low-income students to stay in school and go to college.

Develop a Key Constituency Chart which will:

1. Identify the influential groups in your school community.

2. Identify the main contact persons from the above groups who will work with you.

3. State the possible interest each group has in your school.

4. Determine the current attitude each group has toward your school and education.

5. Describe the type of involvement you desire from each of these groups.

6. List the challenges you can expect from each group.

You may use the following chart as a guide or design one of your own.

Name of group	Contact person	Nature of interest in school	Current attitude toward school/ education	Desired involvement	Challenges

WORKING AGAINST COLLABORATION: UNDERSTANDING THE GOVERNANCE STRUCTURE OF NEW YORK CITY SCHOOLS

The governance structure of the New York City school was pertinent to the way in which QUP operated during its tenure, creating both opportunities and obstacles. Some of the major outcomes of QUP are remarkable given the centralized/decentralized nature of the education system. The elementary/middle/junior high schools were under the jurisdiction of 32 community school districts and were governed by elected boards. The high schools were grouped into five geographically larger districts covering New York City boroughs. Also, there were several special districts for alternative schools and schools serving severely disabled students. This split in responsibility for the New York City public schools complicates the achievement of one of the major purposes of the QUP—collaboration between levels of schooling. It must be noted that since 2003, the current configuration of organization of the school system has changed. New York City mayor is in charge of the public schools. In 2003, the districts were grouped into ten regions, each encompassing several elementary and middle school districts, and part of a high school district. In 2007, Mayor Michael Bloomberg and Chancellor Joel I. Klein announced the dissolution of the regions effective June 2007 and the introduction of School Support Organizations (Hemphill, 2010). In fact, the reorganization of the public school system works against building effective partnerships. These changes have centered more around the issue of accountability and control and less on schools grouped together to increase collaboration among those of the same level and between the various sectors. Meanwhile, public higher education institutions in New York are governed by the Board of Higher Education, and in New York City, by the City University of New York, which comprises 24 college and professional schools.

REFLECTIVE EXERCISE 2.2

Working with Community-Based Organizations

Many educators are part of communities in which they live or spend considerable time.

1. With which community-based organization do you volunteer your time?
2. Why did you select this organization(s)?
3. If possible, how can your involvement with this organization(s) impact your work with your school?
4. Share with your colleagues some of the promotional materials from these organizations.

CONCLUSION

The "model" of operating principles that was to become the hallmark of QUP was developed during these initial planning meetings. This meant that all those who had a stake in systemic change needed to be at the same table as equals, from the beginning and throughout the process—ignoring the traditional hierarchy and status of positions associated with most institutions. The following chapter continues the conversation of building community with those involved and it focuses on the organizational structure that makes it possible to effectively implement a collaborative program.

KEY TERMS

- Key constituents
- Collaboration
- Effective partnerships
- Governance structure
- Institutional leaders

CHAPTER 3

Creating Structures for Community Involvement

LEARNING OBJECTIVES

After reading this chapter you will be able to:

1. Describe the programmatic needs of a collaborative program
2. Assemble a team of leaders to plan and implement the program
3. Develop strategies to keep the team members engaged in the goals and objective of the collaborative
4. Assess and select activities to sustain the work of the collaborative

---

INTRODUCTION

Developing effective partnerships for schools demands a clear understanding of the governance characteristics of participating collaborators. For this to happen, there must be an organizational structure that allows for the development of mutual trust and respect among members of the partnership. Such a structure permits cross-dialogue among the educational institutions and community-based organizations involved in the partnership. This chapter not only describes the organizational structure of two grant-funded programs, but explores the unique arrangement between a higher education institution and a high school that facilitated the success of at-risk high school students. Readers will learn from these examples in order to build their own planning teams, develop strategies to keep team members focused on the mission of the partnership, and select activities that sustain partnership efforts.

Educational Leadership Constituent Council (ELCC) Standards

This chapter meets the needs of advanced academic programs in preparation for educational leadership:

Standard 1.0: Candidates who complete the program are educational leaders who have the knowledge and ability to promote the success of all students by facilitating the development, articulation, implementation, and stewardship of a school or district vision of learning supported by the school community.

Standard 3.0: Candidates who complete the program are educational leaders who have the knowledge and ability to promote the success of all students by managing the organization, operations, and resources in a way that promotes a safe, efficient, and effective learning environment.

Standard 4.0: Candidates who complete the program are educational leaders who have the knowledge and ability to promote the success of all students by collaborating with families and other community members, responding to diverse community interests and needs, and mobilizing community resources.

Standard 6.0: Candidates who complete the program are educational leaders who have the knowledge and ability to promote the success of all students by understanding, responding to, and influencing the larger political, social, economic, legal, and cultural context.

(National Policy Board for Education Administration, 2002)

★   ★   ★

It is clearly evident that programs that address the total child seem to be the best solution to addressing student retention and high school completion. Also, given the pressures confronting today's children and youth, schools cannot solve these problems alone. However, the importance of higher education institutions in school reform is often underrated. Discussions around school improvement and increasing student academic achievement often leave colleges and universities out of the equation, and if they are to be considered, it is usually for staff training and teacher professional development. The larger community, too, can be part of these discussions as they can provide the setting for curriculum development, teaching resources, student internships, and other innovative initiatives.

So, how can education leaders create a structure to make this happen? The following are examples taken from the Middle College experience, LaGuardia/QUP GEAR UP and the Queens Urban Partnership. The common denominator of these collaborative programs was the school–community partnership philosophy espoused by LaGuardia Community College, which assumed the role of broker by developing linkages and partnerships with the public schools, universities, businesses, and community-based organizations. This college served as a community-wide educational clearinghouse for innovative programs that served to strengthen the school system while ensuring that high school students will eventually enter the doors of a college.

REFLECTIVE EXERCISE 3.1

Institutional Adaptation to Student Retention

You are a principal who has been recently asked by the Department of Education to prepare a plan for a new high school that will be located on a college campus. The following areas need to be considered:

1. What is the mission of this school?
2. What does its organizational structure look like for the high school and for the college?
3. Describe its scope and sequence.
4. What criteria will be used in the hiring process of the faculty?
5. How is the school funded?
6. How will your plan be different if you were working with high schools that were not located on the college campus?

This chapter proposes three types of structures that facilitate collaboration with school–college–community partnership programs.

INSTITUTIONAL ADAPTATION BY A HIGHER EDUCATIONAL INSTITUTION: THE MIDDLE COLLEGE MODEL

The Institutional Adaptation to Student Retention model (Carter, 2004) can be used as a framework for school–college collaborative programs that are housed in higher education institutions and, specifically, for those that wish to address the high school dropout problem. Collaborative programs are often seen as "outsiders" by the very education sectors they are attempting to assist. Adopting this model sends a clear message: school–college collaboration is integral to the operations of a college and, while attending to their own needs, higher education must embrace the issues confronting elementary and secondary education (Carter, 2004).

Middle College is housed in a community college and is an example of a long-term, sustained collaborative. To effectively implement the Middle College model, broad collaboration between the school system and LaGuardia had to occur and it did. The formative years brought college and school faculty and administrators together to jointly plan for the workings of the school. One researcher aptly sums up the school's success in maintaining the different governance structures:

> The success of MCHS at LaGuardia depended on attaining flexibility in the midst of a bureaucratic urban school system, obtaining cooperation between jurisdictions that barely communicated with each other, and implementing a comprehensive plan within a community college that simultaneously pursued multiple functions.
> (Wechsler, 2001)

The key elements of Institutional Adaptation to Student Retention model combined to increase high school graduation and college-going rates are the Policy Environment, Institutional Mission, and Management Strategies. This model is not only applicable to collaborative programs between a community college and a high school, but can be adapted to any senior college or university wishing to partner with the school system.

Policy Environment

The policy environment of the early 1970s when Middle College and LaGuardia Community College were formed contained some issues that are still present today: access, retention, and persistence in schools and colleges. LaGuardia was expected to develop innovative solutions to urban educational problems. Since the early years of the open admissions policy did not swell the population of the City University of New York colleges, something had to be done to ensure that students would enroll. Many students, however, were not graduating from high school but were dropping out. Clearly, this was not only a "school system problem" but one that focused on all sectors of the education system. The high school dropout problem entails systemic reform and would bring together policymakers from all sectors to address the issue.

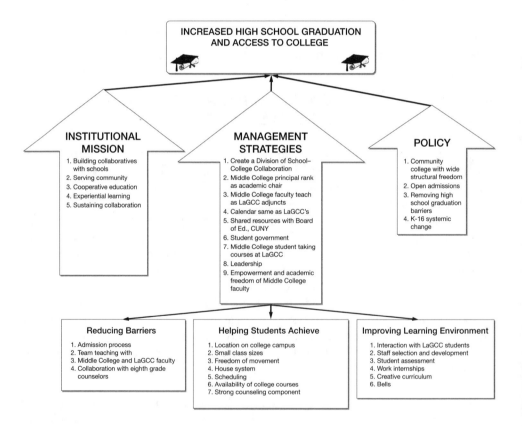

Figure 3.1 A Model of Institutional Adaptation to Student Retention

Source: Carter, H. (2004). A case study of Middle College High School, 1972–2003: An effort to improve the persistence of at-risk students in high school and to facilitate their access to college. UMI: 3124943.

Working with an at-risk population can push administrators to develop alternative paths to student assessment. The Institutional Adaptation to Student Retention model highlights the importance of student assessment. In reference to this issue, Middle College was able to obtain waivers from New York State for student exemption from Regents examinations, a prerequisite for a high school diploma. Instead, Middle College students engage in portfolio assessments and the school still maintains high graduation and college going rates.

Institutional Mission

A special burden falls on higher education institutions to work with and to assist schools in the successful transition of their students. The mandate of community colleges to serve as a link between the school system and higher education best describes the reason for the creation of Middle College at LaGuardia Community College. In addressing the problem of high school dropouts with the Middle College model, the institutions involved need to see collaboration as essential to their mission. The focus of LaGuardia was pragmatic: it aimed to assist the non-traditional student in accessing higher education. Also, in dealing with at-risk students, schools need to foster a climate of expectations that children will succeed and that they are willing to implement innovative curriculum and student-centered teaching strategies. For example, Middle College's decision to use portfolio assessment to evaluate academic competency, its 70-minute classroom periods, cooperative teaching methods, and student-centered curriculum are examples of attempts by the school to create an environment better suited to at-risk students.

Realizing that their goals cannot be achieved alone, community colleges and schools are becoming increasingly interdependent. A significant part of the mission of the community college is the collegiate function. Serving as the nexus between the school system and the senior colleges, community colleges can assist students in the acquisition of the baccalaureate degree. Community colleges in partnering with other educational sectors can assist in improving students' academic achievement and in progressing along the education pipeline. Additionally, community colleges can carry out their mission by collaborating with businesses, social agencies, and community organizations in the community. Similarly, senior colleges and universities need to have students entering their doors ready to engage and succeed in college level work. Often ignored in the debate on high school dropout is the large number of students who enter college and do not complete their studies. In a report conducted by the American Institutes for Research, the writers cautioned about the costs to society of students who failed to graduate from college. For example, in looking at a student cohort who entered college in Fall 2002 having full-time status seeking a bachelor's degree but failed to graduate six years later, the cost to the nation was approximately:

- $3.8 billion in lost income
- $566 million in lost federal income taxes and
- $164 million in lost state income taxes.

It must be noted that these estimated losses are for one year and for one cohort of students. Since the losses for these students accrue year after year, these estimates understate the overall costs of low college graduation rates (Schneider & Yin, 2011).

Leadership and Management Strategies

Effective programs that aim to address student retention should be collaborative with a distinctive process and an organizational structure that facilitates the attainment of program goals. One of the management strategies is commitment from top leadership. Leaders have the capacity to commit institutional resources, to provide legitimacy to the project and underscore its importance, and to remove bureaucratic barriers to collaboration. The early years of Middle College brought leaders of higher education and the school system together in the creation and implementation of the school. Additionally, the school benefitted from the presence of two effective principals who, while ensuring that the ideals of the Middle College model be upheld, left their mark on the school. Successive principals each added a distinct management function that altered the role of the principal in executing various strategies essential to the model. The challenge is for institutions to maintain these commitments from top leadership when those leaders leave. The structure of the guidance component, changes in the curriculum, and emphasis on portfolio assessment made significant improvement in student participation and graduation rates. Another change in management was the process of recruitment dictated by the New York City Department of Education. In the initial phases, recruitment was done by interviews with guidance counselors. More recently recruitment has been included in the overall city-wide choice provided to eighth grade students. The challenge is for institutions to maintain these commitments from top leadership when those leaders leave.

Many of the aspects of the management of this type of model—security, maintenance, and the use of college facilities—fall under the direction of the college administrators. Also, the school's calendar matches that of the college and Middle College students have the opportunity to take courses at LaGuardia. Although effective leadership is central to the working of a collaborative, the rank and file have to be committed to the program's goals. Management strategies, as they are outlined in the Institutional Adaptation to Student Retention model, encourage innovation and flexibility in instruction and promote an environment that is positive to both students and faculty. Middle College faculty are empowered and they enjoy academic freedom, a privilege usually associated with college faculty. They also have the opportunity to work with their counterparts at the college, allowing both faculties to share knowledge of incoming students.

REDUCING BARRIERS

While the policy environment and institutional mission provide the setting for the development of the Model of Institutional Adaptation to Student Retention, it is the management process that determines its effectiveness. Reducing barriers is a major goal in any student retention plan that involves two entities with different governance structures. The student recruitment process involves articulation between the school system and the college, specifically between the eighth grade middle school counselors, counselors at the college high school, and the high school division of the public school system. For example, at Middle College students are selected based on their at-risk nature and their ability to benefit from the goals and objectives of the school. For students to benefit from this type of high school retention-college access program, the last phase of going to college must be central to their everyday experience. Location on a college campus and access to college resources, adopting the college scheduling with the absence of bells, and high school and college faculty team teaching, removes the fear of college, promotes confidence, and academically prepares students for the rigors of college work (Carter, 2004).

Helping Students Achieve

A high school college collaborative model that attempts to retain students in school and prepare them for college has to focus on organizational structure and student needs. The maturity of today's high school students means that teenagers want more freedom and less restriction (Lieberman, 1986). Location on college campus and its non-restrictive environment provides high school students with the opportunity to make their own decisions. Students choose their classes, including college courses and have an individualized program plan that shows their progress and the courses needed to graduate. Knowing how to manage freedom requires a support system. Counseling and small class size allows students to feel accepted and bond to adults. Students see themselves staying in school and graduating with a high school diploma. These are all key elements of Middle College and are part of the Institutional Adaptation to Student Retention model.

Improving Learning Environment

At-risk students achieve in an environment that is engaging and motivating. Exposure to college students benefits high school students as they are forced to engage in college life and become motivated to graduate from high school and enter college. High school college collaborative models such as this one should have staff with experience teaching at various levels or, at least, who have an eye on the entire educational continuum. Selection of staff with counseling experience and opportunities for professional development in creative curriculum is also necessary for work with this type of population.

THE TOWN COUNCIL OF THE QUEENS URBAN PARTNERSHIP

The goal of the Queens Urban Partnership was to provide programs and services that prepare students to handle successfully the numerous hurdles and transitions from school to college to acquire a baccalaureate degree. QUP's change agenda for curricular reform directly attacked the principal cause of lower rates of college admissions for minority and immigrant candidates—namely, reading and writing achievement. The leaders of the program embraced the identity of a town taking as a key goal open and ongoing communication often lost in large-city bureaucracies of urban education (QUP Evaluation Report, 1996). Every effort and area of the QUP reflects this town concept (see Figure 3.1). Nowhere, is it more pronounced than in the Partnership's administrative structures.

Management Group: Executive Committee, Co-Directors, Project Director

From its inception, the QUP assumed as a central aim the development of collaborative relations among key partners to break down bureaucratic walls. To this end, the Executive Committee, the central QUP administrative structure, functioned as a town council. Drawing on both a collaborative and linear model, the QUP Executive Committee connected each of its key institutional leaders not only with other leaders, but with their essential constituencies—students, teachers, parents, and the wider community. The committee was made up of the:

- Project Director
- Co-Director, Superintendent, Community School District 25
- Co-Director, Superintendent, Queens High Schools
- Associate, Community School District 25
- Director of Funded Programs, Queens High Schools
- Special Assistant to the President, LaGuardia Community College (also serves as the Project Advisor)
- Special Assistant to the President, LaGuardia Community College (Language Specialist)
- Director of Collaborative Programs, LaGuardia Community College
- Dean of the School of Education, St. John's University
- Associate Dean of the School of Education, St. John's University
- Program Evaluators
- Dean of the School of Education, Queens College (early years only)
- President, Community School Board District 25.

When the Superintendent of the Queens High Schools left, her replacement automatically became a member of the QUP. Internal policy shifts at Queens College resulted in the administration at Queens College not providing a replacement when the Dean left. The Executive Committee invited the Dean of St. John's University and his associate to become members of the Partnership and they both quickly became viable members of the Partnership activities. The Executive Committee remained stable in its membership over the ten-year life of the project, a reflection of the enthusiasm of the separate sectors for the Partnership and the trust and rapport at the heart of this unique cross-sectoral forum (QUP Evaluation Report, 1996).

The project director oversaw the program, arranged meetings, supervised financial allocation, and maintained records. Other responsibilities included representing the Partnership and coordinating the evaluation efforts. The co-directors, the two school superintendents, had on-site responsibilities. They assisted in the selection of the team leaders and team participants and set policy. They represented the project to the Executive Committee and kept them informed of progress as well as convening meetings and eliciting suggestions from community participants. In the planning proposal to the Ford Foundation (QUP, 1992), an Institutional and Community Advisory Group comprising the local government officials, college presidents, and the Deputy Mayor of New York were to be an integral part of the QUP. This group was to disseminate broad base information on the project and served as consultants in areas of expertise

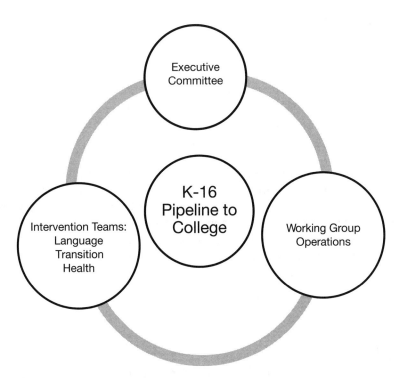

Figure 3.2 Queens Urban Partnership Town Council Structure

and influence. The group did not meet and the Executive Committee assumed many of its functions.

Language, Transition, and Health Teams

The initial point of intervention with the students was a focus on literacy. In each of the target schools, language teams were coordinated and developed by four members: one from elementary school, one from middle school, one from high school, one from college. There were four teams, each led by a team leader, who reported to the language specialist who served on the Executive Committee. As the project progressed, QUP determined that several other key issues were barriers to student success in school, including their emotional and physical health, and the systemic issue of successfully maneuvering through the key transition points in school; movement from elementary to middle school, middle to high school, and high school to college. Health and Pupil Personnel Services teams were developed to include representatives of the QUP participating institutions.

GEAR UP GOVERNANCE STRUCTURE

While the funding for Middle College was institutionalized and that of the Queens Urban Partnership long term, LaGCC GEAR UP had six years to implement its grant activities. As with short-term grants, especially those funded by the federal government, there is often a rush to implement activities as soon as possible. There is no planning year provided by federal government grants as with grants from private foundations. GEAR UP established a governance structure comprised of representatives from the three school districts and the participating middle schools, the Queens High School Office and the three GEAR UP high schools, LaGuardia Community College, and the service providers. A Coordinating Council serving as an advisory board and three Site Planning teams were created to plan and provide feedback about the program. This structure allowed for cross-dialogue among the various sectors of the education system and the community—a rarity in urban education. The project contributed a model of school support staff enhancement that allowed it to carry out its mission within large, often bureaucratic settings.

REFLECTIVE EXERCISE 3.2

Report from the First Meeting of the GEAR UP Coordinating Council

This report provided raised questions that normally surround a collaborative project in its initial phase:

1. Are we reaching this student population and their parents as much as we need to? Do the students know of the program's services?
2. Does the program know who among the eighth grade cohort needs what services (e.g., English Language Learners; social skills and mentoring; health; tutoring; librarian)?
3. Is the assessment qualitative as well as quantitative? Will an increase or a decrease of scores be attributed to GEAR UP?
4. How can the outreach librarians effectively reach parents, tutors, and mentors, and identify what students and parents need?
5. There is need for a formal line for dissemination of information to parents.
6. As students leave the intermediate schools, how will it be possible to keep the intermediate schools engaged in GEAR UP?
7. How will this year prepare for the move to high schools next year (e.g. space for the Site Counselors; transitional meetings between the Site Counselors and Counselors at the high school)?
8. The GEAR UP Legacy: what aspects of school reform should GEAR UP concentrate upon?

(QUP, 2000)

(See Appendix B for the complete minutes of the first governance meeting of the QUP Coordinating Council.)

Reflective Exercise 3.2 represents a portion of the minutes of the first meeting of the QUP Coordinating Council and serves to identify the concerns and issues usually associated with the beginning stages of implementing a grant. Appendix B illustrates a typical agenda of an advisory board such as the QUP Coordinating Council.

Site Planning Team

The Site Planning Team was the pulse of the program in the GEAR UP schools, as it provided necessary feedback, made recommendations, and customized the GEAR UP activities to the needs of the cohort. There were three teams with a structure that allowed for the cross-dialogue among the various sectors of the education system and the community-based organizations. Each Site Planning Team comprised Principals of each Intermediate/Junior High Schools who worked with LaGuardia faculty/administrators, participating High School faculty/administrators, Queens Borough Library, Queens Child Guidance Center, as well as with parents. The team also allowed for the middle and their respective feeder high schools to engage in dialogues and planning of non-GEAR UP initiatives, efforts that were hoped would be continued when funding ended.

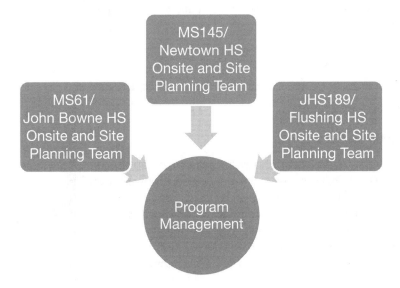

Figure 3.3 GEAR UP Onsite Teams and Site Planning Teams

Onsite Teams of Social Workers and Guidance Counselors

Counseling was one of the distinguishing features of GEAR UP's work with the at-risk population. From its inception, the program focused on the importance of counseling in assisting students to persist through middle and high school and to enter college (GEAR UP, Annual Performance Report, 2005). Three teams, each consisting of one guidance counselor and one social worker, were assigned to work with the GEAR UP student cohort. These onsite teams were integral members of the Site Planning Teams. They moved with the cohort from middle school and onto high school, identifying students' needs through classroom visits, communication with teachers and counselors, individual and group counseling, and data analysis. These findings were brought to the monthly meetings with program staff at LaGuardia so that necessary interventions were planned and implemented.

GEAR UP: BUILDING A TIMELINE FOR COLLABORATION AND STUDENT PROGRESS THROUGH GRADES

The success of GEAR UP depended heavily on its ability to move the student cohort from middle school through high school and into college in the expected six-year timeframe. GEAR UP had to ensure that its student cohort remained on track to graduate on time. The program leaders developed a plan of action with the onsite team of counselors and social workers, along with the Site Planning Teams working together to meet the needs of the student cohort. Table 3.1 shows this plan.

While it became clear that not all members of the student cohort would graduate on time, GEAR UP created a customized program for students on track to graduate on time and those not on track to graduate. Details of this customized plan are highlighted in Chapter 10.

PORTFOLIO BUILDING 3.1

A Focus on Black Boys

You are a new principal of a middle school (or high school) whose Black male students are performing at lower rates than their counterparts. Your superintendent agrees to a Black Male program at your school, but only if you include a community partnership component. You have a meeting with community officials to address their concern for the academic status of this population and other at-risk students.

1. Which groups will you invite to this meeting and why?

2. Which groups would object to this meeting and why?

3. How would you address their concerns?

4. Prepare an agenda for this meeting.

5. How will you evaluate the program's effectiveness?

Table 3.1 Action Plan for Student Progress through Grades

Year	Focus	Activities
1 Seventh grade	• Entrance of GEAR UP into intermediate schools • High school selection process for students and parents • Introduction to careers and colleges	Full-time and part-time staff hired; advisory board confirmed; monthly Site Planning Teams and program staff meetings. Academic activities implemented with the student cohort; professional development begins. Evaluation surveys for students, parents, and teachers take place. Staff program activity logs collected monthly every semester and in the summer.
2 Eighth grade	• Preparation for eighth grade tests • Successful completion of middle school • Introduction to careers and colleges	Advisory board meet quarterly; Site Planning Teams and program staff meet monthly. All academic activities implemented with the cohort including visits to target high schools. Professional development continues. Evaluation surveys for students, parents, and teachers take place. Staff program activity logs collected monthly every semester and in the summer.
3 Ninth grade	• Transition to high school • Retention of students moving on to the tenth grade • Closer monitoring of ninth grade cohort by onsite staff to avoid dropout problem • College prep	Onsite staff enter high school with cohort; absorbed into guidance department. Advisory board and Site Planning Teams meet monthly. All academic activities implemented with the cohort. Professional development continues. Evaluation surveys for students, parents, and teachers take place. Staff program activity logs collected monthly every semester and in the summer.
4	• College prep intensifies • Retention of students moving on to the eleventh grade	Advisory board meets quarterly; site planning teams and program staff meet monthly. All academic activities implemented with the cohort; new college prep activities introduced; visits to local colleges. Professional development continues.
5	• College prep intensifies; onsite staff meet with each student to develop a personal college prep plan • Retention of students moving on to the twelfth grade	Program staff, Site Planning, and advisory board continue to meet. Student activities and professional development occurs. Onsite staff conduct in-school groups with cohort; visits to colleges and college fairs increase; extra academic supported provided to ensure cohort are on time to graduate.
6	• Transition to college • College selection, application, and financial aid process • Cohort graduates and progresses to college	Program staff, Site Planning Team, and advisory board continue to meet. Student activities and professional development occurs. Onsite staff conduct in-school groups with cohort; extra academic support provided.

PORTFOLIO BUILDING 3.2

Creating a Management Plan for a Community Partnership Program

The objectives of a proposed Community Partnership Program can only be achieved through both the cooperation and accountability of each sector of those charged with its implementation.

1. Design a Management Plan that is:

   - clear as to the tasks to be performed
   - calls for collaboration
   - has central guidance
   - allows for initiative and resourcefulness as needed.

2. In the Management Plan, include an Advisory Board, Program Staff (see Appendix J for sample job descriptions), and Site Planning Teams. How are these groups coordinated?

3. Construct a timeline of activities for each year of the Community Partnership Program.

LESSONS LEARNED

1. Identify Key Staff as Early as Possible

The hiring of program staff needed to be priority before implementation of activities in the first year of the program. Although some grants do not require a planning period, ample time has to be devoted to carefully recruit project personnel. The emphasis on implementing activities in the Fall semester of the first year when an organizational structure is not yet in place can create much havoc and undue stress.

2. Include the Second in Command in Decision-Making Groups

The practice of including the "second in command" from the two school districts added to the stability of the membership, and gave further assurance that implementation would take place. LaGuardia was represented by several influential positions, though not necessarily by positions that are generally assumed to be major decision makers, i.e. President or Provost. Each member reflects the policies of the institution he or she represents, though all are committed to the goals of the QUP.

3. Include Evaluators in Program Planning

Hired evaluators were integral committee members and met regularly to discuss the required services for students. One of the main benefits of having grants supported by external funding is that there is more flexibility in adapting program offerings.

4. Develop an Evaluation Plan

Collaborative project objectives are greatly facilitated by a systematic, comprehensive, and timely project evaluation. An evaluation that is suitably tailored to the objectives of the project, gathers significant information at key intervals, and quickly disseminates that information to project personnel will allow the partnership to achieve and maintain consistently high levels of performance. Collaborative projects should secure the commitment of an independent evaluation firm to design and conduct a thorough evaluation of project activities. An evaluation plan should consist of multiple methods intended to gather information on project effectiveness, e.g. surveys, focus groups, interviews, and questionnaires. The intent is to provide project staff with valid and reliable data on how the project functions in order to support project improvement, as well as to report on project outcomes. This dual focus of the evaluation provides staff with information that helps them to determine which aspects of the project have been particularly effective and which aspects of the project could benefit from improvement. Evaluation plans that focus on collaborative projects, as those described in this book, should utilize qualitative and quantitative sources of data, including (a) students; (b) parents; (c) teachers; (d) program participation and attendance records; (e) school records; (f) city test scores; and (g) state test scores. A sample evaluation plan is provided (see Appendix E) for consideration by educators who wish to develop collaborative programs in their schools. The plan included both process and outcome evaluation guidelines and proves to be an effective tool to reassess the program and make necessary modifications.

5. Maintaining the Semblance of Neutrality: Team Meeting Location

The GEAR UP teams met each month under the guidance of the GEAR UP Project Director. They were held at the participating schools and at the offices of the community partners. Each partner hosted a meeting to ensure that no one institution would "dominate" the discussions and decisions. No meetings of the teams were held at LaGuardia Community College due to logistical difficulties. It was decided that the location of the college would make it difficult for the school staff to attend meetings immediately after school. GEAR UP leaders were sensitive to the needs of its partners, particularly the length of the school day, distance between schools and the extra-curricular demands placed on school staff. Governance meetings that brought the Coordinating council and the Site Planning Teams together at the beginning and at the end of the academic year were held in a conference center at a local hotel (see Appendix D for meeting schedule). The reasons for the choice of a conference center were clear. GEAR UP wanted to maintain the perception of neutrality that a non-partner site would give; the conference center could accommodate the numbers of participants; and school and college staff needed to be treated as professionals. In addition, the Site Planning Teams ensured, through the exchange of information at their meetings, that the connections between various levels were maintained as the cohort moved from the middle school through the high school.

CONCLUSION

A major challenge for partnerships is to ensure that collaboration is not something that remains on the periphery but is integral to the overall working of the school or college. This is important for long-term collaboratives. Staffs from the school, community-based organizations, and those at the college must be considered equals and integrated into the organizational structure of the partnership. For example, colleges that view building collaboratives with schools as part of their institutional mission need to have an organizational structure that supports the relationship, for example, a department of Academic Collaboratives housed in the Division of Academic Affairs. This allows for the sustainability of long-term programs and sends a message: systemic reform initiatives or, at least, partnership efforts with the school system are seen as essential and beneficial to the wider community, if not the college itself. The following chapter focuses on the difficulty many students have in transitioning from middle to high school. It suggests various strategies students, their parents, and teachers can employ as they progress on to high school completion.

KEY TERMS

- Governance structure
- Site Planning Teams
- Coordinating council
- Town council
- Sustainability

CHAPTER 4

High School Bound: Transitioning from Middle School to High School

LEARNING OBJECTIVES

After reading this chapter you will be able to:

1. Examine the issues facing middle school students
2. Propose various strategies to assist middle school students, their parents, and teachers in selecting an appropriate high school
3. Assess the most effective strategies to meet the needs of middle school students as they prepare to transition to high school
4. Support the needs of middle school teachers so that they can better serve their students
5. Design a high school Bound program for your school

INTRODUCTION

Transition from middle to high school is often accompanied by a decline in grades, failing courses, and increased absences (Barone, Aguirre-Deandreis, & Trickett, 1991). Low-performing students may have more difficulty coping with the transition, and have a narrower range of support, than higher-performing students (Newman et al., 2000). This chapter looks at innovative strategies educators can employ to ensure that:

- teachers and administrators are empowered to make decisions about the middle school students
- middle school students are prepared to progress to high school and beyond
- families are re-engaged in the education of young people.

This chapter addresses problems students face at the transition point from middle school to high school and the daunting nature of the high school choice process. Readers will learn how to create a High School Bound program, which brings together counselors and teachers from both the middle and high schools to plan middle schools students' smooth transition to high school.

Educational Leadership Constituent Council (ELCC) Standards

This chapter meets the needs of advanced academic programs in preparation for educational leadership:

> Standard 2.0: Candidates who complete the program are educational leaders who have the knowledge and ability to promote the success of all students by promoting a positive school culture, providing an effective instructional program, applying best practice to student learning, and designing comprehensive professional growth plans for staff.

> Standard 4.0: Candidates who complete the program are educational leaders who have the knowledge and ability to promote the success of all students by collaborating with families and other community members, responding to diverse community interests and needs, and mobilizing community resources.
>
> (National Policy Board for Educational Administration, 2002)

★   ★   ★

Potential high school dropouts are identified as early as the middle grades. Undoubtedly, there is a pressing need for better middle school education. Middle grade students exhibit a range of physical, intellectual, emotional, and social development unmatched in other grades. To meet these developmental demands, their teachers must engage in staff development that increases their knowledge and skills, challenges their beliefs and assumptions about education, provides support and coaching to develop comfort with new practices, and engages them as active partners in the study and reform of the school culture. However, few teachers have the specialized preparation to teach at the middle school level. As we know, teacher expertise, content knowledge, pedagogical skills, and an understanding of the learning process are the most important factors in determining student achievement (Armour-Thomas et al., 1989).

At both ends of the spectrum, students will be facing far more stringent standards, both in exiting high school and for admission to college. Students in the middle schools will need a great deal of assistance in preparing for these conditions in order for them to have a reasonable chance of pursuing a postsecondary degree. As state education systems increasingly require students to take and pass stringent examinations to earn a high school diploma, students in public middle schools, too, must achieve the necessary standards, particularly at the eighth grade level if they are to progress on to and be adequately prepared to graduate from high school on time. Since high school dropouts are usually identified as early as the middle school grades, more attention needs to be paid to the experience of middle school students particularly as they prepare to move on to high school. It is widely acknowledged that schools at all levels desperately need reform, redirection, and support if they are to fulfill their mission to prepare students to complete their high school education and proceed to postsecondary education.

The lack of sustained and continuous interaction between middle school, high school, and college students, parents, faculty, and administrators results in the inability of parents to make thoughtful choices about their child's high school or college.

REFLECTIVE EXERCISE 4.1

For some children, the early adolescent years mark the beginning of a downward spiral in school-related behaviors and motivation that often lead to academic failure and school dropout.

(Eccles, Lord, & Midgley, 1991, p. 521)

The junior high school, by almost unanimous agreement, is the wasteland—one is tempted to say cesspool—of American education.

(Silberman, 1970, p. 324)

1. What are your thoughts on the above descriptions of America's middle schools? Do you agree or disagree with these descriptions?
2. Describe your experience in dealing with middle school students and their teachers.
3. If you teach in a middle school, how has your teacher preparation program positioned you to work with students at your school?

THE MIDDLE SCHOOL STUDENT

Hayes Mizell, a nationally respected critic of America's middle schools, stated:

If all students in the middle grades are going to achieve at significantly higher levels, they will have to participate in very different and more effective educational experiences than is now the case. The majority of sixth, seventh and eighth graders continue to attend regular public schools. Most of these schools have yet to demonstrate that they can provide the very different and more effective educational experiences that enable all students to perform at higher levels.

(Mizell, 1992)

Despite the outdated quote above, students' plight from middle school to high school is still, unfortunately, relevant. Eighth grade students are usually excited and concerned about going to high school. Although they want the freedom associated with high school and the opportunity to get involved in extracurricular activities, eighth graders express concern about getting lost in the high school and getting bad grades (Cognato, 1999; Maute, 1991; Mizelle, 1995; Phelan, Yu, & Davidson, 1994; Wells, 1996).

In revisiting the 1989 Carnegie Council Turning Points report, there are strategies that school leaders can employ in working with young adolescents. Suggestions from this landmark publication include:

- creating smaller communities for learning
- teaching an academic core program
- ensuring success for all students by eliminating tracking
- empowering teachers and administrators to make decisions about the experiences of middle school students
- staffing middle grade schools with teachers with expertise in teaching young adolescents
- reengaging families in the education of young adolescents
- connecting schools with communities.

ARTICULATION PRACTICES FOR STUDENTS TRANSITIONING INTO HIGH SCHOOL

Facilitating young adolescents movement from middle to high school requires programs that focus on the transition period (Cognato, 1999; Felner, Ginter, & Primavera, 1982; Hertzog & Morgan, 1999; Hertzog et al., 1996; Mac Iver, 1990) as well as middle school programs that challenge and support students (Belcher & Hatley, 1994; Bry & George, 1980; McAdoo, 1999; Mizelle, 1995; Oates, Flores, & Weishew, 1998).

REFLECTIVE EXERCISE 4.2

High School Bound for Students

You are an eighth grader getting ready to choose a high school.

1. What career do you see yourself pursuing in the future?
2. Do you want to go to college?
3. How will you make the decision about which high school to attend?
4. How can your current school help you make this decision?
5. How can your parents help you make the decision?
6. What concerns do you have about going to high school?
7. How can those concerns disappear?

In large public school systems, such as New York City's, there are often large communication gaps at the points of transition and articulation between the middle school and the high school. Despite attempts at reorganizing the public school organizational structure to make it more streamlined and manageable, school faculty do not regularly exchange information about the needs of their students, curricular sequence, and high school graduation requirements. Establishing a forum for this communication would create a context not only for useful appraisal but also for the development of new activities and initiatives.

REFLECTIVE EXERCISE 4.3

I urge the next generation of middle school educators to help save the ninth grade. The middle school concept has, too often, not been able to fulfill its announced intention to make the transition to high school a smooth and successful experience. In fact, the transition to high school has never been more treacherous nor the consequences more personally disastrous for so many. All over America, thousands and thousands of ninth graders are and have been painfully failing . . .

We can no longer allow all the good work you do in middle schools to evaporate in the first six weeks of high school.

(George, 1999, in Middle School Journal, 2000, p. 57)

- You are a middle school principal whose eighth grade students are getting ready to go to high school. What short-term and long-term strategies will you put in place to ensure that their choice of and transition to high school is smooth and effective for them, their parents, and teachers?

A FOCUS ON THE LAGCC/QUP GEAR UP PROGRAM

When programs are in place to support students during the transition from middle to high school, students have better educational outcomes, with fewer students retained on grade. The LaGCC/QUP GEAR UP program, a grant funded by the United States Department of Education, offered various initiatives to assist middle school students to progress through high school and onto college. The central features of successful transition initiatives include:

- creating smaller learning communities or cohorts of students who spend time together
- providing greater support from teachers and counselors who can serve as liaisons between students, families, and school
- providing information to students and parents about high school
- providing students with social support
- bringing middle and high school together to learn more about one another's school.

At the beginning of the grant period, the LaGCC/QUP targeted three middle schools in high needs communities in Queens, New York. In the New York City public school system, middle school students have various options available to them after graduating. They can attend the local feeder high school; apply to a specialized high school in New York City; or apply to a private school. Most students choose the first option, but many also attend other public high schools in the city. The LAGCC/QUP moved with the majority of the original seventh grade cohort to the three local feeder high schools: Flushing, John Bowne, and Newtown high schools. A portion of the original cohort remained at JHS 189 for the ninth grade as the school provides for students from grades 7 through 9. However, for the middle school students moving over to the targeted high schools, the journey took them to schools where there were severe gaps. These included overcrowdedness, high dropout rates of around 20 percent, and lower graduation rates than other schools in New York City with 55 percent of students graduating with their cohort (GEAR UP Third Year Evaluation Report, 2002).

It must be emphasized that the LAGCC/QUP GEAR UP program did not only focus on the middle to high school transition, but included an early college preparation component which meant that transition must have a longitudinal view encompassing all the educational sectors. More importantly, was the point that everyone in the school building—students, teachers, guidance counselors, and administrators—must be involved in the transition process. Transitioning affected students, their teachers, and the curriculum. The following table lists those objectives of the LAGCC/QUP GEAR UP that pertain to the transition process.

Descriptions of the specific services offered to middle school students, their parents and teachers, and receiving high school teachers are outlined below.

HIGH SCHOOL BOUND

The High School Bound program was designed for eighth grade students (from the LaGCC/QUP GEAR UP cohort) to gain an understanding of how their high school experience will be different to their middle school experience. Eighty students participated in this program at the three feeder high schools. Students had the opportunity to experience English Language, Arts, and math classes team-taught by middle school and high school teachers. They met with ninth grade guidance counselors who talked to them about the expectations of high school and graduation requirements. During the last session of the program, students were allowed to reflect on the experience and received feedback on how they could improve their academic performance. Students recorded their self-assessments in their LAGCC/QUP GEAR UP High School Action Plan books. About 35 percent of the students reported that the classes were somewhat more difficult than they expected. However, the majority of students found the classes challenging but manageable (GEAR UP program Annual Performance report, 2001).

The middle school and high school teachers who participated in the program spent three hours, over the course of two weeks, planning the math and English program. Overall, participating teachers felt the experience was a positive one for the students. They thought students benefitted from attending the classes at the high school, interacting with high school students, guidance counselors, and other high school faculty who addressed them and gave them a chance to ask questions about some of their concerns. The teachers themselves felt that their most valuable experience was team-teaching with other teachers. For some of the high school teachers, it was their most valuable experience working in this manner with middle school teachers. High School Bound was an opportunity for students to become familiar with the high school campus and environment. They also participated in a career component, which gave them an opportunity to begin to think career goals and the related educational requirements. It was also an opportunity for teachers across grade levels to learn from one another.

Table 4.1 GEAR UP Transition Plan

Objectives	Activities	Target Group	Results
1. Coordinated the services and resources of schools, school districts, postsecondary institutions, community-based organizations, and employers to increase positive relationships among key leaders within each educational institution and the community to improve student performance; articulation between grades.	Mini Seminars Cross School Dialogues Instructional Strategies Seminars	Students Teachers, Guidance Counselors Administrators Teachers, Guidance Counselors, Administrators	4,424 students have participated in Mini Seminars since 1999. Six site planning meetings were held each year at each of the three high schools.
2. Coordinated the services and resources of schools, school districts, postsecondary institutions, community-based organizations, and employers to provide various opportunities for middle school students to visit high schools and colleges to learn about school and college choice and admission.	High School Bound College Bound	Students, Teachers Guidance Counselors	High School Bound and College Bound has provided high school and college visits for 1,433 middle school and high school students since 1999
3. Coordinated the services and resources of schools, school districts, postsecondary institutions, community-based organizations, and employers to foster cross-educational level and inter-agency dialogue through the development of teams of teachers, counselors, administrators, and social workers.	Instructional Strategies Seminars Cross School Dialogues Mini Seminars	Students, Teachers, Guidance Counselors, Administrators	Since the beginning of the grant period, over 500 teachers, administrators, counselors, and social workers have participated in these activities. Surveys indicate increased coordination and satisfaction.

Source: LAGCC/QUP, Final Report, 2006

MINI-SEMINARS

Mini-Seminars brought middle school staff and students together with faculty from LaGuardia Community College and professionals from a variety of fields. Presenters worked closely with the middle school faculty in planning the seminars, which were intended to extend and enrich the classroom curricula, develop communication skills, and help students look toward the future. The seminar series included: Theater and Communication, Oral Speaking, Developing a Sophisticated Reader, and What Do I Want to Be When I Grow Up.

MENTORING AND COUNSELING

LAGCC/QUP GEAR UP funded the salaries of three Guidance counselors and three social workers to provide additional support to the LAGCC/QUP GEAR UP student cohort and to provide additional support to the participating schools. Using groups or individual sessions, the counselors and social workers worked with students on various issues such as problem solving, family problems, relationship building, and critical thinking.

SUMMER ENRICHMENT PROGRAM

Involvement in the transition programs illustrated by GEAR UP provides many lessons for educators seeking to prepare students, their parents, and teachers to move through the various educational sectors.

PORTFOLIO BUILDING 4.1

High School Bound Program: What Shall We Do in the Summer?

The following is the contents of a newsletter used to advertise a Summer Enrichment Program for the GEAR student cohort.

This year GEAR UP will sponsor a Summer 2001 Enrichment Program at LaGuardia Community College for 120 students from IS61, IS145 and JHS189. Forty students from each school will attend classes from July 9 to August 3, 2001.

The academic as well as the artistic components of the program will revolve around the theme "Exploring New York City." English Language Arts and math classes, computer workshops, counseling and mentoring sessions, dance theater, and folklore classes are all designed to allow students to explore and appreciate the rich culture in our city.

One day a week students will have an opportunity to learn outside the classroom and will engage in a series of neighborhood walking tours throughout the other boroughs. Every Friday, students will go on a trip to New York City where they will visit sites like Ellis Island and Central Park. They will also participate in a multicultural walking tour, walk over the Brooklyn Bridge and learn more about its history, and view "Across the Sea of Time" at the Sony Imax Theater.

Our summer faculty comprises of middle school and high school teachers from GEAR UP feeder schools as well as GEAR UP counselors and social workers, LaGuardia Community College faculty and staff, professionals from various artistic disciplines, college students and high school seniors.

The program is free for GEAR UP participants and breakfast, lunch, and transportation will be provided. This should be a wonderful opportunity for students to explore different aspects of New York as well as their own cultures and communities.

LESSONS LEARNED

1. Inadequate Preparation of Middle School Teachers

Unfortunately, the statistics about middle grade teachers can be as troubling as the results their students get. Students' success is reduced without teachers who are experts and prepared to teach the middle grades (Cooney & Bottoms, 2002; Jackson & Davis, 2000). Since the U.S. middle school movement is relatively new, most middle grade teachers were prepared in college for either elementary or secondary school. Educational researcher Gilbert Hunt (2003) calls for more specialized preparation for both teachers and administrators who work in middle schools. He further states that most middle school teachers were trained in secondary education where the emphasis was on subject matter, while others were trained in elementary education, which is student centered but lacking in a content foundation. Hunt also raises a key point in the discussion on middle school reform: "the lack of uniform agreement as to just what should be accomplished at the middle level in terms of student performance" (Hunt, 2003, p. 214). He listed several goals of the middle school, one of which was focusing on high school preparation.

2. Exchanging Information across Grades: Cross-GEAR UP Schools Dialogues

While staff development is necessary for deepening the mastery of skills needed to work with young adolescents, middle school teachers needed to collaborate with their peers in the other sectors to prepare students for high school and beyond. It was with this in mind that the designers to the LaGCC/QUP GEAR UP project convened teachers and administrators to focus on issues relating to curricular content, scope, sequence, and pedagogy. Teachers and guidance counselors across the feeder pattern identified the needs of students at each step in the educational spectrum and made recommendations to their schools. Teams were organized around one of the following academic disciplines: English Language Arts, Mathematics/Science, Counseling, and Social Studies. The most frequently cited positive outcomes of the dialogues included:

- having the opportunity to communicate with educators from different educational levels
- being able to communicate professional concerns with other educators
- hearing perspectives from people in other schools in one's field
- sharing best practices with one another.

(GEAR UP Final Evaluation Report, 2003)

While collaboration with teachers and administrators across sectors is crucial to assisting middle school students transitioning to the high school, it was the gains made by the counselors' dialogues involved with this program that led to the most immediate and promising outcomes. Administrators from the middle and high schools brought together their respective guidance counselors and parent associations to plan on how best to serve parents and students at their schools. This association was expected to be ongoing:

> This simple idea will have a far-reaching impact for the students on both the junior high school and the high school level. It is one more avenue in uniting the school levels for the benefits of students. It is also one more example of school counselors from different levels cooperating for the benefit of all.

(Cross GEAR UP Dialogues School Counseling Report, 2003)

3. Involving Parents in the Transition Process

It is imperative that parents be involved in the transition from middle to high school. Students whose parents are involved in their high school experiences are less likely to drop out of school (Horn & West, 1992). The challenge for educators is to keep parents involved in the transition activities at their schools through various activities. Like their children, parents, too, need support in sending their children off to high school. For many parents in large urban cities, the high school choice process can be confusing and intimidating. Schools must include parents in the transition activities including the application process and visits to high schools.

REFLECTIVE EXERCISE 4.4

High School Bound for Teachers

You are an eighth grade teacher whose students are concerned about going to high school.

1. How will you assist them in making the best choice of high school?
2. How will you utilize time in class to deal with this issue? Give examples.
3. Once they have selected a high school, how will you prepare them to enter a new school?

REFLECTIVE EXERCISE 4.5

High School Bound for Parents

Your eighth grade son/daughter is getting ready to choose a high school.

1. What do you see as the perfect high school for your child?
2. How do you go about choosing a high school?
3. List the factors that are most important in helping you decide.
4. What role should your child's current school play in your decision?
5. After a decision is made, how can you prepare your child for high school?

PORTFOLIO BUILDING 4.2

Design a High School Bound Program for Your School

Using the guidelines presented in this chapter, design a High School Bound program for the sending middle school and receiving high school.

CONCLUSION

Transitions between schools, while exciting and full of possibility, usually present particular difficulties for students. The transition into high school can be challenging in urban schools, where many young people have difficulty navigating the larger high school. Many middle school students exhibit physical, emotional, intellectual deficiencies making the transition to high school even more daunting. On the other hand, many middle school teachers are not adequately prepared to teach this segment of the school population making it impossible to assist students who are struggling. Collaborative initiatives between middle school and high school staff can assist both the middle school teacher and student. Colleges and universities can also be helpful as students may ultimately get to their doors and need to be prepared to succeed.

KEY TERMS

- Transition
- Articulation practices
- Feeder pattern
- Teacher preparation for the Middle School
- Longitudinal view of education

CHAPTER 5

Bridging the Gaps: Higher Education Institutions and the School System

LEARNING OBJECTIVES

After reading this chapter you will be able to:

1. Describe the relationship between schools and colleges
2. Discuss elements of successful school–college collaborative programs
3. Analyze effective strategies to develop and maintain collaboration
4. Appraise the academic and social impact of those strategies on student achievement
5. Create institutional activities applicable to specific schools

INTRODUCTION

Postsecondary education is now a prerequisite to academic and economic success. Employers are increasingly demanding a skilled workforce. Those without academic credentials find themselves in low-paying jobs and irregular employment. Minority populations, especially those in large urban cities, are particularly vulnerable. The failure to educate large numbers of minority youth, particularly blacks and Hispanics, and their exclusion from productive employment is catastrophic to society. This "minority-majority" population is growing at a rapid rate and is persistent in our schools. It is in the interest of employers that the minority population receives the type of education that allows them to succeed economically. But higher education institutions also depend on all students to persist through the educational pipeline. This persistence of students enables higher education institutions to keep their doors open. Clearly, this means getting involved early in the education of students, preferably at middle schools as potential dropouts are usually identified at that time. This chapter explores the relationship between the school system and higher education institutions, characteristics of effective school–college partnerships and highlights an exemplary school–college collaborative model: Middle College High School. The school was created to increase high school retention, improve graduate rates at the secondary level, and attract adolescents to higher education. However, for most "traditional" schools, college preparation usually begins in the tenth or eleventh grades. This was not the case of the schools participating in the GEAR UP program where program planners designed a six-year plan to get school students ready to graduate from high school and enter college prepared to succeed.

Educational Leadership Constituent Council (ELCC) Standards

This chapter meets the needs of advanced academic programs in preparation for educational leadership:

> Standard 4.0: Candidates who complete the program are educational leaders who have the knowledge and ability to promote the success of all students by collaborating with families and other community members, responding to diverse community interests and needs, and mobilizing community resources.

> Standard 6.0: Candidates who complete the program are educational leaders who have the knowledge and ability to promote the success of all students by understanding, responding to, and influencing the larger political, social, economic, legal, and cultural context.
>
> (National Policy Board for Education Administration, 2002)

★ ★ ★

BRIEF HISTORY OF SCHOOL–COLLEGE COLLABORATION

Traditionally, many higher education institutions remain remote in their interaction with the school system. The prime activities and values of universities are often removed from public schooling. Also, even within these institutions, education departments or colleges are often separated from other departments by attitudes and values echoing these larger separations (Daly, 1985). During the mid-1980s' wave of public school reform, the need for closer school–college collaboration became more apparent ushering in one of the most rapid periods of growth in school–college partnerships. Calling for educational institutions to form relationships with one another for the common good of students, the 1973 Carnegie Report reminded educators of the need to consider the connection between students' problems in college and their prior experiences in elementary, middle, and high schools. Apart from preparing teachers for elementary and secondary schools, colleges and universities have not been eager to enter partnerships designed to enhance cooperation between the two sectors. In many cases, high schools have been left without any sense of what the colleges expect their students to know (Carnegie Foundation, 1973).

Beginning with the nineteenth century, there have been many attempts to bring the two sectors together. The Committee of Ten (National Education Association, 1893), which promoted a national dialogue on the contents of high school curriculum and the College Entrance Examination Board in 1890, offered uniformed entrance examinations based on negotiated requirements (Wechsler, 2001). Another attempt to integrate the systems by focusing on improving the high school curriculum was proposed by faculty of the University of Chicago during the late 1920s and the early 1930s. Building on this work and a grade 11–14 component at the University, then president Robert M. Hutchins moved toward offering high school sophomores a college program (early college), which resulted in achieving the baccalaureate degree. Interestingly, Hutchins projected that junior colleges would become the acceptable education of the United States and suggested that they implement the "early college" model. Opposition to this reform came from the President's Commission (1947), which voted for a 12–2 configuration, as the State will hesitate to disturb the organization of the high schools. Similarly, the membership of the North Central Association of Colleges and Secondary Schools preferred to keep the junior college as an institution with separate jurisdiction and a faculty separated from the local high schools (Geiger, 1970).

By the 1960s, the feeble attempts at cooperation came to a halt as colleges and universities were caught up in the social issues surrounding this decade, including free speech and war protests. The ushering of the civil rights movement pushed many colleges and universities to expand their programs for minorities and women, while school districts were meeting the challenges of desegregation. What emerged was a high school curriculum that mirrored the college in its fragmentation. Ultimately, there was little effort for both sectors to connect curriculum.

THE COMMUNITY COLLEGE

The community college, more than any other segment of postsecondary education, was at the forefront of the post World War demographic expansion that changed the face of American higher education (Brint & Karabel, 1989). The two-year colleges not only represented an American innovation in the reform of higher education, but were part of a great surge in social reform spanning from the 1890s into the First World War. Cohen and Brawer commented that the community college "was founded to serve as a link between the lower school and establishments of higher learning" (Cohen & Brawer, 1989). The community college served as the major point of entry into higher education for America's low-income youth, underrepresented ethnic minorities, and new immigrants. It knew the needs of the community was well suited to work with the school system, and was central to the restructuring of public education to this day. One of its underutilized strengths in urban school reform is its ability to share resources across educational levels. While they have had a long history of working with other institutions, there is a sense that community colleges cannot fully carry out their mission without stronger and more sustained collaborations.

To collaborate between the sectors, educators need to understand the problems of diverse cultures of the two education sectors. Cooperation is usually easier with community college–university partnerships because the cultures are similar but it is more difficult between high schools and universities. Professionally the focus of the community colleges is pragmatic: it aims to assist the non-traditional student in accessing higher education. The emphasis of the four-year colleges and universities is more theoretical and abstract than that of community colleges. Clinicians had clearly established that underprivileged and high-risk students desperately needed a connection with the future. The connectedness is established by bringing them to school on the college campus. The governing structure of two-year college is less hierarchical than the four-year college. Therefore, the community college fosters a spirit of informality and collegiality that increases the integration of high school faculty and administrators into the mainstream of the college (Lieberman, 1986).

Community colleges are the most responsive to social, political, and economic forces and seek out relationships with other institutions in their communities, including the local school districts, business firms, community-based organizations and social agencies. These relationships in many cases benefit the parties involved, permitting the leverage of scarce resources, cost reduction, and exchange of skills. The institutional partners sustain the collaboration by leveraging their own resources. Other collaboratives survive through a combination of public and private funding. Community colleges realize that the key elements of their mission cannot be reached without sustained collaboration between various institutions. For example, efforts to improve student achievement, access to higher education, and a reduction in the numbers of high school dropouts bring some community colleges into long-term relationships with school systems. Issues of access and student achievement are not housed in any one sector but extend along the educational pipeline. Community colleges are a vital part of these discussions.

REFLECTIVE EXERCISE 5.1

In what ways do colleges and universities need to work with elementary, middle, and high schools?

> If colleges and universities are going to fill their classrooms they will have to get involved in the work of teaching and learning that takes place in the public schools; they will have to recognize that education is all one system and what happens at one level has direct implications for the next level.
>
> (Pew Charitable Trust, Duhl, 1990)

PRINCIPLES OF SUCCESSFUL SCHOOL–COLLEGE COLLABORATIVE PROJECTS

Very different cultures guide the school and college sectors. These differences lead to a significant lack of understanding as each distinct culture tends to distrust the other. This divide further supports the 1986 Carnegie Report, which emphatically stated that if educators need to be more serious about transforming the quality of schooling across the educational continuum from K–12 to graduate study, it will require a much greater degree of substantive cooperation between schools and colleges than has been the case so far.

Researchers Gomez et al. (1990) state that for cooperation to occur, innovators need to understand the governance characteristics of the school system and higher education institutions. These include the following:

1. A clearly articulated and accepted statement of mutual self-interest and common goals as a necessary starting point for building a successful collaborative.
2. Collaborative activities that develop mutual trust and respect among members. Each participant must understand the unique experience and perspective that others bring to the collaborative and demonstrate a willingness to work together on a professional basis.
3. Successful collaboratives stress the involvement of all parties in decision-making.
4. Given the many complex issues that could be addressed, it is important to establish a clear focus.
5. A corollary to establishing a clear focus is the need to set a meaningful agenda and focus activities in accordance with this agenda.
6. Because collaboration is often seen as peripheral to core functions, it is necessary to have both the commitment and involvement of top leaders from each of the participating entities: leaders provide legitimacy to the undertaking, underscore its importance, and have the capacity to commit resources.
7. Other characteristics include fiscal support, long-term commitment, dynamic nature, and information sharing.

In addition to the above characteristics, the Carnegie Report (Maeroff, 1987) cites five basic principles of collaborative projects:

1. Educators from both levels must agree that they have common problems. Education is a seamless web, and communication between the sectors is required.
2. For effective collaboration to be achieved, the traditional academic "pecking order" must be overcome. Colleges and universities have had—for many years—a "plantation mentality" about the schools. Higher education set the ground rules and the schools were expected passively to go along. For example, faculty committees that do not consult school administrators and teachers make college admission requirements in isolation. In addition, schools of education unilaterally develop programs for teachers whose "real needs" are not adequately considered.
3. Serious cooperation will occur only if school and college people agree to focus on one or two specific goals.
4. Participants must get recognition.
5. The focus must be on action, not machinery. While resources are important, they should not become the preoccupation of school and college planners.

The above principles are useful for programs that bring the school system and higher education institutions together. Lundquist and Nixon (1998) called for community colleges to develop a partnership paradigm: a modeling of collaborative relationships, an emphasis on student development, the development of community partnerships, and the creation of new types of planning and resource allocation. They emphasized the need for a new organizational culture in community colleges if college personnel are to respond effectively to their communities. This partnership paradigm also promises benefits to the college and the community "more powerful than those any single department in the college or single institution in the community can realize" (Lundquist & Nixon, 1998). Maeroff (1987) emphasized the need for increased collaboration between the sectors:

The jurisdictional boundaries separating schools and colleges are crossed successfully only when institutions on both sides of the line are amenable. It is not easy to build incentives for cooperation if one institution considers itself the winner and the other the loser. In all of this, a special burden falls on higher education. The nation's colleges and universities must, in tangible ways, affirm the essentialness of the nation's urban schools.

(Maeroff, 1987)

LESSONS LEARNED

THE MIDDLE COLLEGE EXPERIENCE

Middle College is housed in a community college and is an example of a long-term, sustained collaborative. Middle College is located in one of the four buildings owned by LaGuardia Community College. It was the first of the three high schools created by the college; International High School and Robert Wagner High School are the other two. Middle College unites the New York City's Department of Education with LaGuardia Community College of the City University of New York and is an example of the commitment of a higher education institution to partnering with the school system. The school's success in maintaining the different governance structures is aptly summarized:

> The success of MCHS at LaGuardia depended on attaining flexibility in the midst of a bureaucratic urban school system, obtaining cooperation between jurisdictions that barely communicated with each other, and implementing a comprehensive plan within a community college that simultaneously pursued multiple functions.

(Weschler, 2001)

Much can be learned from this school that unites the school system with a higher education institution in a unique program to address the needs of potential dropout students. While Middle College is located on a college campus, not all high schools are structured in the same manner. However, there are key strategies to building effective collaborative programs that the experiences of Middle College could provide. The following lessons serve as a guide to anyone seeking to bring different systems together.

1. Sharing of Responsibility

To effectively implement the Middle College model, broad collaboration between the school system and LaGuardia Community College had to occur, and it did. One of the tangible benefits of a collaboration that is as close as LaGuardia Community College and Middle College is that problems of responsibility are shared by both the high school and the college. The success of a high school–college collaborative demands an academic and administrative partnership between the college and the public high school. LaGuardia adopted the role of a "caring parent" (Cullen & Moed, 1988): providing advice, assistance, and resources enabling the school to develop an identity of its own and to experiment with non-traditional practices.

2. Creative Funding Arrangement and Shared Resources

The funding for Middle College reflects the joint relationship that different governing entities need to implement a collaborative program. In the original planning stages, funding for Middle College was provided by the Carnegie Foundation and the Fund for the Improvement of Postsecondary Education. Various funding models were negotiated giving either the Board of Higher Education or the New York City Department of Education control over the school. State policy prohibited the high school division from sending money for secondary education through a college level governing body. Additionally, state funding must go to the New York City Department of Education, which would pay the salaries of teachers. Historically, funds could go to a senior college, which had a laboratory school for elementary and secondary teachers. Community colleges were not permitted to have a school of education, which prohibited them from receiving funding for schoolteachers. Middle College planners opted for New York City Department of Education funding for teachers, with the Board of Higher Education contributing money for space, security, and supplies, and for LaGuardia faculty teaching high school courses.

The joint funding arrangement allowed the school to implement one of its main features: small class size. Middle College class size runs from 16 to 25 students, with an average size of 20 compared to 34 students in the regular high school. The relatively low student to faculty ratio at a reduced cost is feasible for two reasons: shared resources and cooperative education. Middle College uses the library, the gym, the cafeteria, and the lounges of the college. Classroom spaces are shared; the college uses them after 3 p.m. Also, gifted and able students take college classes, freeing instructors and reducing class size. The main monetary saving and economic factor is the cooperative education program, which enables at least one-third of the students to be out working on sites at any given time. The internship program substantially reduces class size.

The most significant impact of this funding arrangement was a change in the program design. The school would not serve students in grades ten to fourteen, but rather would become a high school serving grades nine to twelve. The ability for students to earn both a high school diploma and an Associate degree did not come to fruition until the year 2002 with the introduction of the Early College program, which is financially supported by private funding.

An attempt to depart from the funding arrangement took place in 2000, when Middle College decided to become a charter school. This followed the passage of legislation that defined this particular change as essential to maintaining the fiscal health of the school, altering its relationship to its public funding sources. When the request for student insurance, formerly covered by LaGuardia, was denied, the school decided to return to its initial arrangement that proved to be the easier of the two choices of operating within dual governance structures.

3. Developing a Relationship with Leaders of Collaborating Institutions

The relationship between the schools and colleges can be jeopardized by a college's superior attitude to the schools. There can be a tendency for colleges to want to fix the schools. Leaders provide legitimacy to the collaborative as seen by the involvement of administrators from both the school and the college working closely together to implement the Middle College model. To be effective, collaboration has to be institutionalized and part of the organizational structure and culture of both entities. For this to occur, there needs to be personal connections, individual initiatives, and commitment of like-minded individuals. Active involvement of the college and school administrators is important for practical and symbolic reasons and necessary to maintain the goals of the collaborative program. However, executive administrators cannot unilaterally create and sustain partnerships or mandate faculty and student involvement. For example, college administrators need to identify faculty leaders who will sustain partnerships and include collaboration as part of their scholarly work. They have access to college faculty and their participation strengthens the idea that collaboration with high schools is valued and an important academic goal of the college. School faculty, too, need to be supported in their efforts to work with college personnel.

REFLECTIVE EXERCISE 5.2

Collaborative Programs and their Benefits to School and College Faculty

1. Imagine you are school principal who is about to meet the dean at a college with whom you want to establish a collaborative program.
2. Describe the benefits and incentives this program will bring for both school and college faculty.
3. What obstacles do you foresee and how can you overcome them?

4. Motivating At-Risk High School Students To Go to College

College is not a reality for many at-risk students. One of the key features of the Middle College model is the location of the school on a college campus and the impact that has on student academic performance. The identification and affiliation of the teenage student to the college is both emblematic and intentional. The designers of Middle College saw the "power of the site" as one of the critical factors in working with an at-risk population. Additionally, they felt that access to college facilities would foster contact and communication with older students. They saw the location enabling the high school to create a culture infused with communication, trust, academic achievement, and cooperation, which is very different from current high school cultures and the adolescent destructive peer culture. The lasting impact was that by watching college students, they could identify and see the importance of continuity in higher education, which fueled their motivation to attend college.

5. Blending In with College Students

Students at Middle College do not want to be considered immature, or be easily identified from the LaGuardia students because of their behavior. The environment of the school is non-restrictive and both college and high school students seem to co-exist peacefully. Despite their high-risk history, Middle College students are treated as college students in a school that shares the facilities and mission of a community college. Interviews with the students by the author revealed that they did not want to be distinguished from the college students. They wanted to blend in, supporting the premise used by the program founders that a

15-year-old has more in common with an 18-year-old than with a 12-year-old. This was further supported by observations by the author of college and Middle College high school students in one of the college cafeterias. The only indicators that differentiated college students from high school students were the color of their identification cards. Relationship-building between the generations was critical to academic success and important in developing student attachment to significant adults.

6. Having More Access to Freedom than in a Traditional High School

Access to more freedom was cited as a reason why students enjoyed the climate of the school, why they chose Middle College, and why they remained in school. The idea that they are treated as college students, that they move around freely, and call adults by the first name immediately distinguished the school as different from other high schools.

The indirect benefit of the "power of the site" was the pressure students placed on themselves to stay in school (Carter, 2011). They were able to see and understand options. The presence of college students provided an opportunity to model their behavior and to plan to progress to college. For many students, the pressures of real life—family members and friends who dropped out of school, and not seeing college as a reality—were always present, but many said they did not want to make the same mistakes their peers and their parents made. However, some students abused the freedom given to them and began to cut class, one of the main behaviors of potential dropouts. Some of the student interviewees reminded me: Middle College students are still teenagers and can engage in truant behavior.

7. Creating a Professional Supportive Working Environment for High School Staff

The location of Middle College on a college campus is not only beneficial to the school's students but to their teachers. The school creates a richer learning environment for students by placing emphasis on a professional supportive working environment for their staff. Because the governing structure of two-year colleges is less traditional than the four-year college, the community college fosters a spirit of informality and collegiality that increases the access of high school faculty and administrators into the mainstream of the college. That exchange facilitates mutual and professional development of learning. Most faculty in other public high schools have no experience with the environment that permeates college faculty relations. For example, Middle College provided faculty with their own individual office space. Average high school faculty generally have less responsibility in the overall management and feel they have less independence in the direction of the institution. Additionally, small class size, in most cases 15–20 students, allows for experimentation and creativity in their curriculum and pedagogy and more time with their students. There is greater decision-making in curriculum content. Various teachers create courses they wish to teach, and these studies are included in the curriculum with administrative approval.

8. Teachers Have a Longitudinal View of the Learning Process

Exposure to college faculty and college students benefit school faculty as they get an idea of what the college expects and what high school students need to know. Middle College faculty who teach at LaGuardia have a longitudinal view of the learning process (Carter, 2011). They see what their high school students can become and how best to prepare them for college. Overall, placing a high school on a college campus raises the status of high school faculty.

9. Opportunity to Teach at both the High School and the College

Middle College faculty have the opportunity to teach at LaGuardia, a decided attraction because of the considerable increase in status. At Middle College and at LaGuardia, faculty have the option of being employed and at both levels. In more traditional areas, it is unusual that higher educational institutions offer teaching opportunities to the high school faculty; or that the secondary establishment uses the concept of adjuncts as a less expensive way of delivering part time instruction (Carter, 2011). In times of dwindling resources, the availability of positions at the collegiate level is limited. Many highly qualified faculty opt to go to the high schools where they have security. The overlap creates a pool of talent that can enrich both institutions. Apart from financial advantages, both high school and college faculties gain professional stimulation. When high school faculty are exposed to college faculty and college students they have a sense of what the college expects, a decided asset to continuity in curriculum planning.

PORTFOLIO BUILDING 5.1

Learning From Best Practices

1. Conduct an internet search on one or more school–college collaborative programs in your city or state.
2. Select a program that you think best fits your school.
3. How would you apply the essential features of that program to your school?
4. Construct a Master Plan to present to the college or university with which you wish to partner.

PORTFOLIO BUILDING 5.2

Creating a High School on a College Campus

- Submit a plan to the State Education department to develop a high school on a college campus which includes a source of financing, faculty recruitment, and curriculum.

PREPARING FOR COLLEGE: THE SEVENTH TO TWELFTH GRADE PLAN

Not all schools have an embedded culture of college preparation as seen by the Middle College experience. Many teachers and administrators are concerned about bringing students up to the grade level capacity that they are supposed to have, and early college preparation plans are not their main focus. Improving the academic performance of the student cohort was one of the main objectives of the GEAR UP program. The schools participating in the LaGCC/QUP GEAR UP had the opportunity to enhance their educational programs primarily through the benefits of external grants and school administrators who saw the benefits of transitioning to college not only during the high school years, but as early as the seventh grade. Unlike Middle College, which began with funding from private foundations and sustained with primarily public funds, GEAR UP was a six-year grant funded initiative. With a limited period of time and funding, the challenge for the leaders of the grant was much more intense. The goals and objectives of the grantor and grantee were finite: to significantly increase the number of low-income students who are prepared to enter and succeed in postsecondary education. Together with the GEAR UP staff, the school administrators created a grades 7–12 plan for preparing students for college. Samples of the flyers, meeting agendas, and workshop materials are provided in Appendix F

The single most important indicator of success for any GEAR UP program, and the first critical step on the way to college, is graduating from high school. For the LaGCC/QUP GEAR UP, this indicator reflected a resounding success. Eighty five percent of seniors graduated from the target high schools (GEAR UP internal report, 2006), a significantly high percentage considering that only about 50 percent of students in New York City schools graduate each year. Other academic outcomes also indicated that students were well prepared for college:

- The dropout rate for GEAR UP students was an extremely low 1 percent, compared with 17 percent of students in their high schools the previous year.
- More students in the GEAR UP cohort were accepted into and planned on attending four-year colleges than non-GEAR UP students in the previous year in their high schools.
- A large percentage of GEAR UP students had taken challenging classes, including Advanced Placement courses.
- Nearly two-thirds of the students attributed their plans to attend college to GEAR UP, an increase from less than half of the students in 2002.

The program positively impacted school staff as well. When it began in 1999, teachers and counselors had a passing and formal knowledge of each other's schools. Six years later, there was an improved knowledge of each school's challenges, discussion, and development of approaches.

LESSONS LEARNED

Middle College was created around the same time as LaGuardia Community College with both entities "growing up" together. It was developed to address some of the academic problems that the City University of New York, of which LaGuardia is part, faced in dealing with under prepared students in the onset of the open admissions policy. This type of school had to connect key curricular and organization features to its host institution and to the structure of public education (Houle, 1996). LaGuardia Community College was ideally suited to house a Middle College as its "mission and structure promoted innovation and flexibility" (Lieberman, 1989). The LaGCC/QUP GEAR UP, however, had a different origin and purpose. It was designed in response to a proposal submitted by the United States Department of Education. LaGuardia, with its long history of collaborations with schools and community organizations, took the lead in submitting a proposal and was awarded a $9 million grant to work with various schools and organizations. The coming together of different entities, each with a separate culture and environment, meant that for the success of the grant to occur, there had to be a clearer understanding of collaboration and major adjustments to the schools who were allowing external partners to enter their premises. However, by the sixth and final program year, the LaGuardia Community College/Queens Urban Partnership GEAR UP had become an integral part of the three targeted high schools. The following reflects the lessons learned.

1. A Clear Understanding about the Proposed Services and Their Implementation

School administrators need to be involved in the planning of the program, particularly activities that would impact their personnel and building during the school day. Specifically, the subject Assistant Principals are an important group as they were better able to indicate to their teaching staff the benefits of their involvement in the academic offerings of the program.

2. Support of Teachers

The support of teachers is crucial as they are the main vehicle through which students are referred to GEAR UP services. While the on-site staff had access to the classroom, teacher buy-in was critical to student participation in the program's activities. More communication with the classroom teacher and GEAR UP onsite staff was needed to better connect students with the appropriate intervention.

3. Improved Program Coordination and Use of Resources at the College

LaGuardia Community College has established an impressive array of school/college collaborative programs, which serve a large number of Queens' students. Prior to GEAR UP, these programs operated, for the most part, independently, recruiting their own students and faculty and providing services. The GEAR UP program was able to draw upon the resources of several LaGuardia programs, e.g., College Now and College Connection, which enabled high school students to take LaGuardia Community College courses tuition-free, the Liberty Partnership Program, and College for Children/Programs for Teens, which offered a range of enrichment and resources, coordinating them on behalf of the GEAR UP student cohort. Benefits accrue from leveraging mutual resources and GEAR UP was confident that would continue.

4. Increased Knowledge of College Choice and Selection

Via its College Portfolio project, GEAR UP left behind a series of lessons, to be implemented by the English high school faculty during the first two weeks of each semester, which centered on self-reflection and goal-setting with respect to postsecondary plans; identifying talents, strengths, skills, and interests; relating talents and strengths to a variety of careers; career preparation; examining the range of educational programs within the City University of New York, the State University of New York, and private colleges. These lessons and activities were developed for grades 9–12. They are a useful source of information for students, particularly as they approach their senior year and the college application process. They, in addition, enabled students to think about college and begin to consider their choices earlier in the high school grades than was currently possible.

5. Increased Knowledge of the Role of and Programs at the Community College

GEAR UP enabled high school faculty and counselors to learn more about community colleges, the kinds of programs and opportunities they provide for students as well as the increased faculty attention, which are often available to students in comparison to larger senior colleges. In addition, GEAR UP planned day visits to LaGuardia, which provided information about careers. Faculty spoke of the opportunities, demands, and challenges in various fields. LaGuardia students shared their experiences of transitioning to college and lessons learned. GEAR UP designers believed that activities such as this can be sustained and continued and that activities featuring the Senior Colleges can be developed as well.

6. Leveraging Resources through Coordinating Programs

Implementing and sustaining collaboratives often require educators to draw upon the resources of other programs with similar missions. Benefits accrue from leveraging mutual resources. As these programs are bound by limited grant funds and time considerations, maximizing its efforts can be achieved through working with similar programs. LaGuardia Community College established an impressive array of school/college collaborative programs, which served large numbers of Queens' school students. Prior to GEAR UP, these programs operated, for the most part, independently, recruiting their own students and faculty and providing services. GEAR UP was able to draw upon the resources of these LaGuardia programs, e.g., College Now and College Connection, which enable high school students to take LaGuardia Community College courses tuition-free, the Liberty Partnership Program, and College for Children/Programs for Teens, which offers a range of enrichment and resources, coordinating them on behalf of the GEAR UP student cohort.

CONCLUSION

Colleges and universities have played a critical role in the transition of American society from an agrarian to post-industrial social system. However, despite this, higher education institutions have lagged behind in changing their goals, organizational character, and operations to match contemporary needs. Many of them do not see themselves as agents of change, and often adhere to the traditional postures in teaching, research, and management. If the educational prospects for at-risk students are to be improved, both schools and colleges must change the way in which they operate. Given that the current system is not working for many young people, particularly minorities, it is crucial for educators at all levels to find ways to reach those students who are currently falling between the cracks. Although the relationship has not always been smooth, both educational sectors recognize the need for cooperation.

In order to overcome problems in the education system, higher education institutions and the school system must work together and work differently. For this to occur, higher education institutions need to see the education system as one continuum and recognize the interactions of different levels. Whereas the primary responsibility for student achievement rests within each individual system, elementary and secondary schools need to increase graduation rates and improve basic education and colleges need to expand access and retention; the two sectors have much to learn from each other. Being part of a team for "significant change" was exciting and appealing for both GEAR UP and Middle College educators, as some of their daily efforts were frustrating and unsuccessful. Since participants were chosen, but at the same time volunteered, they participated actively. The interchange of faculty across levels of schooling was often an eye-opener to faculty; the mutual "blame game" disappeared replaced by practical solutions and mutual flexibility.

Another key factor in the success of students involved in collaborative programs is the involvement of parents. This remains to be one of the most major challenges for educators. The following chapter explores GEAR UP's attempt to work with parents and involve community-based organizations in improving the experiences of families.

KEY TERMS

- Minority-majority population
- Seamless web
- Early college
- Non-traditional student
- Power of the site
- Leadership

CHAPTER 6

Parents and Community Building in Urban Areas

LEARNING OBJECTIVES

After reading this chapter you will be able to:

1. Discuss the issues faced by parents in the education of their children
2. Employ various strategies to involve parents in the college preparation process
3. Differentiate which strategies of parental involvement work best for your school
4. Design a plan to involve parents in your school

INTRODUCTION

Very often the last constituent who gets called to the table in the planning of school programs is the parent. Despite complaints about the lack of involvement by parents in our schools, educators have not quite figured out how to effectively engage this key constituent as partners in their children's education. This chapter looks at a program's attempt to involve parents in the early college preparation process, highlighting the expectations and fears parents have about their children's path through high school completion and postsecondary plans. It also shows how schools can collaborate with community-based organizations in meeting the needs of families.

Educational Leadership Constituent Council (ELCC) Standards

This chapter meets the needs of advanced academic programs in preparation for educational leadership:

> Standard 2.0: Candidates who complete the program are educational leaders who have the knowledge and ability to promote the success of all students by promoting

a positive school culture, providing an effective instructional program, applying best practice to student learning, and designing comprehensive professional growth plans for staff.

Standard 4.0: Candidates who complete the program are educational leaders who have the knowledge and ability to promote the success of all students by collaborating with families and other community members, responding to diverse community interests and needs, and mobilizing community resources.

(National Policy Board for Education Administration, 2002)

★ ★ ★

The importance of parental involvement in student retention and success cannot be underestimated. Federal legislation defines parent involvement as:

The participation of parents in regular, two-way, meaningful communication involving students' academic learning and other school activities. The involvement includes ensuring that parents play an integral role in assisting their child's learning; that parents are encouraged to be actively involved in their child's education at school; that parents are full partners in their child's education and are included, as appropriate, in decision making and on advisory committees to assist in the education of their child.

(NCLB, 9101(32))

If parents have such an important role in deciding their children's progress in school, schools must, in turn, have an important part to play in determining levels of parent involvement (Epstein, 2001). The effort to include parents is particularly important as students grow older, and in schools with high levels of poor and minority students. Middle and high schools tend to be more impersonal than elementary schools and students are taught by several teachers, meaning parents no longer have one contact in the school who knows their child well (Rutherford et al., 1997).

But research also shows there are ways that middle schools (and high schools) can overcome such impediments. Organizing a middle school so that at least one person knows each child well, keeping a "parent room" in the building, and sponsoring parent-to-parent communication and events are key parts of an effective parent-involvement program in the middle grades (Berla, Henderson, & Kerewsky, 1989). Joyce Epstein, one of the foremost leaders in parent involvement, claims that for parents to be involved to develop and grow, it must be significantly integrated into a school's program and community. She developed a framework of six types of parent involvement that schools can use to guide their efforts. It says schools can:

- help families with parenting and child-rearing skills
- communicate with families about school programs and student progress and needs
- work to improve recruitment, training, and schedules to involve families as volunteers in school activities

- encourage families to be involved in learning activities at home
- include parents as participants in important school decisions
- coordinate with businesses and agencies to provide resources and services for families, students, and the community.

(Epstein, 2001)

A report from the Southwest Educational Development Laboratory states that students stay in school longer, perform better, and like school more when families and community groups work together to support learning. The report, an amalgamation of research on parent involvement over a ten-year period, also claims that, regardless of family income or background, students with involved parents are more likely to:

- earn higher grades and test scores, and enroll in higher-level programs
- be promoted, pass their classes, and earn credits
- attend school regularly
- have better social skills, show improved behavior, and adapt well to school
- graduate and go on to postsecondary education.

(Henderson & Mapp, 2002, p. 7)

James Comer's School Development Program, or as it is better known, the Comer Process, is intended to improve the educational experience of poor minority youth. The Comer Process was developed in 1968 by James Comer, a child psychiatrist at the Child Study Center of Yale University, the Comer School Development Program. It is based on Comer's belief that a child's success is contingent on the relationship between school and family (Goldberg, 1990). Through his initial work in the New Haven public schools, Comer and his colleagues developed a process to reconnect schools and their communities and reallocate power in decision-making between parents and school staff. The result was clear: an improvement in students' overall development and academic achievement.

Focusing on elementary schools in New Haven, Connecticut, with low standardized test scores and high teacher and student absenteeism, Comer and his colleagues developed an organizational and management system centered on child development themes. The hope was that this would encourage teachers, administrators, and parents to collaborate to address children's needs (Comer et al., 1996).

Parents are the main element in the Comer Process or Comer Model. As Comer states it, "In every interaction you are either building community or breaking community. The mechanisms . . . are secondary" (Comer et al., 1996, p. 148). To accomplish this, the model embraces a collaborative, consensus-building, no-fault approach to problem solving (Ramirez-Smith, 1995). Participating schools are organized by management group around the following:

- School Planning and Management Team
- Student and Staff Support Team
- Parents Team
- a comprehensive school plan
- Staff development activities

- assessment
- a no-fault attitude toward solving problems
- decision-making by consensus
- collaborative participation that does not paralyze the principal.

(Comer et al., 1996)

REFLECTIVE EXERCISE 6.1

Involving Parents in Their Child's Education: The Comer Process

Conduct an Internet search on the Comer Process:

1. What role does the school play in a child's development?
2. Why is the community important to the child's developmental process?
3. Give examples of how the schools can use the Comer model.
4. What are the challenges of the model?
5. Using Comer's guidelines, how can you improve your school?

PREPARING PARENTS FOR THEIR CHILDREN'S ACCESS TO COLLEGE: EFFORTS OF THE GEAR UP PROGRAM

Students' aspirations and plans to go to college are heavily influenced by their parents. In fact, parental encouragement is the most positive predictor of students' plans after high school (Stage & Rushin, 1993). Recognizing this fact, the LaGCC/QUP GEAR UP program was designed to encourage parental involvement with their children and in the program in numerous ways. The program for parents of the GEAR UP cohort was designed on the following principles:

- Parents must be respected.
- Schools must make an effort to effectively inform parents.
- Parents are seen as partners in their children's education.
- Parents are involved in the governance of the school.
- Parent involvement is reciprocal.

(McLeod, 1996)

The following represents GEAR UP work with this important constituent as stated in the GEAR UP Proposal for Funding from the United Stated Department of Education (1999).

GEAR UP Parent Involvement Plan

The initial Parent Involvement plan was for GEAR UP to build on existing services the schools provided for parents and to expand them exponentially. These included after-school and Saturday programs in English as a Second Language, Computers, substance abuse prevention/intervention, and college and financial aid workshops. The

Queens Borough Public Library, one of the participating partners, also provided services for parents. One of the primary services GEAR UP provided to parents was guidance on how to navigate the New York City educational system. The choices parents make, from elementary through high school and on to college, affect their children and GEAR UP assisted them in that process. Parents also served on the Site Planning Teams, which provided feedback and planning of the services available to the GEAR UP student cohort.

To supplement the existing services for parents, GEAR UP personnel designed a comprehensive year-round plan for parents, which included classes and workshops for financial aid and college awareness, citizenship classes, counseling services, survival skills, and literacy skills. Beginning in the seventh grade, the GEAR UP cohort parents were guided through a series of activities and workshops to better help them make choices for their children. Deciding which high school their seventh graders will apply to in the eighth grade was one of the first of these choices, considered by guidance personnel, administrators, and students themselves, to be extremely critical, and often an unnerving experience. As a large number of GEAR UP parents were non-native English speakers, the available information can be confusing or overwhelming. GEAR UP rectified some of this by providing special parent workshops in their native language using the services of the public library. Seventh graders were required to complete the new state requirements for graduation from high school. In response to this and the intimidating high school application process, GEAR UP planned to offer a series of workshops, visiting speakers, and visits to area schools for parents and students. These information sessions were also designed to assist parents and students to make an informed choice of a high school. In addition, parents were given the opportunity to visit high schools with their children before the application process was completed.

Finally, the seventh and eighth grade years are also timely moments for students to begin thinking about their postsecondary plans. With the goal of early college preparation in mind, GEAR UP provided parents and their children with college, career, and financial aid information beginning in the seventh grade and continuing throughout the six-year tenure of the cohort. Parents were also encouraged to accompany students on trips to visit area colleges and universities. The following is a sampling of workshops offered to parents.

Financing a College Education

The goal of this workshop was to introduce GEAR UP parents and students to the four major types of financial aid available to college students: grants, loans, scholarships, and work study.

How to Fill Out Financial Aid Applications

The goal of the workshop was to assist GEAR UP parents and students in the completion of financial aid applications. Federal forms for financial aid are often seen as barriers to students, many of whom do not take advantage of all opportunities because the paperwork seems too overwhelming. Students were asked to bring in their applications, along with other necessary documentation, and were given individual assistance in completing the forms. Individual financial aid counseling was provided on an appointment basis as needed.

College Opportunity Workshops

The college opportunity workshop was designed to help parents and students understand the opportunities available to high school students. Areas covered included the role and differences between community college and senior college programs, admissions requirements, costs, financial aid, and scholarship opportunities at various local colleges and universities.

College Fairs

GEAR UP parents and students participated in LaGuardia Community College's Transfer Fairs. Over 50 colleges and universities come on campus to allow LaGuardia students the opportunity to speak with four-year college representatives about their courses and programs. Staff from the Financial Aid Office at LaGuardia Community College, College Board, and New York State Higher Education Services Corporation conducted the workshops several times during the tenure of the GEAR UP grant.

Citizenship Workshops

Non-native parents who are permanent residents were invited to meet with experts regarding the steps toward citizenship status, including completing the citizenship application.

Intergenerational Technology Classes

These Saturday Parent and Child classes allowed parents to learn alongside their children with a focus on mastering the skills both parent and students alike will need to negotiate technological advances.

Queens Borough Public Library Workshops

As one of the participating partners in the GEAR UP program, the Queens Borough Public Library provided a seminal link for parents, students, teachers, and the community. Building on existing parent workshops at the Library, GEAR UP targeted specific offerings to assist parents who did not speak English as a first language and those parents who wished to improve their reading and writing skills. Other workshops included coping skills, which enabled parents to assist their children in college selection and financial aid, with resident specialists who provided instruction in English, Spanish, Korean, and Chinese.

Services of the Queens Child Guidance Center

Another partner in the LaGCC/QUP GEAR UP program provided services for parents of the student cohort. The Queens Child Guidance Center, a multi-service agency, supplied each of the GEAR UP middle schools with a social worker. The social worker conducted workshops helping parents to understand the critical role they (parents) have in their child's education. Topics included information about the public school system, adolescent development, communicating with teenagers, and homework help.

The social worker engaged parents for guidance or family therapy sessions. Finally, in families where substance abuse, child abuse, or domestic violence was suspected, the social worker addressed these issues directly and, as necessary, encouraged parents to seek specialized treatment. The social worker also acted as a referral resource and liaison between parents and other social services they needed.

REFLECTIVE EXERCISE 6.2

Involving Parents in Their Child's Education: Linguistically and Cultural Diverse Families

Download the article Involving Hispanic Parents in Educational Activities through Collaborative Relationships by Alicia Salinas Sosa.

1. Describe the communities in which the schools exist.
2. How did the schools involve parents?
3. What were the challenges faced?
4. What can "mainstream" schools learn from the strategies used in the article?

IMPACT OF GEAR UP ON PARENTS

Perhaps the most challenging aspect of the LaGCC/QUP program offered to the participating schools was the involvement of parents of the student cohort. Attendance in the activities listed above was, for the most part, under prescribed. Those parents who attended the workshops represented students who were themselves heavy users of the GEAR UP services. GEAR UP employed the services of an external evaluator to track the number and types of services and activities offered to students, parents, and teachers. Surveys were mailed to 1,044 parents of participating GEAR UP students in English, Spanish, and Chinese (see Appendix I for sample survey). The survey asked about parents' hope for their children's educational future, and their knowledge of the college process, including its costs. Only 3 percent of parents responded. Response to the surveys, however, improved somewhat and for the 2004–2005 period, 196 parents completed the survey (Capital Assessments, Inc., 2006). The surveys informed GEAR UP staff about the type of activity or service parents were interested in or saw as important. More so, the responses of these surveys supply school leaders with an insight into how best to work with parents and their children on the college preparation process. The surveys provided valuable information about parent outcomes throughout the course of the grant. For example, most parents had high educational aspirations for their children, and almost all talked to their children about attending college. By 2005, the majority of parents surveyed felt that they had adequate information to prepare their children for college and many had discussed financial aid options with someone. The fear of college being unaffordable was removed.

Parents reported varying degrees of involvement with GEAR UP activities and their children's education (see Figure 6.1).

- Compared to the prior year, slightly more parents reported that they had a special meeting with a teacher or counselor to assist their child to do better in school (39 percent versus 34 percent the previous year).
- Sixty-three percent (63 percent) of parents had contact with GEAR UP staff during the school year; 41 percent met GEAR UP staff on Open School Night and 22 percent reported having telephone contact with GEAR UP staff.
- About 55 percent of parents attended a workshop to learn about the different ways to pay for their child's/children's college education.
- Also, 67 percent of parents reported going to a parent-teacher meeting to discuss their child's progress compared to seventy-three (73 percent) the previous year.

(Capital Assessments, Inc., 2006)

Parents expressed high hopes about their children's future. Most of them hoped that their children would be able to attend at least a four-year college. Also, parents were always concerned about the affordability of college (see Figures 6.2 and 6.3).

- Ninety-four percent (94 percent) of parents hoped their child would attend at least a four-year college, with almost half of those parents (45 percent) looking toward graduate school as well.

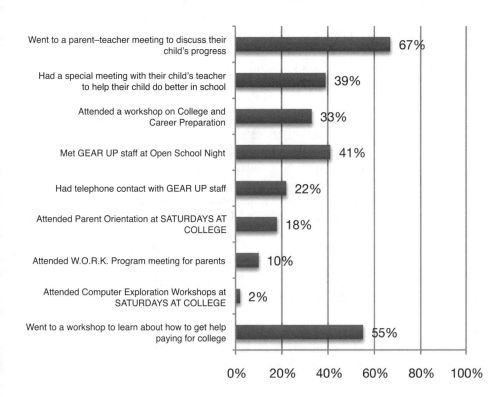

Figure 6.1 Parent Involvement with GEAR-UP Activities and their Children's education

Source: 2005 CAI Parent Survey

- Almost three-quarters (73 percent) of the parents felt that their children would be continuing their education after high school.
- The most common reason parents felt would prevent their children from attending college was the cost (21 percent) of attending college.
- Only 2 percent of parents felt that their children's grades would hold them back.

(Capital Assessments, Inc., 2006)

As shown in Figure 6.1, compared to the year before (2004), there were definite changes in parents' perceptions about the affordability of college, with more parents seeing college as a definite option.

- Almost three-quarters of the parents (70 percent) felt that college would be either "probably" (35 percent) or "definitely" (35 percent) affordable. This was an increase of 22 percentage points from last year.
- The remaining parents (30 percent) either felt unsure (22 percent), doubted (4 percent), or felt that they definitely would not (4 percent) be able to afford college.

(Capital Assessments, Inc., 2006)

As the majority of the GEAR UP students were in their senior year of high school in 2004–2005, parents took much initiative in discussing and planning for college with their children. More parents than ever before had taken the time to speak with their children about attending college. Also, many spoke to someone about the college application process. There was also a substantial increase in the number of parents who spoke to someone about the possibility of receiving financial aid to help pay for college.

- Ninety-nine percent (99 percent) of the parents reported that they spoke to their child about attending college (see Figure 6.4).
- Three-quarters of the parents (75 percent) reported that they had spoken with someone about how to apply to a college (see Figure 6.5).
- Sixty percent (60 percent) of the parents reported that they had spoken to someone about the financial aid options that might be available to their child. This increased from 23 percent in 2004, a gain of 37 percentage points (see Figure 6.6).

(Capital Assessments, Inc., 2006)

Repeating this positive trend, in 2005 more parents felt that they had enough information to help their child prepare for college (see Figure 6.7).

- Sixty-seven percent (67 percent) felt that they had enough information to help prepare their child for college. This was an increase from the last year, when only 21 percent felt prepared (see Figure 6.7).

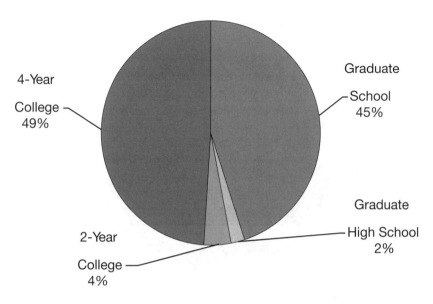

Figure 6.2 How Much Education Do You Want Your Child to Get?

Source: 2005 CAI Parent Survey

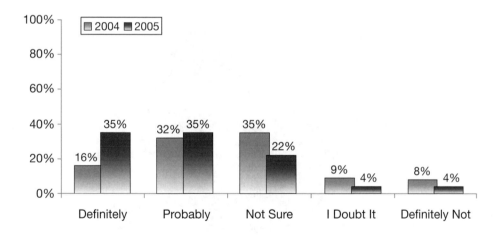

Figure 6.3 Parents' Expectation of the Affordability of a College Education

Source: 2005 CAI Parent Survey

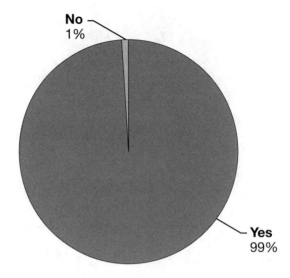

Figure 6.4 Have You Talked with Your Child About Attending College?
Source: 2005 CAI Parent Survey

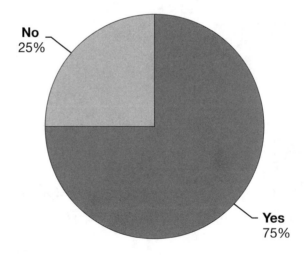

Figure 6.5 Have You Talked with Someone About How to Apply to a College?
Source: 2005 CAI Parent Survey

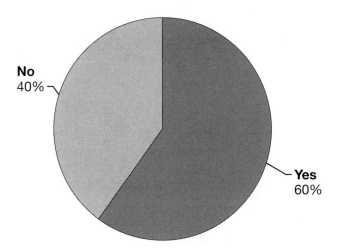

Figure 6.6 Have You Talked with Anyone About Financial Assistance for College?

Source: 2005 CAI Parent Survey

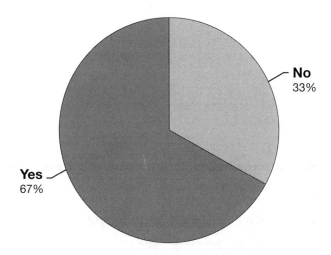

Figure 6.7 Do You Feel You Have Enough Information about How to Prepare Your Child for College?

Source: 2005 CAI Parent Survey

Familiarity with college entrance requirements also increased substantially during the 2004–2005 school year.

- Whereas in 2004 year only 45 percent of parents reported being familiar with the entrance requirements for a four-year college, in 2005, 76 percent said that they were familiar with the requirements. This represented a gain of 31 percentage points.
- The same applied for community colleges. In 2004, only 36 percent of parents responded positively when asked about their familiarity with the entrance requirements. In 2005, 67 percent reported positively about their knowledge about this higher education institution, a gain of 31 percentage points.

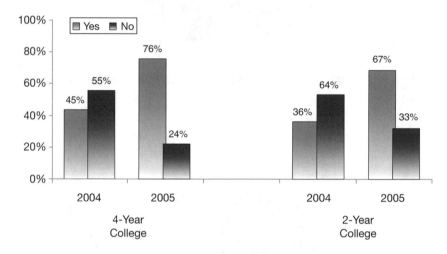

Figure 6.8 Are You Familiar with College Entrance Requirements?

Source: 2005 CAI Parent Survey

PORTFOLIO BUILDING 6.1

Design a Parent Involvement Plan for a School

Engage community partners in the development of a Parent Involvement Plan.

1. What were the lessons learned from the GEAR UP programs that will shape the plan for parental involvement?
2. How can you apply elements of the Comer Process to your plan?
3. What types of professional development should be made available to the school staff to support this plan?
4. Describe the professional development workshops for parents to assist them in engaging in their child's academic and social progress?

LESSONS LEARNED

Overall, the majority of the parents (91 percent) were either very satisfied (60 percent) or satisfied (31 percent) with the GEAR UP program. Clearly, the programs efforts at increasing parents' knowledge about and attitudes toward college paid off. However, while this information on parental involvement in the college process is positive, it was the goal of the GEAR UP program to get parents involved in the college process when their children were in the earlier grades. This did not happen and proved to be one of the most challenging efforts for the program staff. To involve parents earlier in the college process, educators can do the following.

1. Reconfiguring the Parent–School Relationship

Schools usually dictate their relationship with parents. Often, parents are expected to attend pre-arranged meetings or to participate in activities that they were not involved in planning. When the role of parents as social participants is transformed to academic partners, only then can we see more parents being involved in improving the academic achievement of children. This change in mindset is even more imperative when schools engage in preparing students for their postsecondary careers.

2. Encourage Parents to Talk about College with Their Children

Even if parents did not attend college, they should have regular conversations about their children's postsecondary plans. To support this effort, high schools can host college choice and financial aid workshops targeted to middle school and ninth grade high school families.

3. Ensure that Students Take the Appropriate Courses in High School

High school educators must ensure that students take the appropriate courses if they are to enter and succeed in college. Typically, there should be a plan to take, at least, algebra, geometry, two years of a foreign language, science, history, and English. However, students who enroll in a rigorous course of study in high school are much better prepared to succeed in college. Parents must be made aware of this and support their children's effort to take rigorous courses, including Advanced Placement courses, pre-calculus, calculus, and physics. Also, possessing computer skills is a decided advantage for college, as well as mastering speech and debating techniques.

4. Have Written Policies on Parent Involvement

Parents' attendance at the GEAR UP college preparatory workshops offered in the ninth and tenth grade were poorly attended. Schools can instill written policies that show parent involvement as an important component of the college preparatory and high school graduation process. School district leaders can support school policy by providing funding for resources for college preparatory workshops and materials.

5. Develop a "Parents as Partners" Approach

When parents are part of the planning process of school programs they are more likely to be involved in their child's education. Early college preparatory programs such as GEAR UP usually organize activities about college as early as middle schools. Since attending high school is a logical step toward college access, activities bringing middle schools, high schools, colleges, and parents together to plan for student success benefit families in a meaningful way. GEAR UP established a governance structure that included Site Planning Teams that met monthly to plan and provide feedback about the program. This structure allowed for cross-dialogue among school staff, parents, site counselors, public librarians, and social workers. The Site Planning Team made recommendations regarding the customization of the GEAR UP activities and the needs of the cohort and included the voice of the parent.

6. Dealing with Families' Immigration Status

Many members of the GEAR UP cohort were first generation immigrants representing Queens county, the most diverse community in the United States. GEAR UP attempted to conduct several Citizenship Application Workshops with the objective of alerting parents on the importance of obtaining legal residency so that their children are positioned to apply for financial aid. The workshops also provided assistance to those pursuing citizenship through referrals to special community programs. The attendance was abysmal. It became clear that parents wanted a separation between school and their immigration status. GEAR UP's leaders abandoned this initiative.

7. Matching Programs with the Most Appropriate Partners

The community partners, Queens Child Guidance, and the Queens Borough Public Library, were collaborators in many of the activities offered to parents of the student cohort. These organizations had a history of serving this constituent, worked with adult learners, and, in many ways, were better suited than schools to organizing workshops for families on coping skills, adolescent development, reading and writing, and citizenship.

CONCLUSION

Despite all best intentions by school leaders, effective parental involvement in education is the most challenging aspect of school improvement. Nevertheless, it is an area that must be addressed by embracing parents as partners and engaging community organizations. While schools cannot do it alone, there must be a sense of what they can do to improve parental involvement while recognizing there may be areas beyond their capacity. Effective partnerships are built when partners recognize these differences.

One key constituent in creating opportunities for parents and schools to work together to improve the academic experiences of students is the private foundation. The following chapter explores the connection of this constituent with school reform and provides samples of programs that existed primarily due to this funding source.

CHAPTER 7

Private Foundations in School/College Partnerships

INTRODUCTION

Private foundations have been at the forefront of the education reform debate for decades. Whether they are providing seed money for new ideas or supporting long-term initiatives, these institutions are key players in addressing issues facing our schools. This chapter takes the reader through the inner workings of grant-makers from understanding how grants are made; reading program descriptions; viewing actual grants; and writing an actual grant proposal. Additionally, readers develop budgets and explore how a school leader can leverage resources using grants to fill the gaps in services provided to schools.

Educational Leadership Constituent Council (ELCC) Standards

This chapter meets the needs of advanced academic programs in preparation for educational leadership:

> Standard 3.0: Candidates who complete the program are educational leaders who have the knowledge and ability to promote the success of all students by managing the organization, operations, and resources in a way that promotes a safe, efficient, and effective learning environment.

> Standard 4.0: Candidates who complete the program are educational leaders who have the knowledge and ability to promote the success of all students by collaborating with families and other community members, responding to diverse community interests and needs, and mobilizing community resources.

> Standard 6.0: Candidates who complete the program are educational leaders who have the knowledge and ability to promote the success of all students by understanding, responding to, and influencing the larger political, social, economic, legal, and cultural context.

> (National Policy Board for Education Administration, 2002)

★   ★   ★

With the rising costs of education and research, funds from private foundations to educational institutions has become increasingly more important. Private foundations in the United States control over $628 billion in assets (National Center for Charitable Statistics, 2007) and made more than $44 billion in charitable contributions in 2007 (Foundation Center, 2007). Education continues to receive the largest share of grant dollars, with elementary and secondary schools receiving 30 percent of the share. Private foundations are responding to what has become a pressing need in K–12 education throughout the United States. However, for some inexplicable reasons, school personnel seldom consider the opportunity that private foundation funding can provide for innovative programs. Conversely, higher education officers recognize that state and municipal funding only cover obvious and routine costs. Unfortunately, there is no provision for seed money or for funding new ideas. Many new programs or practices get their start through application to private foundations, but many school leaders are unfamiliar with these procedures.

CREATING MIDDLE COLLEGE HIGH SCHOOL

Middle College High School at LaGuardia Community College was funded with foundation funding from inception to opening day and later for national replication. With grants of $95,000 from the Carnegie Corporation and $175,000 from the Fund for the Improvement of Post Secondary Education, the originators of Middle College responded to a charge from the City University of New York to do something to keep adolescents in high school and attract them to college (Carter, 2004). In March 1971, LaGuardia Community College proposed a new educational concept, Middle College, to provide an integrated high school–college program directed to the needs of urban high school youth. The Carnegie Corporation had published a small monograph on school–college collaboration in 1969 that suggested some academic coordination between secondary schools and community colleges. Unfortunately, no branch of the educational spectrum of kindergarten through college offers any funds for innovation so a dean of the college, having read the Carnegie Report, initiated an idea for a new educational institution: a "middle college" that would combine the usual high school years with the two years of the community college built on the college campus. The goal was to improve the high school attendance rate and attract the under achieving student to college admission.

The school had its educational roots in Simon Rock's Early College, which was viewed by its creator, Elizabeth B. Hall, as a model for public education. The Carnegie Commission on Higher Education in a 1973 report, *Continuity and Discontinuity*, recommended "middle colleges" as an idea to improve the relationship between schools and colleges:

> [These schools] . . . might well appeal to a sizable number of students and institutions today and provide an excellent answer to curriculum overlap and discontinuity between school and college. The middle college concept should be seriously explored by large numbers of private liberal arts colleges.
>
> (Carnegie Commission, 1973)

The Commission also saw friction between faculty from the schools and the college often as a result of a perceived distrust, "academic elitualism" of the schools and lack of intellectualism in the schools. This was the report, along with "the works of G. Stanley Hall, Leonard Koos, Ralph Tyler, and the Four-School Committee on reconfiguring secondary and higher education" (Wechsler, 2001, p. 29) that the chief designer of the school, Janet Lieberman, used to propose a middle college aimed at at-risk students. Together with LaGuardia Community College, Joseph Shenker, and other colleagues, Lieberman took three years to develop a plan that was an adaptation of the original Simon's Rock Early College that awarded associate degrees to high school students. Lieberman had another idea:

> instead of designing a four-year middle college for students with other options, she asked if a deft adaptation of the idea might increase the aspirations and abilities of students with little chance for postsecondary education, or who even were "at-risk" of dropping out of high school.
>
> (Wechsler, 2001, p. 19)

While Simon's Rock catered to average and above-average students, Middle College focused on a group that had little chance for postsecondary education—the "at-risk" student. The logical sponsor was a New York City community college, particularly one that was new and committed to working with non-traditional students (Wechsler, 2001). A new policy introduced by the City University of New York, open admissions policy, and a new resolve for colleges to work closely with the public high schools, encouraged the designers to forge ahead with the plan.

In March 1971, LaGuardia Community College proposed a new educational concept, Middle College, to provide an integrated high school–college program directed to the needs of urban high school youth. The following needs were identified:

1. Large numbers of underachieving students drop out of high school lacking adequate skills and life goals.
2. Many high school graduates who enter the City University of New York (CUNY) via the open admission policy were not equipped to study at the college level.
3. Many urban youths who complete high school were unprepared for the world of work.

(LaGCC Middle College Plan, 1973)

It is important to understand that innovation requires planning, and planning takes money so the first approach to educational reform is money for planning, and the obvious donor was the foundation that had already studied the problem of the school–college relationship. After many sessions with the New York City Board [now Department] of Education central office and regional superintendents to explain the concept and to receive tentative approval, the designer of the program had acquired permission to apply for funding. A letter of application went to five foundations: the Carnegie Corporation was the one that responded and a site visit was arranged where the program officer toured the community college and met with the president, students, and faculty. The Carnegie Corporation grant to Middle College covered planning year salaries, faculty curriculum developer, and a counselor. It is a truism in fundraising that once the institution has acquired the initial funding, it is easier to get additional money. The Middle College concept received funding a year later from the Fund for the Improvement of Secondary Education, and in later years from the Ford Foundation, the Gates Foundation, and other sponsors.

STRATEGIES TO DEVELOPING AND SUBMITTING PROPOSALS FOR FUNDING

Success in acquiring funding requires a careful study of the existing sources, a multi-faceted approach, and a thorough but simple explanation of the planning process. Educators frequently have elaborate excuses for not applying for foundation funding, but experience illustrates that foundations are seeking good ideas, which are practical and achievable with goals that match those of the foundation. The following serves as a guide to educators seeking foundation funding of programs to improve the experiences of students as they prepare to complete high school and progress onto college.

1. Conduct a Needs Assessment of the School

School leaders should conduct a Needs Assessment (see Portfolio Building 1.1) of their schools before deciding on the proposal.

2. Research Potential Funders

An essential part of the proposal process is to think creatively in researching and matching the mission of the proposed program and needs of the school to the types of programs supported by the foundation. The following exercise allows the reader to consider which foundation best suits the needs of the school.

REFLECTIVE EXERCISE 7.1

Selecting a Foundation

How do you select a foundation that best matches the needs of your school? Review some of the foundations below.

Organization: Bill & Melinda Gates Foundation
Grant Program(s): Early Learning, High Schools and Scholarships
URL: www.gatesfoundation.org

Profile: The foundation has invested more than $4 billion in scholarships and building high-quality, high-performing schools and systems, supporting more than 2,600 schools.

Organization: The Eli and Edythe Broad Foundation
Grant Program(s): $2 Million Broad Prize for Urban Education, The Broad Super-intendents Academy, The Broad Residency in Urban Education, numerous grants in K–12 urban public education.
URL: www.broadfoundation.org

Profile: Since 2000, the foundation has invested more than $400 million to improve student achievement in dozens of urban areas by developing strong leaders, efficient school district practices, professional teaching conditions, competition, and best practices. Each year, it also awards the $2 million Broad Prize for Urban Education to large urban American school districts that demonstrate the greatest improvement in student achievement and reduction in income and ethnic achievement gaps.

Organization: The IBM International Foundation
Grant Program(s): Reading Companion, ¡TradúceloAhora!, KidSmart
URL: www.ibm.com/ibm/ibmgives/grants

Profile: IBM's primary mission is to improve teaching and learning in public schools through innovative technology. Since the launch of Reading Companion and ¡TradúceloAhora! in 2006, it has invested millions of dollars to provide Reading Companion voice recognition software to more than 750 schools and nonprofit organizations worldwide and free automatic translation software to more than 600 schools and nonprofit organizations in the United States and Latin America. The KidSmart program has been used by more than 100,000 teachers and millions of students worldwide during the last decade.

Organization: The Intel Foundation
Grant Program(s): Intel Education Grants, Volunteer Matching Grants
URL: www.intel.com/community/grant.htm

Profile: The Intel Foundation contributes millions of dollars annually to schools, educational institutions, communities, and selected nonprofits where the company operates major facilities. Over the past decade, Intel has invested significantly more than $1 billion in cash and in-kind contributions worldwide.

Organization: The Lowe's Charitable and Educational Foundation
Grant Program(s): Lowe's Toolbox for Education
URL: http://toolboxforeducation.com/

Profile: In 2008, the foundation contributed more than $4.1 million to schools in all 50 states. Since 2006, it has donated nearly $15 million to more than 3,500 K–12 schools, offering opportunities to 1.5 million schoolchildren and districts for enhanced learning, safe recreation, and parent interaction.

Organization: The NEA Foundation
Grant Program(s): Green Grants, Student Achievement Grants, Learning & Leadership Grants, and Closing the Achievement Gaps Initiative
URL: www.neafoundation.org

Profile: Over the past decade, the foundation has awarded more than 2,000 individual and team grants to public educators, totaling over $5.9 million. This year, it's targeting green grants and those that promote science, technology, engineering, mathematics teaching and learning. Closing the Achievement Gap grants, offered by invitation only, also create local partnerships that help improve achievement rates for poor and minority students. The foundation's website offers an instructional video that guides educators through the online application process.

Organization: Staples Foundation for Learning (SFFL)
Grant Program(s): Staples Foundation for Learning
URL: www.staplesfoundation.org

Profile: Staples Foundation for Learning was launched in August 2002. Since its inception, it has contributed more than $14 million in grants to nonprofit organizations across the United States.

Organization: The Toshiba America Foundation (TAF)
Grant Program(s): The TAF provides grants to K–12 math and science teachers. Each fall, K-6 teachers can receive up to $1,000 while grants of up to $5,000 are offered to 7–12 teachers throughout the year. Grants exceeding $5,000 for grades 7–12 teachers are also available twice a year—applications due Feb. 1 and Aug. 1.
URL: www.taf.toshiba.com

Profile: The TAF's mission is to promote quality science and mathematics education in U.S. schools. Grants are made for hands-on, inquiry-based, classroom projects designed by either individual teachers or small teams of teachers.

Organization: The Wallace Foundation
Grant Program(s): Leadership for Learning
URL: www.wallacefoundation.org

Profile: As one of the largest, private, nonprofit supporters of public education, Wallace has invested nearly $530 million over the past 16 years in school improvement efforts. Since 2000, the foundation has focused on strengthening education leadership to improve student achievement. It commissions research and offers grants to school districts in 22 states and State Departments of Education to develop more effective leadership policies and practices.

Organization: The Walton Family Foundation
Grant Program(s): School District Improvements and other initiatives
URL: www.waltonfamilyfoundation.org

Profile: In 2007, the foundation made grants and program-related investments totaling more than $241 million. Its K–12 educational reform initiatives support four goals: to increase the number of children who have access to public charter schools; to empower low-income students to attend private schools; to improve student achievement in specific urban schools districts (Albany, NY, Columbus, Ohio, Milwaukee, Wisconsin, and Washington, D.C.), and to raise the performance of Arkansas schools while preparing students for postsecondary education and industry careers.

Source: *Money Makers: Districts that land the big grants get to pursue the best projects.* By Marty Weil.

3. Analyze a Request for a Proposal (RFP)

A request for a proposal is an invitation by funders to submit a plan for supplying service to individuals or institutions. Educators seeking funding for a specific program can use the RFP as guide for brainstorming with partners and for the actual writing of the proposal (see Portfolio Building 7.1).

4. Prepare to Write the Proposal

After the initial research of possible foundations are made, the following questions must be addressed and serve as a checklist for writing the proposal:

*   What is the project's goal?
*   How do the goals of the proposal relate to the school's structure and vision/mission?
*   What is the sponsoring organization?
*   What special qualifications does the organization bring to this project?
*   What other organizations are involved, if any? How will they contribute to the work?
*   How does the proposed project relate to the applicant organization's mission?
*   Whom will this project serve?

PORTFOLIO BUILDING 7.1

Writing a Grant Proposal

The purpose of this project is to develop a proposal for funding to private foundations for your school/district. You will utilize the School Needs Assessment Profile and the Key Constituency Chart developed earlier.

Who Is Involved?

The Partnership projects must be based on a partnership (new or existing) between:

- at least one degree-granting institution of higher education
- at least one school district on behalf of one or more schools each with a seventh grade and the high school
- at least two additional community organizations, such as businesses, professional associations, community-based organizations, faith-based organizations, family organizations, parent groups, state or local agencies, philanthropic organizations, religious groups, and other public or private organizations.

Program Activities

Partnership projects are required to provide early college preparation and awareness services through mentoring, counseling—including financial aid counseling and information about opportunities for financial aid, and activities and information regarding fostering and improving parent involvement in preparing students for college, college admissions and achievement tests, and college application procedures—outreach, and supportive services for participating students.

Evaluation of Program Performance

Your proposal must explain your project's overall objectives. These objectives must be clear and measurable, and be outcomes-oriented (i.e., related to achieving specific, desirable results of your services for participants) rather than process-oriented. For example:

Objective 1: Increase the academic performance and preparation for post-secondary education for students.

Objective 2: Increase the rate of high school graduation and participation in postsecondary education for students.

Objective 3: Increase students' and their families' knowledge of postsecondary education options, preparation, and financing.

Selection Criteria

The selection criteria are as follows:

1. Need for the project
2. Quality of project resources
3. Quality of project personnel
4. Quality of the management plan
5. Quality of the project evaluation
6. Adequacy of resources.

Modeled after the GEAR UP (Gaining Early Awareness for Undergraduate Programs) proposal, U.S. Department of Education, 2000.

- How long is the projected program going to exist?
- Describe the significance of the proposal.
- List some goals and specify how they will be met.
- Write the objectives.
- Relate the activities to the objectives. Write activities that will accomplish the objectives.
- What are the intended outcomes, and how will the project achieve them?
- What is the geographic scope of the proposed project?
- Why is this project important to pursue at this time?
- What is the total cost of the project? What amount do you seek from the Foundation, for what period of time? What resources will others provide?
- Assess the school's mission, organization, and resources and discuss with co-planners or, if identified, partners.
- Create a budget. Specify line items: personnel, activities, equipment, direct and indirect costs, and matching funds (see Appendix K for a sample budget).
- Design an evaluation plan.
- Discuss the role of external evaluators.
- Plan a management structure for the project.
- Think ahead about sustaining the project when funding ends.

5. Bring the Partners together to Plan

Whether planning meetings are called by a school leader or a college administrator, it is an important part of the proposal process. The first meeting may not necessarily mean that all the "right" partners are identified, but serves to match the school's needs with those of the partners' and is an opportunity for participants to commit personnel, ideas, and resources to develop the proposal and prepare for anticipated funding. This is the first in a series of many meetings and the above checklist of questions can serve as talking points for these meetings. The following agenda highlights the main areas for consideration for a proposal to fund a collaborative program (see Box 7.1).

6. Organize by Institutional Need and Capacity

The information below describes various discussion items for the meeting of administrators described above from the school system and community-based organizations who want to submit a proposal for a Community Partnership Proposal to prepare students for college success. Two groups were formed, educators and community-based organizations, and each addressed the following questions.

Guided Questions for the Middle School/High School/College Group

1. How will these suggested ideas and activities improve the academic performance of your students?
2. How can the number of students participating in academically rigorous courses (e.g., the Community Partnership Guidelines specifically highlight eighth grade Algebra) be increased?
3. Are you in the process of developing smaller learning environments? If so, how would Community Partnership activities operate within the structure you are creating?
4. Community Partnership targets the entire seventh grade and ninth grade cohort. Of students in the cohort, where is the greatest academic need so that the Community Partnership can insure that students are transitioning to high school, graduating in four years, and entering college well-prepared?
5. Will the activities proposed be helpful to your students?
6. If we cannot fund them all out of the Community Partnership proposed budget, to which would you assign the greatest priority?
7. How would you integrate these ideas and activities into your school day? What would you prefer be done after school? On Saturdays?
8. What benefits will such a network bring to your school and what else would you like to see incorporated into this plan?
9. Are there other ideas/activities you would like to suggest?
10. Once students have transitioned onto the high school, how will the intermediate school sustain those special classes, resources, and activities that have proved to be effective?

Guided Questions for Community Partners/College Group

1. What possibilities do you see for your role in this proposed plan of activities and objectives?
2. Looking back at the activities you have done with the participating schools, what should be continued? What new activities should be considered?
3. In what other ways can your organization support student achievement?
4. Do you have this capacity and experience?
5. What are the costs involved?

BOX 7.1   Meeting to Develop a Community Partnership Proposal

Thursday, March 10, 2012
The James-George Hotel
9:00 a.m.–3:30 p.m.

AGENDA

9:00–9:30 a.m.	Welcome, Introductions, and Our Purposes Today
	School Principals, College Personnel, and Community Partners asked to say a few words about how collaborative programs have made a difference/been useful to their institutions
9:30–9:45 a.m.	Brief Summary of the proposed Community Partnership
	Guidelines
	Focus on mission, approach, kinds of activities permitted, in-kind budget, and per student budget
	Key considerations in developing a winning proposal
9:45–10:00 a.m.	Reflections on the Community Partnership Evaluation:
	What the Data Says
	What were the strengths? What were the weaknesses? (Academic Change, College Awareness, Professional Development, Sustainability)
10:00–10:20 a.m.	Suggested Proposal Priorities and Activities
10:25–11:30 a.m.	Small Group Reactions and Discussion
	a. Middle School/High School/College
	b. Middle School/High School/College
	c. Middle School/High School/College
	d. Community Partners/College
11:30 a.m.–12:15 p.m.	Sharing Feedback and Reactions to the Proposed Plan
12:30–1:00 p.m.	LUNCH
1:00–2:00 p.m.	Professional Development
2:00–2:45 p.m.	Management Plan
2:45–3:15 p.m.	Wrap Up
	Next Steps and Deadlines for
	Data and Forms
	In-kind budget narrative

Guided Questions for Professional Development Plan

1. What topics should be emphasized?
2. How can Community Partnership more closely relate professional development to classroom practice and outcomes?
3. Should technology professional development be included, and if so, how will the schools support it?

Guided Questions for Management Plan

1. How can we insure that administrators and teachers are well-informed about the Community Partnership?
2. What is the most effective mechanism for insuring discussion of emerging issues, planning the year's (or quarter's) activities, problem-solving, and brainstorming?
3. What management structure should be used?

Linking Program Objectives to Activities

A program's objectivities are non-effectual if they cannot be carried out by meaningful, evaluative activities. Community Partnership X is a fictitious collaboration of schools, college, parents, business, and community-based organizations. A proposal was developed based on three objectives:

Objective 1: Increase the academic performance and preparation for postsecondary education of students.

Objective 2: Increase the rate of high school graduation and participation in post-secondary education for students.

Objective 3: Increase student and family knowledge of postsecondary options, preparation, and financing.

To fulfill these objectives, the school principal looked at prior successful activities to see if they could be expanded or adjusted to meet the requirements of the proposal. The following were activities geared toward preparing students for high school graduation and college success and are guided by the objectives identified below.

Objective 1: Increase the Academic Performance and Preparation for Postsecondary Education of Students

In School Activities

To meet this objective, Community Partnership X concentrated on activities that increased proficiency in reading, writing, and mathematics. These include the following:

- *The Welcome Academy*: This is a cross-institutional learning community that paired college and intermediate school faculty in an in-depth exploration of a theme. Targeted to intermediate-level ESL students, who have the greatest difficulty passing the Regents examinations, the Welcome Academy provided continuous instruction over the academic year and engaged faculty in giving students feedback on their writing and developing writing and reading assignments that emerge from intermediate and high school course content.

- *Young Authors*: This unique program brought together the public library and students during the school day with authors. The program is offered in middle and in high schools during the Fall and Spring semester. It is implemented in collaboration with the public library, which purchased the selected books for students to read, and thoroughly discuss within selected English and other classes. Students met the author at their library and learned about his/her experiences as a writer. In conjunction with the Young Authors activities, the Public Library, and Community Partnership X initiated another activity, cross-age tutoring, which enlisted students to read to younger students once a month either in the same school, a nearby elementary school, or the neighborhood library.

- *Mini-Seminars*: Mini-seminars were held during the Fall and Spring semesters in the middle and high schools involved in Community Partnership X. Mini-seminars engaged college, middle school, and high school faculty in joint planning around a topic of interest that was developed in 5–7 sessions. The school faculty role was to prepare classes for the college faculty's visits through preliminary readings, writing assignments, discussions, and opportunities to raise questions. In some cases, a mini-seminar culminated in a trip to the college or a museum or business so that students can apply what they have learned. These seminars not only exposed students to college faculty, but also began a dialogue that enhanced and enriched course content, introduced students to ideas and topics not raised in the basic curriculum, and encouraged them to think about college options. Topics included, but are not limited to, the following: Developing A Sophisticated Reader And Story Ownership; Career Preparation: What Do I Want to Be When I Grow Up?; Critical Thinking across the Curriculum; Reading and Writing Skills Assessment; and Theater and Communication.

After-School Activities

- *Peer Tutoring/Peer Mentoring*: This activity targeted students who were operating on the "margins"—they were not performing well academically and may be exhibiting behavior problems as well. Such students in the cohort were referred to this activity by a guidance counselor, teacher, or a social worker. Peer tutoring/mentoring was provided weekly for two hours and consisted of 45 minutes of tutoring/homework assistance, a snack, and another 45-minute period devoted to a mentoring activity. While many of the weekly topics emerged from the experiences and concerns of the students, the aim of this activity was to strengthen student participants' analytical and interpersonal and conflict resolution skills, enabling them to become better planners for their futures. The peer tutors/mentors were college students or high school students from the feeder high schools. Peer tutors/mentors were trained social workers who also supervised them at the schools.

- *Book Club*: One book club for the seventh grade cohort in the middle schools is planned. Social workers will identify pertinent issues surrounding the emotional and social needs of young people and will partner with a literacy specialist and/or a public librarian to bring students together to read and analyze two to three books each semester.

- *Eighth Grade Prep*: One class per intermediate school for eighth grade English Language Arts Prep—either after-school or on Saturday—was offered. Students were referred by teachers or guidance personnel as well as it being open to all students who wish to attend. Conducted by a middle school faculty member for four sessions, each for two hours, students were prepared for the English Language Arts and Mathematics Exams administered to all eighth graders.

- *College for Me Program*: Credit-bearing college courses, collaboratively developed by high school and college faculty, were offered to students in the eleventh and twelfth grades. In addition to these classes, College for Me offered a Saturday Theater Program, and e-Choose, an opportunity for 150 tenth graders and over 400 eleventh and twelfth graders to participate in a virtual community consisting of their classmates, the college adviser, a College for Me high school faculty member, a college faculty member, and a former college student. Through assignments and dialogues on Blackboard, students explore the college selection and admission process.

- *College Connection*: College Connection enabled high school juniors and seniors to take college courses on-campus in the late afternoon weekday hours and on Saturdays on a tuition-waived basis. New students also participate in a Mentor Hour designed to expose students to resources at the College—especially the library—to the role of the course syllabus in a college course and to the importance of time management.

- *College Board*: Beginning with a yearly customized program for the cohort, its teachers and parents, the College Board offered an array of services to the cohort beginning in the seventh grade through the twelfth. My Road is the Web-based tool that enables students to explore majors, careers, and colleges. It included a validated personality test that provides a detailed report of the student's personality type that the student can use to explore careers and majors that fit his or her personality and strengths.

- *CollegeEd*: CollegeEd empowered students through grade-appropriate knowledge and information, as well as through self-exploration and skill building and was available to the entire cohort from grades 7 through 12. Teachers were trained by the College Board to utilize the materials into their specific subject area. Parent workshops provided a background on the college application process, course requirements, and academic planning, as well as financial aid and scholarship possibilities. The Preliminary SAT Scoring Service (PSSS), a testing service administered to tenth graders, which provided comprehensive, personalized feedback on academic skills and access to the skills needed for the SAT test. Also, the Preliminary SAT/National Merit Scholarship Qualifying Test was a diagnostic assessment for all eleventh grade students that gives them practice for the SAT and helps identify their academic strengths and weaknesses—giving the students, their parents, and their teachers an understanding of the instructional focus they need in order to prepare for success in college.

Saturday Activities

- *Saturday Enrichment Classes*: These enrichment classes were interdisciplinary, engaging students in reading, an examination of American culture, utilizing internet research and the computer lab. High school students attended college classes. Examples of classes included Adventures in Literature and the Arts; American Culture and Theater; Immigration and Theater; American Culture and Dance; Mathematics and Jazz.
- *Regents Prep*: Classes were offered to the cohort when in high school according to the schedule of Regents examinations, i.e., Math A (tenth grade); English Language Arts (eleventh grade); Global Studies (tenth grade); Science (tenth grade); U.S. History and Government (twelfth grade). Each of the five Regents Prep met for three two-hour sessions.

Summer Activities

- *Summer Program*: A summer program for 100 students, four weeks, five days from 9:00 a.m.–2:30 p.m. was offered at the college with Fridays as trip days. The theme-based summer program included reading, writing, and mathematics activities, academic and college counseling. Programs included Exploring Your City; Leadership, which culminated in a trip to Washington, D.C.; and a Summer Internship Experience.
- *Summer Youth Employment Program (SYEP)*: The purpose of the SYEP is to provide youth with summer employment and educational experiences that build on their individual strengths and incorporate youth development principles. These principles included engaging the talents and interests of youth, developing their skills and competencies, and providing positive adult role models. Students applied directly to this program, which is funded by the Department of Youth and Community Development.
- *Other Summer Opportunities*: Weekend and week-long camp activities offered through State programs.

Objective 2: Increase the Rate of High School Graduation and Participation in Postsecondary Education for Students

Improving academic performance is clearly related to increasing the rate of high school graduation. In order to graduate high school, students must accumulate high school academic course credit and pass the required state examinations. Community Partnership X paid considerable attention to preparing students carefully for high school so that they were knowledgeable of high school program options and expectations, and prepared to make a smooth transition to the ninth grade.

- *The Community Partnership X Network*: The high school admissions process in many large urban cities forces students to submit large numbers of applications for admission in many high schools. One of the unexpected effects of this process, however, has been to weaken the "feeder" relationship between intermediate schools and the zoned high schools. It is difficult for students to understand their options and make informed choices. As a result, many students are enrolled in high schools that do not suit their needs, making it more difficult for them to persist and/or meet the graduation requirements. The Community Partnership X Network increased familiarity with the high schools and involved high school and middle school faculty in the joint development of special seminars and enrichment activities scheduled into the seventh and eighth grade school day. These activities were centered on the educational options that each of the high schools offer. Through seminars, students were introduced to high school faculty, who co-taught these seminars. They also made several visits to all of the high schools. Community Partnership X also held workshops for parents, explaining the high school admissions process to them, and hosting evening visits to them as well.

- *Peer Mentors:* In order to promote the entry of a greater number of cohort students into postsecondary education, the Community Partnership X team provided college counseling in school, after school, Saturdays, and during the summer. Counselors met with students regularly every year, and intensively in the eleventh and twelfth grades, to discuss students' plans and refer students to appropriate Community Partnership X services and the College Adviser, with whom the Community Partnership X on-site team coordinated closely. In addition, in the junior and senior year, Community Partnership X offered two evening Financial Aid Workshops per semester for parents and students, and also provided assistance with completion of the FAFSA.

Additional Saturday Activities Offered in the Tenth, Eleventh, and Twelfth grades

SAT Prep Workshops, A College Conference, College Fairs (Community Partnership X's staff team accompanied students and parents to local college fairs), and six Senior Year Workshops assisted in the completion of the FAFSA, financial aid, and the college essay.

Other activities designed to foster entry into postsecondary education included day visits to colleges from the eighth to the twelfth grades. These included college prep workshops; symposia around topics that have been studied in high school classes; community college and senior college samplers; visits that highlight particular careers (e.g., Allied Health); and the accompanying educational programs. Students had an opportunity to interact with college students and faculty, to tour facilities, observe classes and laboratories in session.

Objective 3: Increase Student and Family Knowledge of Postsecondary Options, Preparation, and Financing

To increase both students and families' knowledge of these options, requirements, and financial resources, the following activities were implemented.

- *21st Century Scholar Certificates*: All students received 21st Century Scholar Certificates, which provided them and their parents with information on their eligibility for financial aid.

- *Parent Workshops*: Community Partnership X's work with parents began in the Spring semester of the eighth grade. The program staff worked with the central office appointed Parent Coordinator at each school and the College Board to provide workshops centered on college preparation, college choice, and financial aid. Program staff organized college visits and seminars for parents in the ninth and tenth grade, enlarging these efforts as the cohort moved into their last two years of high school.
- *Resource File*: Working together, Community Partnership X partners coordinated and published a Resource File for the cohort's parents, which provided information on high school programs and special educational options available at each of our partner high schools, and high school graduation requirements. The file also detailed the services and programs for parents and students, which are offered by Exeter College and our Community Partnership X partners.
- *Workshops for Immigrant Families*: Community Partnership X called upon staff in Exeter's financial aid office, the Princess Borough Public Library, and local community-based organizations to provide workshops for parents on the importance of obtaining legal residency so that their children are positioned to apply for financial aid.

7. Link Activities to Program Staffing

A major component of successful collaborative programs is the hiring of skilled personnel with job functions that support the program goal of creating effective partnerships. Detailed descriptions of the roles of the project director, assistant director, guidance counselor, and other program staff are listed in Appendix J.

8. Develop a Budget

A budget is a major component of a grant proposal and serves as a financial plan for the proposed program. It outlines the grant activities and illustrates how the grant will be conducted and managed. A good budget must be complete and provide details on all the costs of personnel, supplies, and program activities. A sample budget is provided in Appendix K.

CONCLUSION

Many innovations in education began with funding from private foundations. With diminishing funding coming from federal, state, and local government agencies, it is imperative that school leaders seek other sources of supporting special program at their schools. For example, the Gates Foundation has funded several early college high schools that are located on public college campuses and graduate high school students with associate degrees. These schools offer students a regular high school curriculum through the tenth grade, high school and college courses in the eleventh and twelfth grades, and a final year of full-time college. This attests to the importance of private foundations and outside funding of collaborative programs that allows public funded institutions to be innovative, flexible, and to realize their dreams. The challenge, however, is the continuation of these initiatives when private funding ends and the commitment of higher education and the school system to institutionalize these programs.

Central to the development of a grant proposal is the selection of key personnel who will ensure that the project goals are implemented. The following chapter introduces the reader to the classroom teacher and support staff who are crucial to the success of grant-funded programs. These personnel have access to the students who are in need of the grant services and prove to be influential in selecting and retaining program participants.

CHAPTER 8

The Importance of the Classroom Teacher and Support Staff in Collaborative Programs

LEARNING OBJECTIVES

After reading this chapter you will be able to:

1. Employ effective strategies to promote student success
2. Distinguish the various needs of at-risk students
3. Prepare at-risk students academically and socially to progress successfully through high school
4. Engage school staff to work in diverse educational settings

INTRODUCTION

One of the most promising strategies for improving schools is giving teachers more control of schools and of what occurs in the classroom. However, no promising changes can come about without the support of the teacher. Whatever the policy, no amount of "legislative learning" will improve the schools unless teachers are ready for it. This chapter focuses on the experiences of teachers, administrators, social workers, and guidance counselors who participated in a study of Middle College High School and the GEAR UP program, both housed at LaGuardia Community College. It also introduces the reader to strategies that address the needs of the teacher, counselor, and the student serving as models for school leaders who wish to engage their staff in collaborative efforts.

Educational Leadership Constituent Council (ELCC) Standards

This chapter meets the needs of advanced academic programs in preparation for educational leadership:

> Standard 2.0: Candidates who complete the program are educational leaders who have the knowledge and ability to promote the success of all students by promoting a positive school culture, providing an effective instructional program, applying best practice to student learning, and designing comprehensive professional growth plans for staff.

> Standard 4.0: Candidates who complete the program are educational leaders who have the knowledge and ability to promote the success of all students by collaborating with families and other community members, responding to diverse community interests and needs, and mobilizing community resources.
>
> (National Policy Board for Educational Administration, 2002)

★   ★   ★

Sadly, teachers are often blamed for the problems in the education system. When students fail, it is the teachers' fault. The results, released in the annual Metropolitan Life Survey of the American Teacher, show that the morale among our teachers is the lowest it has been in 20 years. Discourse around linking teacher evaluations to student test scores, coupled to cuts in student support systems have resulted in large numbers of the nation's teachers feeling demoralized. With so many frequent attacks on the teaching profession, it is not surprising that almost 33 percent are prepared to leave the profession after only five years of employment (Metropolitan Life, 2012).

The assault of our teachers by critics misses an important point in the education reform dialogue: teachers and counselors are central to the academic and social success of students. The empowerment of teachers is essential to school reform. Researcher Paul Terry, in an article entitled *Empowering Teachers as Leaders*, claims that a successful school is one where the leader produces an environment conducive to empowerment and applies the "creative energy of teachers toward constant improvement." He continues: "Empowerment translates into teacher leadership and exemplifies a paradigm shift with the decisions made by those working most closely with students rather than those at the top of the pyramid" (Terry, 2000).

Empowerment is further supported when teachers believe that there is an atmosphere of trust and mutual respect in the school that allows them to thrive as professionals. This will only occur in an environment where teachers feel comfortable with their colleagues and school leadership and where they can make decisions that matter in their classroom and in their schools (Rebora, 2008).

In most schools, and even many colleges, guidance is separated from teaching. Guidance counselors work with students, referred by teachers, usually for academic failures or misbehavior, and the encounter is one on one. Although the areas of behavior, learning, and achievement are deeply related at a fundamental level, the contacts are separated, and often decisions are made without consultation of the student or his family: seemingly, non-related nor integrated with the classroom. Today's world and the significance of the students' behavior and peer group influences contradict this separation. The community of the school is a formative factor in both achievement and attitude and the teacher's role is paramount in the child's development and adjustment. Recognizing these connections, two of the programs highlighted in innovative reforms and in this chapter, Middle College High School and the LaGuardia Community College/Queens Urban Partnership GEAR UP, emphasized two new roles in education: the teacher–counselor and the onsite team of guidance counselor and social worker. In the Middle College paradigm, the designers renamed the position of instructor to "teacher–counselor" and required all teachers applying for employment to have additional experience in counseling training and practice with young people in a community setting. Almost 30 years later, the creators of LaGCC/QUP GEAR UP (many of whom came from LaGuardia Community College, the institution that created the Middle College) recognized the value of this expectation. The onsite team was central to the implementation of GEAR UP in the participating schools. In fact, the team was the first port of call for students, teachers, and GEAR UP program staff.

THE IMPORTANCE OF THE CARING ADULT IN PROMOTING THE SUCCESS OF STUDENTS

Given the current policy climate of accountability, the focus seems to be exclusively on student performance as a measure of school success. Many schools are developing strategies to strengthen student engagement with the intent of improving student performance. Student engagement is defined as a "relationship between the student and school community, the student and school adults, the student and peers, the student and instruction, and the students and curriculum" (Yazzie-Mintz, 2010, p. 1). Strong relationships with students and their peers and adults serve as predictors of student engagement (Perdue, Manzeske & Estell, 2009) and are important for successful academic achievement, persistence, graduation, and school connectedness (Blum, 2005; Klem & Connell, 2004; Morse et al., 2004). When students become attached to teachers and counselors they have a personal stake in meeting the expectations of those adults. This attachment results in "a commitment to stay in school and to reach the goals a high school diploma develops" (Cullen, 1991, p. 32).

THE TEACHER–COUNSELOR ROLE OF MIDDLE COLLEGE STAFF

Eleven teachers, administrators, and guidance counselors from Middle College High School were interviewed for a study that described the characteristics of this school that contribute to its success in retaining students who have been described by middle schools as potential dropouts (Carter, 2004). One of the criteria for selection as a member of the Middle College staff is experience in guidance counseling. The expanded role of the Middle College teacher to teacher–counselor alerts the teachers that the school expects more involvement than the traditional role of subject area specialist. New faculty hired are expected to serve this dual role. The teacher–counselor is responsible for the emotional and academic growth of the student. As teacher–counselors, faculty make phone calls to students who have been absent for more than two consecutive days to inquire of problems and to keep the connection to the Middle College. Students may request wake up calls from faculty to ensure they come to school on time. Additionally, the teacher–counselor is an advocate for students and may represent them to the school's administration or student government. The director of guidance supported this unique role:

> Guidance at Middle College is based on developmental groups but the teacher–counselor was always an integral part. The belief is that students would rather take classes with people they would feel most comfortable with. Guidance counselors support that. If students feels more comfortable with talking to their math teacher, that's fine. Our major concern when hiring is that the teacher is a caring person.
>
> (Director of Guidance, Carter, 2004, p. 75)

Staff training sessions and biweekly family meetings of counselors and house teachers reinforce the expectations of the teacher–counselor role.

The location of the school on the college campus enriches the structure and the support for teachers, helping them to accept their expanded role. Borrowing from LaGuardia's tradition of promotion and tenure review, Middle College established a personnel committee made up primarily of teachers to ensure that new personnel are willing to take on the expanded role of teacher–counselor. The expanded role of the teacher is supported by other structures of the school. For example, the career internship program provides teachers with an opportunity to step out of the classroom for a cycle to supervise students in the field. Teachers are given the opportunity to relate to students outside the traditional classroom setting, to adjust their curriculum, and to assess the employment skills needed for today's workforce. Through the career internship program, the school can build invaluable connections with the community-based organizations and businesses in the Queens area.

The small ratio of students to counselor is essential to developing a positive relationship between student and an adult:

> Guidance is really unseen in larger traditional schools where counselors have a caseload of anywhere from 300 to 600 students. This makes it almost impossible to do the kind of counseling that we have insisted upon doing here at Middle College.
>
> (Guidance Director, Carter, 2004, p. 76)

Like group counseling, one-on-one peer counseling was also central to the guidance program. Counselors' main contact with students was by running groups every day. Individual counseling, including crisis intervention, was also provided to students.

Guidance is included in the institutional program and the students' schedule. The institutional organization features the recognition of the importance of faculty support and advisors. Although Middle College is small in comparison to other New York City public schools, it is made smaller by its division into three clusters. Each cluster is comprised of a house teacher, a guidance counselor, and a house parent. Students stay in a house for three years allowing for continuity and the building of a relationship with the adults. The house teacher monitors students' attendance. Assistance is given in the areas of graduation requirements, academic sequence requirements, and personal needs. Group counseling, provided to all students, is another feature of the clusters. This "institutionalized caring" is evident by the structuring of the guidance program (Cullen & Moed, 1988):

> Everybody cares. Everybody tries to reach out to students in different ways. Our principal runs a house, our assistant principals, everybody runs a house here. Everybody has a homeroom. Everybody has associations and relations with kids. Our secretaries, through internships, get close to kids. Security guards from LaGuardia conducted tutoring sessions. They come with us on our Boy's Harbor Leadership Training weekends. They are there for the evening events regardless if they are paid or not. They're here when we are having school dances. They are here for every event, often sitting in the audience to support the kids. Everybody in this place cares. We reach out to students in a different way. And so, as we change, and as we go through different kinds of metamorphosis as a school, one thing that doesn't change is that we all care.
>
> (Guidance Director, Carter, 2004, p. 77)

REFLECTIVE EXERCISE 8.1

Creating a Teacher–Counselor Program

You are to introduce the teacher–counselor concept to your staff. A meeting is scheduled and you are planning an agenda.

1. How would you encourage the staff that this is best for the school?
2. What are some of the roadblocks you may face?
3. What are the items on the agenda for the meeting?
4. Who will you enlist to assist you in conducting the meeting? Explain.

SITE COUNSELOR AND SOCIAL WORKER: DESCRIPTION OF ROLES AND RESPONSIBILITIES

In order to improve the academic achievement of students so that they can meet rigorous standards, the LaGuardia Community College GEAR UP program placed additional guidance counselors and social workers to work with a student cohort as they progress from middle school on their way to college. Three onsite teams, each comprised of a social worker and a guidance counselor, served the full range of students represented: those whose behavioral and emotional issues were impeding their academic progress; and those needing remedial assistance as well as enrichment. The descriptions below reflects the responsibilities of the onsite counselor and social worker and serve as a guide to school leaders wishing to build collaborative teams of support staff to work with cohorts of middle and/or high school students.

Site Counselor: Description of Roles and Responsibilities

The roles and responsibilities of the GEAR UP Site Counselor included working closely with the school staff. In this capacity, he/she:

- accepted referrals from teachers for GEAR UP students related to a range of academic, personal, and social issues
- met periodically with the school counselor and social worker to determine appropriate actions on referrals and to delegate responsibility for the referral to the appropriate person
- assisted the school counseling staff "in the crunch times," e.g., student admissions in September and February and summer school registration
- kept assistant principal, pupil personnel services, and all school staff advised of all GEAR UP activities
- participated in school-wide committees and activities
- worked closely with the Assistant Principal Pupil Personnel Services and all school coordinators (e.g., attendance, cutting, lateness)
- assists in Annual Review.

Additionally, the GEAR UP Guidance Counselor provided oversight to the GEAR UP cohort. In this capacity, he/she:

- recruited students and teachers for GEAR UP activities
- visited all cohort in order to provide whole class group guidance
- conducted small-group counseling sessions
- interviewed students who are failing their classes, referring them to appropriate GEAR UP, school, and community resources
- made parental contacts by phone and mail
- planned parent workshops, paying particular attention to providing students and parents with information on the benefits of and preparation for a college education, the college admission process, and financial aid
- conferred individually with students and parents
- provided crisis counseling
- conducted orientation programs for students, parents, and staff
- interviewed all GEAR UP students leaving high school for any reason prior to graduation
- documented services on GEAR UP activity logs as per GEAR UP mandates.
  (GEAR UP Internal Document, 2005)

Social Worker: Description of Roles and Responsibilities

The GEAR UP Social Worker conducted social skills groups; helped identify at-risk youth; provided individual group and/or family counseling for youngsters; and conducted parent education workshops. In this capacity, he/she:

- conducted adolescent groups around social skills development and peer relationships

- conducted parents education workshops that are culturally sensitive and language specific
- assessed the needs of at-risk youth
- provided crisis intervention, short-term counseling, parental guidance, and family therapy for adolescents, as needed
- referred youngsters and families to other social services, as needed
- coordinated the Teacher Mentor program
- attended all GEAR UP Site Planning Team meetings and worked together with other school personnel to effectively support youth in the GEAR UP cohort
- completed administrative tasks related to the above duties
- reported to Clinical Administrator and school's Assistant Principal for Guidance
- provided crisis and mediation services as needed
- recruited teachers and students for GEAR UP activities in collaboration with Site Counselors
- planned parent workshops, paying particular attention to providing students and parents with information on the benefits of and preparation for a college education, the college admission process, and financial aid
- participated in school-wide committees and activities
- conducted small group sessions
- other duties as assigned.

(GEAR UP, Internal Document, 2005)

PORTFOLIO BUILDING 8.1

Creating a Resource Guide for Students and Parents

This activity involves the guidance counselor and social worker working together to improve student progress. You belong to a team of guidance counselors representing various levels from the school system and from higher education. You have identified several issues that impact student academic progress as they move from elementary, middle, high school, and into college. Select strategies that can assist students and their parents through the different transition stages.

You are to present your findings and recommendations to the local district office in the format of a *Resource Guide for Students and Parents*.

INVOLVING TEACHERS IN THE TRANSITION PROCESS

Middle grade students demonstrate a range of physical, intellectual, emotional, and social development unrivaled in other grades. In order to fulfill these developmental demands, their teachers must engage in staff development that increases their knowledge and skills, challenges their beliefs and assumptions about education, provides support, and engages them as active participants in the study and reform of the school culture (National Staff Development Council, 1997). The High School Bound program, a GEAR UP initiative, not only benefitted the students who participated, but offered middle and high school teachers an opportunity to learn about each other's educational sectors and the issues they and their students encounter around the transition process. The purpose of the Program was for eighth grade students to gain a realistic understanding of how a high school classroom operates with typical assignments, realistic expectations, and feedback from a team of two high school and middle school teachers to familiarize themselves with their feeder high school. Teachers engaged in typical ways of teaching English and math in the hope that after the experience students will gain some idea of what they

---

PORTFOLIO BUILDING 8.2

Involving Teachers in the Transition Process

Call for Teachers

1. How would you adapt this program to suit the needs of middle school students at your school?
2. How else can classroom teachers be involved in the transition process?

The GEAR UP Program is interested in working with two Middle School Teachers who teach eighth grade students and two High School Teachers who would enjoy working with middle school students in order to facilitate their transition into high school and prepare them for academic achievement.

Duties and responsibilities include:

- (High school staff only) Attending a high school team planning meeting to plan lessons and presentations for both high school visits.
- Participating middle school teachers must communicate with middle school liaison and counselors regarding student recruitment.
- Middle school teachers must recruit 25 students to participate.
- Middle school teachers must take attendance and submit attendance sheets to the GEAR UP office.
- Middle school teachers will escort students to and from the high school for both visits.
- High school teachers must prepare English Language Arts and math lessons.
- Student evaluations must be distributed by middle school teachers to students and completed immediately following the second high school visit.
- Teachers must complete an evaluation of the program.

Schedule: Two visits to the high school will take place after school during the month of June. Each session is two hours long.

Salary: $36.50/hour for 8 hours.

need to do and be prepared before entering high school. Participation in the program was an opportunity for students to become familiar with the high school campus/environment and to meet and speak with faculty and high school students.

The following is a description of roles and responsibilities established for middle school and high school teachers seeking to work with the High School Bound Program.

EXPANDING THE ROLE OF THE CLASSROOM TEACHER TO FACILITATE COLLABORATION

Once the GEAR UP student cohort moved on to the high school and the site counselors and social workers integrated themselves into the schools, it became clear that more assistance was needed. The site counselors and social workers needed to concentrate primarily on academic and personal counseling in classroom presentations, small groups and on a one-to-one basis, recruitment, and data collection. While it was important for them to remain involved and be knowledgeable of what is happening in the tutorial sessions as well as other GEAR UP activities, the supervision of tutorial and other special activities conducted during the school day needed to become the responsibility of other staff. GEAR UP sought to hire faculty who can assume a supervisory role. They were referred to simply as the GEAR UP teachers.

GEAR UP Teachers

GEAR UP worked with a designated number of faculty, who, operating under the direction of their assistant principal, were each responsible for at least three classes of tenth graders. These teachers were to do the following.

- Host the mini-seminars and participate in the planning of these series of presentations with college faculty. These seminars were intended to extend and enrich the classroom curricular, develop communication skills, and help students look toward their future. They also exposed the cohort to presenters comprising of college faculty and professionals from various fields.
- Serve as a primary point of reference for and linkage to the site counselors and social workers allowing them periodically to:
  1. recruit students within classes for GEAR UP activities, including college campus trips
  2. visit classrooms periodically
  3. distribute student surveys and parent permission forms required for assessment purposes.
- Refer students who can benefit from GEAR UP services to the site counselors and social workers.

Other Special Opportunities for GEAR UP Teachers

Faculty were recruited to serve in a variety of special roles for which they were compensated. These roles included, but were not limited to, the following:

- tutor supervisor
- special programs leader (e.g. Regents review, W.O.R.K. Program, parent outreach, poetry club or a writers' club, ESL/Bilingual English conversation circle, other activities)
- mentor teacher. GEAR UP offered paid training sessions to help prepare teachers for providing academic support
- coordinator of college and high school students. College and high school students were available to offer homework help sessions either before the school day or during lunch periods, assuming this was feasible.

LESSONS LEARNED

Both GEAR UP and Middle College highlight the benefits to school staff of collaboration across educational sectors, an often unusual practice in contemporary schools. Also, the success of these programs lay in the determination of the school staff to adhere to the ideals of school reform and innovation practices. The following experiences are insightful to educators wishing to engage school staff in collaborative programs.

1. Selection of School Staff with Experience in Diverse Settings

When selecting staff to work in collaborative programs, educators should look for those with experience in diverse settings. Middle College attracted personnel who had experience outside the education ranks, drawing on practices that were beneficial to various aspects of the school: grant writing, program development, and working with private foundations and community-based organizations. These skills are a vital asset to any school seeking to develop relationships with external partners. The Middle College staff interviewed for this study represented the mathematics, English, social studies and career development, and counseling departments. Two of the teachers had over 20 years' experience, one of whom was at Middle College for most of his career and taught as an adjunct lecturer at LaGuardia Community College. One English teacher also taught media and journalism, musical theater, oral communication, drama, and psychology. She had over 22 years' teaching experience, seven of those years at Middle College. One of these teachers was responsible for mentoring newer teachers and had a reduced workload to accommodate this responsibility. One Middle College teacher worked at alternative detention programs. Another teacher taught in suburban settings. Others had a quite varied experience: they worked at traditional high schools, one in a semi-rural setting and another in a suburban setting. Some had experience in adult education programs such as basic education, GED prep, and English as a Second Language. Some of the teachers and all the administrators taught at the college level. One remarked:

> I have been at Middle College for over 21 years, and before that, I was in a junior high school for another ten. I taught in a traditional junior high school to seventh, eighth and

ninth graders. Besides teaching at Middle College, I teach in the Math Department at LaGuardia Community College for 21 years as a college adjunct. So, I have seen many Middle College students come and go.

(Teacher, Carter, 2004, pp. 73–74)

2. Experience in School Reform

Personnel involved in collaborative programs, such as those described in this book, should have prior experience in school reform initiatives or, at the very least, believe in the concept of applying innovative practices to school improvement efforts. The faculty and counselors at Middle College were all attuned to school reform programs, committed to the goals of alternative education, and clearly met the criteria established for innovative programs by the originators of Middle College. The stated goals and criteria were:

1. commitment to the Middle College concept
2. innovative teaching experience, including interdisciplinary and team teaching
3. evidence of professional competence in a professional discipline of interest to the Middle College
4. demonstrated interest in career guidance
5. evidence of guidance training and counseling skill
6. familiarity with inner-city schools and communities
7. evidence of ability to teach college level courses.

(LGCC Middle College Plan, 1973)

Similarly, one of the main criteria for selection to work as GEAR UP teachers and support staff was the experience and willingness to work with cross-sectoral education groups and with community organizations. For example, English teachers were recruited to prepare innovative curricular that included college awareness content and involving the public librarian and New York authors in reading state-mandated textbooks.

3. Professionalization of School Staff

One of the advantages of working in a school located on a college campus or with collaborative programs that bring school staff together with college personnel is that those at the school level often mirror the culture of independence that is typically not part of many public school settings. Academic freedom, normally the prerogative of college faculty, is clearly evident in Middle College. During the tenure of one of the principals, there was a push for collaboration between high school and college faculty mainly through curriculum planning, teacher exchanges, and team-teaching. This allowed the faculty to assume responsibility for personnel and governance. The result was a culture of independence by Middle College faculty that mirrors that of LaGuardia's faculty. This shared governance model was more typical of college than high school faculty. One faculty member who taught in traditional settings noted how different her Middle College experience was compared to her former school:

As a department, we pretty much function well together as a group. Whatever we have to do, whatever our agenda is we just do it. I mean, in other schools it just wasn't like this. There were staff meetings, we met after school, the principal got up there and spoke to the faculty, then there were department meetings, the department chair said we were going to this, that or the other. There was very little decision making amongst the faculty. I don't know if I am typical but I found a lot of disgruntlement amongst the faculty in those schools. You should see how it is in other places, how top-down and mandated it is in other places. Even this is something that's unusual, very unusual.

(Teacher, Carter, 2004)

4. Development of a Longitudinal View of the Educational Process

Middle College faculty can teach as adjunct college faculty affording them the opportunity to learn about college courses, meet college faculty, and supplement their income. In return, college faculty may teach high school level courses. Additionally, college faculty can gain an insight into the educational problems of a high school and may work together with school personnel to address them. What is clearly evident is that the problem of teaching content courses to students with weak literacy skills is similar at both the high school and college levels. The benefits to Middle College faculty who have the opportunity to teach both in the school and in regular LaGuardia classes was proposed by the program founders in the Middle College Plan. This relationship between LaGuardia and Middle College is further developed through joint staff development by faculty from both levels. Teachers hired were expected to acquire a longitudinal view of the learning process, which will aid in development of improved course content and sequence.

REFLECTIVE EXERCISE 8.2

The Classroom Teacher and Building School Community

You are a frustrated high school teacher whose students enter the ninth grade ill-prepared to cope with the demands of the high school English (or Social Studies) curriculum. Your school received a grant to deal with this problem and the principal asked you to spearhead the initiative. One of the criteria of this grant is to bring together a team of teachers from the elementary, middle, and high school and college levels and community organizations to develop seamless curriculum that will better prepare students to move through the school system and in to college. You must be able to prepare students for the state exams and ensure their readiness to cope with college level English courses.

1. What are some of the common curricular issues that English teachers face in the classroom?

2. Apart from other English teachers, who else can you bring together to work on developing the new curriculum? Explain your choices.

3. How can your principal and other administrators assist you in the implementation of this curriculum?

4. Develop an outline of this curriculum to present to your principal.

---

5. Creating a Sense of Autonomy and Ownership

"Having your own space" was most unusual to Middle College faculty: "In other schools you really couldn't make a phone call or get a phone call. In that sense it feels very comfortable to have a place to work with students privately" (Teacher, Carter, 2004).

Faculty enjoyed a sense of autonomy and school ownership, encouraging them to invest themselves in helping students. Most faculty in other public high schools have no experience with the environment that permeates college faculty relations. Average high school faculty generally have less responsibility in the overall management and feel they have less independence in the direction of the institution. A college administrator saw the professionalization of Middle College faculty, in comparison to their counterparts in the traditional high school, because of the structure of the school:

> If you're smaller [size of the school], you have the space, you can give teachers a certain respect by giving them space to work with students in privacy. If you can control your schedule so that you're not working within a 35 minute or 42 minute [schedule] . . ., but, in fact, you can play with your school schedule, well then that gives you opportunities with curriculum that you otherwise don't have.

Faculty enjoyed a sense of autonomy and school ownership, encouraging them to invest themselves in helping students. Most faculty in other public high schools have no experience with the environment that permeates college faculty relations. Average high school faculty generally have less responsibility in the overall management and feel they have less independence in the direction of the institution. One Middle School faculty member, whose current assignment is to mentor newer faculty, supported the feeling of professionalization that permeates through the school:

> You know I feel personally very able to speak with the administrators about concerns or issues and I feel like you know if I am interested in taking on a larger role in this school, a larger leadership role that that is a possibility.
>
> (Teacher, Carter, 2004, p. 80)

6. Support of the Classroom Teacher

The support of teachers is crucial as they are the main vehicle through which students are referred to GEAR UP services. While the GEAR UP on-site staff (guidance counselors and social workers) had access to the classroom, teacher buy-in was critical to student participation in the program's activities. More communication with the classroom teacher and GEAR UP onsite staff was needed to better connect students with the appropriate intervention.

7. Enlisting School Staff as Liaisons of Change

GEAR UP onsite teams placed a high premium on personal, individual student attention. They also created opportunities for students to interface with high school and college students as well as college faculty so that planning for the future is not as intimidating. Additionally, the onsite teams identified students through their own contact in groups and referrals from the classroom teachers. They sought out youth based on one or more of these risk factors: recent immigration and/or difficulty adjusting to New York and the school, truancy or frequent class cutting, violation of school rules, failing grades, drug or alcohol abuse, poor parental supervision, depression, and other emotional problems.

This important relationship between students and adults was clearly evident between the GEAR UP onsite and program staff and the student cohort. Onsite GEAR UP staff at the three high schools and LaGuardia GEAR UP program staff arranged 30 college admissions and financial aid workshops for students and their parents. In contrast, these high schools would normally conduct about two to three workshops for senior level students. GEAR UP provided additional SAT classes and partnered with the Liberty Partnership Program to accommodate the demand for this service. Also, those who needed additional academic support were encouraged to attend activities offered by GEAR UP and LaGuardia's Liberty Partnership Program. Those needing to accumulate college credit were encouraged to enroll in LaGuardia's College Now and College Connection programs. The GEAR UP Counselor and Social Worker were the primary adults in the cohort's journey from middle school through high school. They assisted students in developing personal action plans based on graduation requirements, academic sequence, and individual need.

CONCLUSION

Collaborative programs can positively impact school staff providing an improved knowledge of one another's challenges, discussion, and development of approaches. Both programs provided direct academic and counseling services to students; they sought to prepare and ease the transition to the next educational level and to enrich the educational experience and to strengthen academic skills. Middle College teachers and GEAR UP counselors and social workers were the primary adults in the students' journey through high school. The benefit of this connection is that students had a personal stake in meeting the expectations of those adults. This attachment resulted in a commitment to stay in school and to reach the goals of a high school diploma and a college degree.

Involvement of school staff in collaborative programs will never occur without the commitment and foresight of the educational leader. The following chapter explores the importance of building a collaborative culture in a school and the role of the leader in developing effective partnerships with other schools and community organizations.

KEY TERMS

- Student engagement
- Attachment
- Supportive work environment
- Teacher–Counselor role
- Faculty empowerment

CHAPTER 9

The Collaborative Leader and Partnership Building

LEARNING OBJECTIVES

After reading this chapter you will be able to:

1. Collaborate with the school staff and the external community by responding to their needs and interests and mobilizing resources to support student achievement
2. Assess school culture and implement appropriate strategies to improve school programs
3. Demonstrate the ability to facilitate an effective instructional program
4. Involve the school staff in managing the organization
5. Analyze effective strategies to develop and maintain collaboration
6. Build collaborative relationships with all stakeholders and policymakers

---

INTRODUCTION

Current research suggests that effective school leaders take thorough steps to understand their school communities and develop partnerships that focus on learning both inside and outside of school (Fullan, 1994). Leaders provide legitimacy to the partnership, underscore its importance, and have the capacity to commit resources (Gomez et al., 1990). This chapter explores the key dimensions of collaborative leadership, including personality traits, group processes, consensus building, motivation, and managing change.

Educational Leadership Constituent Council (ELCC) Standards

This chapter meets the needs of advanced academic programs in preparation for educational leadership:

> Standard 1.0: Candidates who complete the program are educational leaders who have the knowledge and ability to promote the success of all students by facilitating the development, articulation, implementation, and stewardship of a school or district vision of learning supported by the school community.
>
> Standard 2.0: Candidates who complete the program are educational leaders who have the knowledge and ability to promote the success of all students by promoting a positive school culture, providing an effective instructional program, applying best practice to student learning, and designing comprehensive professional growth plans for staff.
>
> Standard 3.0: Candidates who complete the program are educational leaders who have the knowledge and ability to promote the success of all students by managing the organization, operations, and resources in a way that promotes a safe, efficient, and effective learning environment.
>
> Standard 4.0: Candidates who complete the program are educational leaders who have the knowledge and ability to promote the success of all students by collaborating with families and other community members, responding to diverse community interests and needs, and mobilizing community resources.
>
> Standard 6.0: Candidates who complete the program are educational leaders who have the knowledge and ability to promote the success of all students by understanding, responding to, and influencing the larger political, social, economic, legal, and cultural context.
>
> (National Policy Board for Education Administration, 2002)

★　★　★

BUILDING A COLLABORATIVE CULTURE IN THE SCHOOL BUILDING

Twenty-first-century school principals are required to fulfill a variety of roles. As a community leader, the principal shares leadership among educators and community partners and has close relations with parents. As a visionary leader, he or she is committed to the conviction that all children will learn at optimal levels and inspires others inside and outside the school building with this vision:

> We need school leaders who visualize successful student learning, understand the work necessary to achieve it, and have the skills to engage with others to make it.
> (Innovations in Education: Innovative Pathways to School
Leadership, U.S. Department of Education, 2004)

A key approach to improving schools and addressing the needs of all students is the development of a collaborative culture in the school building. School leaders can support collegiality by promoting teacher leadership: encouraging staff to exchange ideas and work together; creating a time and place for professional dialogue and teamwork; and, providing substitute teachers to cover classes for faculty who wish to participate in collaboration activities.

(Peterson, 1994)

Promoting a collaborative culture can also promote a high sense of effectiveness among school staff who can view their efforts and expertise as having a great impact on student learning (Smylie, 1988). This results in higher student achievement and a belief that all students can learn (Peterson, 1994). However, education leaders need to develop structures and activities that support collaboration. These include shared decision-making and site-based management models, regular communication of ideas, inter-disciplinary curriculum projects, collective work on new instructional methods, team teaching, and peer observation and faculty groups (Peterson, 1994). Additionally, a collaborative culture is created through diagnosing the organization and building skill and confidence in staff (Lieberman, Saxl, & Miles, 1988).

REFLECTIVE EXERCISE 9.1

What is My Leadership Style?

1. What is my leadership style? Task oriented or people oriented?
2. How charismatic am I?
3. Do I trust others?
4. Do others see me as trustworthy?
5. How good am I at disciplining others?
6. How good am I at building and leading a team?
7. What is my preferred type of power?
   a. Reward
   b. Coercive
   c. Legitimate
   d. Expert
   e. Referent.
8. How good am I at playing politics?
9. What is my preferred conflict-handling style?
   a. Competing
   b. Collaborating
   c. Avoiding
   d. Accommodating
   e. Comprising.
10. What is my negotiating style?

USING STUDY GROUPS AND SCHOOL LEADERSHIP TEAMS TO BUILD A COLLABORATIVE CULTURE

A school that does not have a culture of collaboration is not ready to receive partnership programs. One way for principals to have their schools "ready" for collaboration is to create and support the practice of study groups. A study group is a group of people who meet regularly to address issues and concerns that they deem necessary. There are various types of study groups in a school setting:

- teacher study groups
- online
- book discussion
- administrator
- student.

Study groups are an important for administrators as it:

- builds a professional community
- develops instructional techniques
- develops group process and communication skills
- develops leadership skills
- addresses an issue of concern
- empowers staff
- reduces teacher isolation
- institutionalizes school and district initiatives (life after)
- sustaining the school's mission and vision.

(Roberts & Pruitt, 2003)

As important as study groups is the effective use of school leadership teams. School leadership team management is usually associated with school reform or a restructuring process that means modifying school governance. Principals using this approach to management allow decision making to include teachers, parents, and the community. School leadership team management should be seen as a process rather than a goal (Roberts & Pruitt, 2003).

IMPLEMENTING AN INNOVATIVE PROGRAM

This section focuses on an interview taken of one of the early principals at Middle College High School who played a significant part of the evolution of this collaborative model. He had far-reaching knowledge of collaborative programs and school reform efforts and, at some point in his career, taught at various educational levels. The goals of Middle College were to reduce the dropout rate by improving students' academic performance, to improve students' self concept, and to enhance college and career options by helping students reach their full potential. The Middle College model encouraged potential dropouts to succeed through a support system that includes visible

REFLECTIVE EXERCISE 9.2

Building Collaborative Groups

Assistant Principal Jones is preparing to convene a meeting to talk about the dismal performance of students in the high school science examinations over the last five years. She wants to build a collaborative science group in response to this problem and has formulated some questions and key talking points. After the group has met several times, she will prepare an outline for a presentation to the principal and to the college president.

1. What strategies would you employ to get teachers/guidance counselors/ administrators interested in your group?
   - utilize data
   - one-on-one conversation.

2. How large is the group?
   - Importance on group composition: include middle school and college faculty/counselors.
   - Administrators may want to include college faculty and staff, dean, college president or representative, district personnel, other principals, including middle school administrators, head of guidance.

3. How often and where will you meet?
   - Who decides where and when to meet?
   - Process of selection is very important?
   - After-school, before school?
   - Incentives to meet: food, stipend, performance appraisal?
   - Rotate meeting sites?

4. How will the leader be determined?
   - expert in the area?
   - skilled facilitator?
   - charisma?
   - administrator group—principal as leader?
   - rotate leadership?

5. What areas will be discussed during the lifespan of the group?
   - Faculty/counselor experiences?
   - Student experiences—focus groups with students?

6. How will you keep members engaged?
   - acknowledge everyone's contribution.
   - celebrate small successes.

7. What topics will be on the agenda for the first meeting?

peer models, small classes, and superior academic and support services. Modeled after the LaGuardia Community College's cooperative education program, students are able to relate school to work opportunities, and to develop motivation and a sense of purpose through a program of internships. The internships are part of the career education requirement and students are allowed to work in schools, colleges, hospitals, and other service organizations. Research indicated that after the first internship, student rates of credit accumulation doubled, especially for the lowest level of achievers (Lieberman, 1989).

As stated in the Middle College Plan, the school was to "graduate students who know how to raise the right questions, gather data, sift, hypothesize, test their hypotheses, and evaluate their conclusions." The creators saw the objectives of the school as:

1. Students who complete the Middle College program will earn the New York State high school diploma and college degree at the two-year level.
2. In comparison with average high school graduates, a higher proportion of Middle College students will have college-level skills by the end of the twelfth year.
3. The rate of retention at both high school and college levels will be higher than average.
4. Through career education and exploration students will acquire broad job skills and life goals.
5. Specific, high goals will be set in all subject areas.

(LaGCC Middle College Plan, 1973)

As an agent of change, this principal was not only involved in a major education reform effort, but was a key player in ensuring that the core values of the Middle College experiment were honored (Carter, 2004).

Learning Each Other's Culture: A Key Element to Effective Collaboration

The school brought together two different institutions that had little experience in collaboration, which seriously hindered the implementation of key components of the model in the early years. However, the staff eventually "attained substantial autonomy and realized more elements of the design by learning how to 'play off' governing bodies and constituencies and by invoking the school's status as an alternative high school" (Wechsler, 2001, p. 54). This position was further endorsed by the principal who was interviewed:

> Being embedded in the college allowed the school to have a free zone, a blurred area of authority not controlled by LaGuardia or the Department of Education. So we're viewed as being I think creative, innovative, high functioning, high performing and there is a kind of hands off because of our being embedded in the college.
>
> (Principal A)

One of the benefits to the free zone was that the school was able to implement its plan:

> Being on a college campus enabled us to blur the boundaries between the high school and the college and also it allowed us to be between the two major institutions and the Board of Higher Ed and the Department of Education and, therefore, construct a free zone. So should anybody question the kind of practices that we put in place we were able to always blame the other institution and that kind of free zone enabled us I think to develop practices that were most appropriate for teenagers.
>
> (Principal A)

Additionally, the placement of Middle College in the alternative superintendency of the New York City Department of Education gave the school staff a high level of independence.

> Well, we successfully negotiated to work very little with the Department of Ed. to be very independent and to just deal with the Deputy Chancellor when we have an issue. That's a big change so I don't respond to all of that bureaucratic paper work at all, which is nice, very nice.
>
> (Principal A)

Living in the "free zone" did not mean that principals had a choice of how to respond to both governing institutions. As Principal A stated:

> I wanted to feel that the Department of Ed. would regard me as certainly one of them but I also wanted the college to feel that I was deeply invested in a role as a member of the college community and so I just made sure that I was attending to both. I made sure that I never missed a chairpersons meeting or a faculty meeting that the president was speaking at the college. It would be very, very rare that I would have to choose between the Department of Ed. and the college.

Working Together to Maximize Resources

However, despite the advantages of its location on a college campus, the principal felt the school was not maximizing its potential. This was exemplified by the school staff's adherence to the traditional way of teaching. One of the key components of the school as specified in the Middle College Plan (1973) was the career education program. However, the field experiences that were to accompany this program were not provided to students:

> The internship program was basically mythic, it never existed, it was like a concept that never got realized for anybody. There were career education courses that they had over at the college but the accompanied experiences in the field never took place. I felt that the school was in pretty serious trouble because of all those reasons.
>
> (Principal A)

Although the school's faculty was competent, he felt that it was "committed in a very traditional kind of way." Also, while there was a good relationship between teachers and students, he felt that teachers needed to be motivated and move away from the familiar, traditional teaching methods and strategies for dealing with an at-risk student population:

> We should be grappling with some of the issues that we're working . . . it seems to me that we all need to be thinking about why it is that the kids are not coming to class, what we can do to make it happen, how we can organize ourselves? You are a wonderful teacher; you have something to share and yet the class doesn't show up. There are outbursts of violence, what do you do about that?
>
> (Principal A)

One way to address the needs of students was to take advantage of the resources at the college:

> I don't think we were taking advantage of the college opportunities. The college was giving us a budget to spend and we tend to spend in very traditional ways. There were very few courses that were taught for our kids. There are very few kids taking courses in the college. There is a lot of unrealized potential . . . And then there's a magnificent campus with all kinds of opportunities, how do we take advantage of it?
>
> (Principal A)

Despite the various professional development opportunities made available by LaGuardia, Middle College faculty did not take advantage of them. Principal A also encouraged his faculty to teach at the college, an immediate possibility as Middle College teachers have adjunct faculty status, a unique feature in public education. Additionally, he chided faculty for not encouraging more students to take college courses.

To confront these issues the director and the faculty organized a Summer Institute to bring the school into alignment with its goals and objectives. The results were telling:

> Well, when we opened up in September we were a different school. We had a different schedule, we had a different sense of energy, we had a different sense of focus, we were much more connected to and looked more like a mini version of the college. The faculty was re-energized. That was crucial, I would say there were very few people who left in the end of that next year at the college that didn't think that the whole thing felt different.
>
> (Principal A)

What really emerged after the Summer Institute and more so during the tenure of this director was academic reform. There was curriculum innovation. The Summer Institute also addressed student governance, involving students in the disciplinary process and changing Middle College's admission system to allow current students to screen applicants and creating a sense of ownership. Principal A focused on developing a stronger relationship with LaGuardia and in making members of the college community more aware of the purpose of the school.

LESSONS LEARNED

The success of collaborative programs demands an academic and administrative partnership with the college, public school system, and community organizations. To effectively implement the Middle College model, broad collaboration between the school system and LaGuardia Community College occurred. The formative years brought college and school faculty and administrators together to jointly plan for the workings of the school. Its success largely depended on its ability to be flexible in the midst of a bureaucratic urban school system that barely communicated with each other (Wechsler, 2001). The lessons of the Middle College experience include the following:

1. Building a Stronger Relationship with the College Partner

Principal A felt that he needed to be more knowledgeable about how the college operated. With a background in higher education administration, he knew that he needed to build a relationship with faculty and administrators at LaGuardia: "I was learning two cultures, it wasn't learning one culture, it was definitely learning two cultures, one was the Middle College culture and the other was the LaGuardia culture."

His attempt to be more connected to the college was further seen by utilizing his rank of a college chairperson, which placed him in meetings with the college administration, including the academic deans. He also felt that he could make a contribution to the college community by making himself available to its members. The response to him was very positive and his contribution was valued. He became the "expert" on working with high school students, an extremely valuable role for college faculty and administrators who wanted to better understand the school system. When there were complaints by LaGuardia about the misuse of the college laboratories by Middle College students, the director hired a laboratory assistant to supervise the Middle College students: "We began to repair some of the ruptures and build some bridges in quiet ways to kind of get the college to understand that we were caring."

This re-emphasized connection with LaGuardia allowed qualified junior and senior students to enroll in college courses and earn both high school and college credits. More LaGuardia faculty taught Middle college students and in return received community service credit, which was counted toward promotion.

2. Commitment to the Ideals of an Innovation

The evolution of an innovation requires leaders who clearly understand and are committed to its mission. Middle College principals were each deeply involved in the evolution of Middle College and had a lasting impact on the life of the school. Principal A had the freedom to shape the school while carrying out the mission of the designers.

3. Continuous Evolution of an Innovation

One evaluation of the school stated that despite its success, it continued to evolve and was replicated by other City University of New York colleges. What was impressive is that this school did not rest on its success even after being replicated nationally (Gregory, 1989). Engaging in innovative programs to improve public schooling of youth who have been disenfranchised by the rigidities of the system usually attracts progressive teachers and leaders. Practitioners such as Principal A often respond positively to the promise of change and relished the satisfaction of participating in new ventures. The trick was to select practitioners when they have had enough experience to understand both the need for change and the parameters of possibility in a large, closely scripted, deeply routinized metropolitan school system.

REFLECTIVE EXERCISE 9.3

You are a principal whose high school recently received a four-year Partnership $600,000 grant to improve student achievement at your school. The grant guidelines requires the school to implement in-school and after-school activities for students, teachers, and parents. You are planning your first meeting of the Action Team.

1. Who should you invite from within and outside the school to participate on the Action Team?

2. How often should you meet? Where would you meet? Explain you rationale.

3. Explain how you would build team morale and team effectiveness.

4. Within the Department of Education parameters, how can you reconfigure the curriculum, staffing, and facilities to implement the grant?

5. How do you plan to institutionalize some of the activities once funding ends?

---

4. Impact of Changes in Leadership

The success of a high school–college collaborative demands the academic and administrative partnership between the college and the public high school. One of the intangible benefits of a collaboration that is as close as LaGuardia and Middle College is that problems of responsibility are shared by both the high school and the college. Originally, the Middle College principal who was given the rank of chairperson participated in activities in the department of Academic Affairs. Changes in the levels of collaboration between LaGuardia and Middle College were often attributed to the changes in the college administration and new policies that were introduced. For example, in the early years of the school, college faculty was given credit for participating in Middle College. When a new dean removed this opportunity, there was no incentive for college faculty to become connected to Middle College. Also, agenda items on the department chairs' meetings did not often reflect the needs of the high school, sending the message that the school is not as central to the academic life of the college as it was in the early stage of the collaboration.

5. A Clear Understanding about the Proposed Services and Their Implementation

School administrators need to be involved in the planning of the program, particularly activities that would impact their personnel and building during the school day. Specifically, the subject Assistant Principals are an important group as they are better able to indicate to their teaching staff the benefits of their involvement in the academic offerings of the program and the overall benefits of collaborating with other school, community organizations, and higher education institutions.

6. Need for New Pathways to Leadership Preparation through Community Engagement

A major criterion for leading schools in the twenty-first century is for educational leaders to perform a variety of roles: visionaries, change agents, instructional leaders, curriculum and assessment experts, budget analysts, facility managers, and community builders (Darling-Hammond et al., 2007). Additionally, schools are affected by the sweeping changes in the global economic, demographic, and technological sectors transforming the job of the school leader. In an era that is more outcome-based and accountability-driven, it is critical that school districts have good quality leaders. Principals and superintendents no longer serve primarily as supervisors. They are called upon to rethink goals and priorities, finances, staffing, curriculum, pedagogies, and assessment methods (Levine, 2005). New expectations for leaders move beyond the traditional requirements of managing school operations. They are now expected to:

- articulate and model core values that support a challenging and successful education for all
- establish a persistent public focus on learning at the school, classroom, community, and individual levels
- work with others to set ambitious standards for learning
- demonstrate and inspire shared responsibility and accountability for student outcomes
- develop a collaborative culture in the school building
- create structures and activities that support collaboration.

Middle College was fortunate to have innovative leaders. Traditional educational administration programs and certification procedures are not producing enough of this type of leader. State laws and regulations for public school principals require a set number of years of teaching experience and completion of college coursework in education administration. They rely on students to self-enroll rather than actively recruiting the best candidates. Many leadership programs are not customized to suit the needs of the candidate and to prepare them for non-traditional school types, i.e. charter schools, small schools, high poverty, low-achieving schools, and schools with large numbers of English Language Learners.

The onus is on Schools of Education to work with the public schools to create this type of leader described above. One strategy is to recruit and engage aspiring teacher leaders with ongoing support, assistance, and sharing of best practices. Leadership students can be placed immediately in schools for an entire year where their content knowledge will have immediate practical application through fieldwork, projects, collaborative inquiry, and ongoing assessment of their performance. Through on-site mentoring and supervision, redesigned college courses and fieldwork experiences, and reflective practice, Educational Leadership programs can train a cadre of professionals who can create conditions for success in their buildings.

Grounded in the belief that all students can learn, this new type of preparation can embrace the community, including school systems, parents, and community-based organizations in creating an environment that supports effective teaching and learning. By adopting this new preparation pathway, the perspective that it "takes a village to raise a child" is embraced. This calls for much needed resources to go into the identification and selection of a cohort of quality and committed candidates and improved and enriched field experiences and preparation of educational leaders.

Another key component of effective leadership preparation programs is the mentoring between current principals and aspiring leaders. Mentoring allows veteran leaders to give back to the field of education and help shape the future by supporting and serving as guides for aspiring leaders. Interdependence and collegiality among seasoned and prospective leaders promote a culture of continuous learning in schools resulting in greater productivity and student achievement (Daresh, 2004). Effective leadership preparation programs build and provide seamless leadership development that extends preparation through a school leader's career. Since this new paradigm targets individuals who have been teacher leaders, it becomes a model for succession planning and sustainability. Connected to this new paradigm is the need to increase knowledge or understanding of educational problems through Roundtable Discussion groups, which provides a forum for educators from the school system and the Schools of Education to present and explore current research, share best practices, present school improvement projects, and allow for constructive feedback.

The Southern Regional Education Board call for the merging of theory and practice through the development of strong working relationships between schools of education and school districts (SREB, 2007). Educational practitioners can work as site mentors and adjunct faculty. This allows for a blend of relevant educational theory and practice in order to create powerful and effective learning experiences for aspiring leaders. While college involvement is critical, school practitioners must also be involved in reforming leadership practice, as they have ways of influencing schools that scholars do not (Ryan, 2003). Additionally, professors of educational leadership contribute to leadership development in significant ways by serving as scholars, teachers, and mentors. Also, college faculty can convene with school practitioners to redesign college courses that will best serve the needs of the twenty-first-century school leader.

CONCLUSION

Possessing a mindset of collaboration does not necessarily occur without proper guidance and support. Schools of Education must prepare the next generation of leaders to view collaboration as a logical component of effective leadership. Leadership is central to the success of collaborative programs. Because collaboration is often peripheral to the core functioning of an organization, it is necessary to have the commitment and involvement of the top leaders from each participating entity. One of the skills of school leaders for the twenty-first century is that they create structures and activities that will support partnerships. Another is to identify the needs of the students in their charge. The next chapter illustrates the need for grant-funded collaborative programs to sometimes go "off script" and tailor its offerings to the needs of students participating in the program.

KEY TERMS

- Collaborative leadership
- School leadership teams
- School culture
- Leadership succession

CHAPTER 10

Keeping Students on Track: Customization through Collaboration

---

LEARNING OBJECTIVES

After reading this chapter you will be able to:

1. Analyze the academic needs of students
2. Design a customized program to meet student needs
3. Select the appropriate academic and social intervention for students to ensure that they are on track to graduate
4. Assess the impact of the academic and social interventions and make the necessary adjustments

---

INTRODUCTION

In this era of accountability, the success of schools is largely determined by test scores and graduation rates. Why, then, should school leaders work relentlessly to retain students who constantly bring down their schools' test scores? School leaders must create and sustain an effective learning environment that meets the needs of the public to improve student achievement. With this in mind, the LaGCC/QUP GEAR UP program worked steadfastly with the leaders of the participating schools to ensure that students who were not on track to graduate on time receive the necessary interventions to put them on the pathway to high school graduation and college entrance. This customization of services for the GEAR UP student cohort brought together higher education institutions, guidance counselors, social workers, teachers, and parents to work with students on their postsecondary plans.

Educational Leadership Constituent Council (ELCC) Standards

This chapter meets the needs of advanced academic programs in preparation for educational leadership:

> Standard 2.0: Candidates who complete the program are educational leaders who have the knowledge and ability to promote the success of all students by promoting a positive school culture, providing an effective instructional program, applying best practice to student learning, and designing comprehensive professional growth plans for staff.

> Standard 3.0: Candidates who complete the program are educational leaders who have the knowledge and ability to promote the success of all students by managing the organization, operations, and resources in a way that promotes a safe, efficient, and effective learning environment.
>
> (National Policy Board for Education Administration, 2002)

★　★　★

Urban school leaders grappling with the diverse needs of students must work hard to hold and prepare them for the future. To do it, they have to draw upon the resources, knowledge, and expertise available within their own schools and in the larger community. School leaders have to expand their reach, creating continuity and links between schools and support systems in the surrounding community. They have to craft a compelling educational program—one that will make knowledge and application and education and work more apparent. The larger challenge is to ensure that all students are prepared to succeed in college and in the workplace.

STUDENTS' RESPONSES TO THE COLLABORATIVE EFFORTS TO KEEP THEM IN SCHOOL AND PREPARE THEM FOR COLLEGE

The GEAR UP program became an integral part of the three targeted high schools and was well regarded in the school community by parents, teachers, and students. The program was associated with many positive outcomes that increased in magnitude year to year, indicating that GEAR UP had a cumulative increasingly strong impact. The following data is obtained through GEAR UP students who completed surveys administered by the external evaluator Capital Assessments Inc. in the 2004–2005 school year and was compared to student data collected in grades nine (2002), ten (2003), and eleven (2004). Clearly, GEAR UP impacted on students' behavior, educational knowledge, and future plans:

- Over the course of the 2004–2005 school year, there were subtle changes from the previous year in students' perception about their academic future. While eight in ten of the students still felt that they would graduate from at least a four-year college, there was a slight increase in the number of students (15 percent) who thought that they would graduate from a two-year college and go no farther. This was up from the 10 percent of students who reported feeling this way in the prior year (see Table 10.1).

- Less than 1 percent of students thought that they would not graduate high school and only 2 percent assumed that high school would be the final point in their education, reflecting a 1-percentage decrease from 2003.
- The percentage of students who wanted to go on to graduate school increased 3-percentage points from 2003.
- As Table 10.2 indicates, the percentage of students who had taken challenging classes has increased from the 2002 to the 2005 academic year.
- As it was in the last year, the largest increases in the percentage of students completing advanced courses were in the areas of Chemistry and Advanced Placement (AP) classes. Sixty-eight percent of students had already taken Chemistry, and 42 percent had taken AP classes.

Table 10.1 Student Predictions about their Academic Future (N=612)

	Percent of Students			
Prediction	2002 (%)	2003 (%)	2004 (%)	2005 (%)
Won't graduate high school	1	2	1	<1
Graduate high school/go no further	4	6	3	2
Graduate high school/go to trade school	5	4	3	2
Graduate high school/go to a 2-year college	17	14	10	15
Graduate high school/go to a 4-year college	49	53	55	50
Graduate high school/go to graduate school	24	21	28	31

Source: 2002/2003/2004/2005 Student Surveys

Table 10.2 Percentage of Students Who Took or Planned to Take Challenging Courses in High School (N=615)

	Spring 2002		Spring 2003		Spring 2004		Spring 2005	
Courses	Took Class (%)	Planning to Take (%)	Took Class (%)	Planning to Take (%)	Took Class (%)	Planning to Take (%)	Took Class (%)	Currently Taking (%)
Mathematics A	38	25	59	12	60	4	80	16
Foreign Language	73	15	79	10	79	5	73	23
Chemistry	7	56	27	43	43	18	58	10
Physics	15	43	8	48	18	31	19	12
Advanced Placement Classes	6	38	10	42	24	36	23	19

Source: 2002/2003/2004/2005 Student Surveys

Students grew increasingly aware of what they needed to do in order to get to college and followed through on this knowledge (see Figure 10.1).

• Nearly all of the GEAR UP students who completed the student survey in 2005 (90 percent) had either taken the SAT exam (78 percent) or were planning to take it (12 percent), and 61 percent had practiced on the PSAT, with another 8 percent of students planning to take the PSAT. In comparison, an average of 31 percent of eleventh and twelfth graders in the three high schools had taken the SAT in 2003–2004.

Although there was a slight dip in the percent of students who took the SAT during the 2004–2005 school year, the general trend over the last four years was that students were taking the SAT in increasing numbers.

Figure 10.2 shows that the majority of students communicated with someone about how to pay for college.

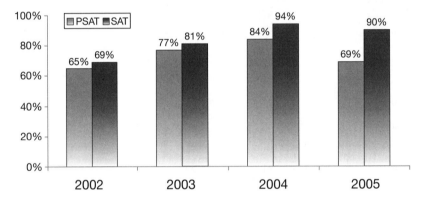

Figure 10.1 Percentage of Students Who Took or Plan to Take the PSAT/SAT Exams

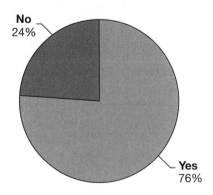

Figure 10.2 Percent of Students Who Were Informed About How to Pay for College

Source: 2005 Student Survey

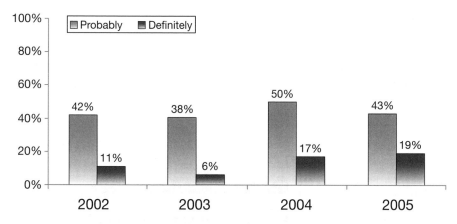

Figure 10.3 Percent of Students Who Felt They Can Afford to Go to College
Source: 2002/2003/2004/2005 Student

- Three-quarters of the GEAR UP students (76 percent) reported that they had spoken to someone about how to pay for college. This is up from last year, when 59 percent of the GEAR UP students reportedly sought this information. With high school graduation approaching, students' impressions of whether or not college was part of their future remained positive (see Figure 10.3).
- A little over half (52 percent) of the students felt that they would "probably" (43 percent), or "definitely" (19 percent) be able to afford college.
- Twenty-eight percent of students reported that they felt unsure about being able to afford college.
- As seen in the past, there continued to be fluctuation in the percent of students who felt that they can afford college.

Figure 10.4 illustrates students' awareness regarding the many different ways to pay for a college education.

- Students showed an increased awareness of several financing options such as Federal Work-Study (55 percent up 16 percentage points), Federal Grants (72 percent up 14 percentage points), and Private/Merit Scholarships (48 percent up 10 percentage points).
- Awareness about state and athletic scholarships decreased slightly from 2004, both down 3 percentage points to 68 percent and 57 percent, respectively.

Continuing the trend of the past several years, the percentage of students who felt that their involvement in GEAR UP changed their plans about going to college increased slightly in 2005 (see Figure 10.5).

- Sixty-four percent reported that their GEAR UP participation changed their plans about going to college. This is up 1 percentage point from the previous year. Thirty-six percent (36 percent) felt that their plans did not change because of GEAR UP, which is down 1 percentage point. Making plans and setting goals for the future are an important part of the high school years. This was not lost on GEAR UP students, seniors in particular.

- In terms of planning for the future, 90 percent of students reported that they had given much thought to the kind of career they would like to have (see Figure 10.6).
- Applying to college is a major step toward achieving career goals. Among the senior class of 2005, 51 percent of students applied to a four-year college or university.

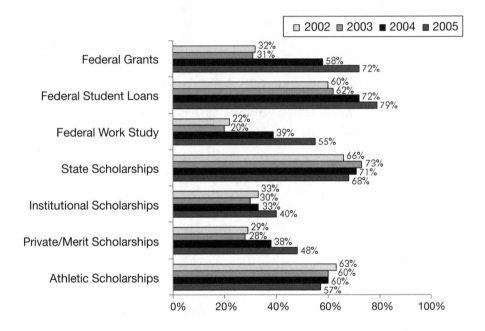

Figure 10.4 Students' Knowledge of Ways to Finance a College Education

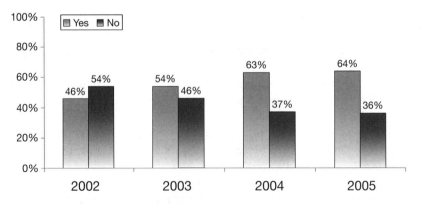

Figure 10.5 Has Participating in GEAR UP Changed Students' Plans about Going to College?

Source: 2002/2003/2004/2005 Student Surveys

Another 19 percent applied to a two-year community college (see Figure 10.7).

• Only 2 percent of the graduating class did not have plans to attend college at all, while 14 percent had not yet applied, but planned to.

Among those who had already applied to colleges, many had already been accepted (see Figure 10.8).

• The majority of students (84 percent) had already received a letter of acceptance from one of their schools of choice, but 16 percent had not. The most frequently cited reason for this was that the students had applied late (74 percent), while some students (22 percent) reported that the schools to which they applied had rolling admissions. The remaining 4 percent stated that the colleges/universities they applied to had a late notification date.

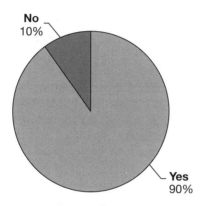

Figure 10.6 Have You Thought about What Kind of Career You Would Like to Have?

Source: 2005 Student Survey

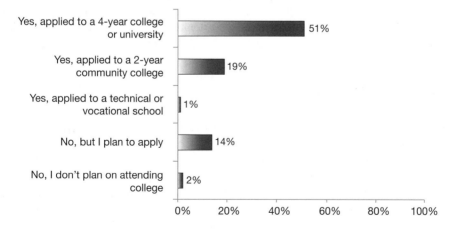

Figure 10.7 Have You Applied to Any Colleges for Next Year?

Source: 2005 Student Survey

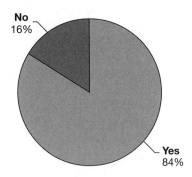

Figure 10.8 Have You Received Notification of Acceptance from Any Colleges?

Source: 2005 Student Survey

GEAR UP stimulated considerable change within the six participating schools. Communication across grades 7–14 increased and the perspectives of faculty, counselors, and administrators have been enlarged. Overall, the above evaluations indicated that the program learned more each year about how best to reach students (their parents and teachers), and most importantly, put those lessons into action to benefit their targeted audience. In the final year of the program, the GEAR UP leaders focused more on a careful appraisal of what student groups among the cohort were served most and least effectively. The evaluation data indicated that they served the high program consumers well: they have higher grade point averages, higher passing rates on Regents exams, and higher average attendance rates than low GEAR UP participants. The program, apparently, had a cumulative impact on students who worked intensively with GEAR UP over the six-year period, remained focused, on-track, and pointed toward college. Nevertheless, too many students were not impacted by the program: the low users of GEAR UP services or those who had serious deficits before GEAR UP entered the participating schools. Ultimately, grants such as GEAR UP are evaluated on their ability to move large numbers of students along a pathway of success. For the program leaders, this was disappointing news, and more efforts were now placed on the "hold-over" student.

THE HOLD-OVER STUDENT

There were a number of students, the "hold-overs," who failed to stay on track. Two hundred and fifty-eight students in the cohort, who entered high school in 2001, did not progress along with their counterparts to graduate from high school on time (LaGCC/QUP Final Evaluation Report, 2005). With respect to size, this group was not inconsequential: nine of the GEAR UP cohort remained in the ninth grade while 46 remained in the tenth grade, 69 in the eleventh grade, and 134 were still in the twelfth grade. What became clear is that the issues surrounding student hold-overs are complex. These are students who do not accumulate sufficient credits from year to year so that they can keep pace with their peers. Their attendance in their daytime classes is quixoticto-poor, resulting in missed assignments and, eventually, failing grades. In response, the high schools developed several options, which include PM School, and night school. Thus, a hold-over student wishing to push toward graduation can easily find him or herself enrolled in classes during the day, the afternoon, and the evening—a case, very often, of too much, too late.

This trend among members of the GEAR UP student cohort clearly supported retention studies that look at one of the most critical issues in the dropout problem: the rate at which ninth graders in public high school reach regular high school graduate status. One study conducted by the Center for Postsecondary Education Opportunity (Morenson, 1999) blamed the standards movement in K–12 education as causing an acceleration of declining high school graduation rates. The Center further stated that the attempt to make the high school curriculum more rigorous resulted in a growing share of high school students lost before graduation through attrition. To further the dropout problem is the rapid population growth rate of minority populations (Justiz, Wilson & Bjork, 1994). "This growth is a cause of concern since high dropout and low graduation rates in school and college, and illiteracy are particularly significant for Native American, African American, Hispanic and Asian American populations" (Carter, 2004, p. 12).

In the cohort's junior year, GEAR UP funded in each of the high schools a PM class for cohort students with junior status. The attendance pattern was inconsistent and erratic. In the senior year, 2004–2005, GEAR UP did not offer PM classes as these were already provided by the high schools. The program did not want to duplicate their efforts nor did GEAR UP leaders believe, based on the previous year's data, that this offering was particularly effective. This student group required a great deal of counseling, much more than our GEAR UP counselors (and certainly more than the schools' Guidance Counselors) have been able to provide. GEAR UP continued to serve the remaining twelfth grade students with college preparation workshops during the Summer and the Fall semester.

A second student group that faced special barriers in financing a college educa-tion was the immigrant students, who are a significant population within the GEAR

REFLECTIVE EXERCISE 10.1

Involving More Black Males in College Prep Activities

Data from the GEAR UP program revealed that the majority of participants were female. The program reviewed the literature; met with those who have run successful programs attracting low-income, minority males as well as experts in the area of school and college retention; and, finally, examined its own recruitment efforts for ways these can be improved.

1. Convene a study group to investigate this problem.
2. What role does mentoring play in your suggestions?
3. How can a social worker be involved in this project?
4. Who, from the community, should be included?

UP high schools. They were hard-working students, who have responded well to GEAR UP activities. Many of them, however, are undocumented. GEAR UP did not know precisely how many since they and their parents preserve that information carefully. Lack of citizenship or legal permanent residency was a barrier toward their attending college since they are unable to apply for financial aid. Over the years, GEAR UP tried to address this through citizenship workshops in the belief that the earlier parents go through the citizenship or legalization process, the greater the likelihood that their children will be able to apply for financial aid. Unfortunately, the senior year of high school was too late to implement this strategy so the program relied upon scholarship searches, which do not require U.S. citizenship or permanent residency as a prerequisite.

CUSTOMIZATION OF SERVICES TO STUDENTS

The collaborative programs described in the previous chapters have all underscored the importance of a community effort in ensuring student success. Despite the pressure to raise school-wide test scores and meeting the needs of all students in their charge, school leaders must categorize their student cohorts with tailor-made student activities. The intention of the New York State education regulators was to raise the academic standards at all levels of education. The old Regents competency tests (RCTs) were being phased out and, beginning with the class entering the ninth grade in 2000, all students were required to demonstrate competency in all areas using the new New York State Regents examinations. Students were now held to higher standards. They had to get higher test scores under the new Regents examination. Whether or not schools would be able to implement new programs of instruction to bring students up to these standards and prepare them to pass these new stringent examinations was another matter. For the at-risk student, the new Regents standards made the attainment of high school completion and graduation much more of a challenge. Recognizing that over 800 out of the 2,300 members of the student cohort did not achieve the expected twelfth grade status by the 2004–2005 academic (the final year of the GEAR UP program) and were not prepared to pass the Regents examinations, GEAR UP worked intensively with this student group, assisting them to accumulate credits and meet high school graduation requirements. Not wanting to shift resources away from the other 1,800 students, the program categorized the program activities to students on track to graduate on time and those not on track to graduate.

The following tables highlight the services to the GEAR UP cohort during the 2004–2005 academic year and are listed by Fall and Spring semesters (see Tables 10.3–10.7).

In addition to gathering assessments of students' behaviors, knowledge, and plans, information was also collected on their academic success. This outcome data, including students' Grade Point Averages (GPA), Regents test scores, and attendance rates from 2004–2005, was provided by the New York City Department of Education for 1,139 students who had parent consent forms on file. These forms required parental permission to collect this information. Additionally, the schools provided the college acceptance data for 1,045 students who completed a survey. The analysis of the data obtained is summarized below.

Table 10.3 Fall, 2004: Services to Students on Track for High School Graduation in 2005

GEAR UP activities for this student group—approximately 1,500 students across all three high schools—emphasized college preparation

Services to Students on Track	Frequency	Timeline	Expected Outcomes
1. Preparing college applications • Saturday and evening workshops for students and parents on the application and financial aid process and on the college entrance essay • Individual and small group assistance • College visits for students and parents	Daily, during the school day, after school, and Saturdays	September–December	• Completed college and financial aid applications • Selection of colleges
2. Enriching and strengthening the academic experience in preparation for college • Authors series hosted by the Queens Borough Public Library • SAT Prep sessions	Monthly, during the school day, and Saturdays	September–December	• Increased emphasis in reading and career preparation enriching their academic experiences
3. Enriching and strengthening student academic skills so that they can complete high school graduation requirements • Regents Prep at the high schools • Newtown High School Saturday Academy	Weekly, after school, and Saturdays	September–December	• Prepared for the Regents Examinations
4. Providing academic and social support to students and families through the GEAR UP site counselor and social worker	Daily, during the school day	September–December	• Increased focus and clarity of goals
5. GEAR UP leveraged a number of programs and resources available through LaGuardia on behalf of GEAR UP student cohort. These include: • College Prep • College Connection • College Now • Liberty Partnership Program	Weekly, during the school day, after school, and Saturdays	September–December	• Gained information on different higher education options: City University of New York, State University of New York, and private institutions • Increased knowledge of the application and college choice process • Completed college-level credit and non-credit bearing courses • Assistance in meeting high school graduation requirements and preparation for the SAT and Regents examinations

Source: GEAR UP End of Year Report, 2005

Table 10.4 Fall, 2004: Services to Students not on Track for High School Graduation in Spring 2005

GEAR UP activities for the student group—approximately 800 students across all three GEAR UP high schools—will emphasize high school completion and college preparation

Services to Students on Track	Frequency	Timeline	Expected Outcomes
1. Providing academic support • PM school (with Supplemental Instructional tutors) • Regents Prep • SAT Prep goals • Academic counseling (transcript review and an academic plan of action)	Daily, during the school day and after school, Saturdays	September–December	• Prepared for the examinations which are part of the high school graduation and college entrance requirements • Increased focus and clarity of goals
2. Providing social/emotional support and individual assistance • Mentoring	Daily/weekly, after school	September–December	• Increased focus and clarity of goals
3. Planning and preparing for college • Participation in college visits (with parents)	Twice a semester	October–November	• Increased focus on college and high school completion
4. GEAR UP will leverage a number of programs and resources available through LaGuardia Community College on behalf of students who will most likely not graduate in the GEAR UP student cohort. These include: • College Prep • College Now • College Connection • Liberty Partnership Program	Weekly, during the school day, after school, and Saturdays	September–December	• Students in College Prep will gain information on the different higher education institutions: City University of New York, State University of New York and private institutions • Increased knowledge of the application and college choice process

Source: GEAR UP End of Year Report, 2005

Table 10.5 Spring, 2005: Services to Students on Track for High School Graduation in Spring 2005

GEAR UP activities for this student group—approximately 1,500 students across all three high schools—emphasized preparation for and transition to college

Services to Students on Track	Frequency	Timeline	Expected Outcomes
1. Preparing for the transition to college • Mini Seminars • College visits for students and parents	Weekly/monthly, during the school day, and Saturdays	January–May	• Increased awareness of the college writing process, college schedule building, and career preparation • Increased focus and clarity of goals
2. Enriching and strengthening student academic skills so that they can meet high school graduation requirements • Regents Prep at the high schools • Newtown High School Saturday Academy	Weekly, after school, and Saturdays	January–June	• Students will pass the Regents examinations I
3. Preparing for a postsecondary experience • Summer Internship Experience • Summer Residential programs	Weekly, for four weeks	July	• Students will be able to explore various careers and have knowledge about college allowing for a smooth transition
4. Provided academic and social support to students and families through the GEAR UP site counselor and social worker	Daily, during the school day	January–June	• Goal setting, problem solving • Referrals to in-school and external resources
5. GEAR UP provided college tuition stipends to students who participated regularly in GEAR UP activities. Eligibility includes attendance and GEAR UP completion of at least four to five activities for students and their parents, an essay, and acceptance into college.	Based on participation in activities	June	• Assist families with the costs incurred in attending college • Students will be more likely to attend college
6. GEAR UP will leverage a number of programs and resources available through LaGuardia on behalf of the GEAR UP student cohort. These include: • College Prep • College Now • College Connection • Liberty Partnership Program	Weekly, during the school day, after school, and Saturdays	January–June	• Students in College Prep will gain information on the different higher education institutions: City University of New York, State University of New York and private institutions • Increased knowledge of the application and college choice process • Completed college-level credit and non-credit bearing courses • Assistance in meeting high school graduation requirements and preparation for the SAT and Regents examinations I

Source: GEAR UP End of Year Report, 2005

Table 10.6 Spring, 2005: Services to Students Not on Track for High School Graduation in Spring 2005

GEAR UP activities for the student group—approximately 800 students across all three high schools—emphasized high school completion and college preparation

Services to Students on Track	Frequency	Timeline	Expected Outcomes
1. Providing academic support • PM school (with Supplemental Instructional tutors) • Regents Prep, SAT Prep • Academic counseling, review and an academic plan of action	Daily/weekly, after school, and Saturdays	January–June	• Successful completion of and high school graduation and college requirements • Move to twelfth grade status • Increased focus and clarity of goals
2. Providing social/emotional support and individual assistance after school • Mentoring	Daily/weekly	January–June	• Increased focus and clarity of goals
3. Planning and preparing for college • Participation in college visits (with parents)	Twice a semester	January–May	• Prepared to select colleges of their choice
4. GEAR UP will provide college stipends to students who participated regularly in GEAR UP activities. Eligibility includes attendance and completion of at least four to five activities for students and their parents, an essay, and acceptance into college.	Based on participation in GEAR UP activities	June	• Assist families with the costs incurred in attending college • Students will be more likely to attend college
5. GEAR UP will leverage a number of programs and resources available through LaGuardia Community College on behalf of students who will most likely not graduate in the GEAR UP student cohort. These include: • College Prep • College Now application and college • College Connection • Liberty Partnership Program	Weekly, during the school day, after school, and Saturdays	January–June	• Students in College Prep will gain information on the different higher education institutions: City University of New York, State University of New York and private institutions • Increased knowledge of the choice process • Completed college-level credit and non-credit bearing courses

Source: GEAR UP End of Year Report, 2005

Table 10.7 Overall Academic Results for Students in the Outcomes Database and All GEAR UP High Schools★★★ 2004–2005

Academic Indicator	GEAR UP Cohort (2004–2005)	Previous Year Student Cohort (Non-GEAR UP) (2003–2004)
Percent of students passing Regents at 65% level	58%★	62%★
Average Grade Point Average (GPA)	72★	Not available
Percent of students graduating★★	85%	50%
Percent of students still enrolled	26%	34%
Percent of students dropped out	1%	17%
Average score on SAT Verbal	396	402
Average score on SAT Math	455	434
Average % Attendance	91%	82%

Notes: ★ Calculations include any Regents Exam taken. ★★ Data obtained from schools: 1,386 graduated out of 1,636 students enrolled in the twelfth grade. ★★★ Data collected based on the 1,139 students with parent consent forms on file.
Source: Student Surveys, 2005

The single most important indicator of success for any GEAR UP program, and the first critical step on the way to college, is graduating from high school. For the LaGuardia Community College/Queens Urban Partnership GEAR UP program, this indicator reflected a resounding success. Other academic outcomes also indicated that the LaGCC/QUP GEAR UP students were well prepared for college (see Table 10.7). Specifically:

- Nearly 85 percent of GEAR UP students graduated from their high schools, compared with 50 percent of students in their schools the previous year.
- The dropout rate for GEAR UP students was an extremely low 1 percent, compared with 17 percent of students in their high schools the previous year.
- The average GPA for students was 72, an increase from 68 in 2003–2004. (No comparison data was available for the high schools as a whole.)
- GEAR UP students had an average attendance rate of 91 percent, compared with 82 percent for all students in their high schools.
- The average SAT Verbal score for GEAR UP students (396) was comparable to that of the previous graduating class (402). Their SAT Math scores (455) were slightly higher than that of the previous year's cohort (434).

The results, presented in Table 10.8, indicate that a higher percentage of GEAR UP students applied to and planned to attend college than in the previous year. In addition, more GEAR UP students were attending a four-year college than their cohorts from the previous year.

All of the student outcome data together indicate that GEAR UP met their ultimate goal of preparing their students to graduate from high school, and apply to and attend college. The results also indicate that they assisted many students in meeting these goals who would otherwise not have met them, as shown from the previous year's data.

Table 10.8 GEAR UP Schools Postsecondary Enrollment

GEAR UP cohort	Percentage of Students Attending College (%)	Percentage of Students Attending a 4-Year College (%)	Percentage of Students Attending a 2-Year College (%)
2004–2005 Graduates (GEAR UP Cohort)★	95	55	40
2003–2004 Graduates	78	38	40

★ Only 1,045 of twelfth graders completed this survey
Source: Student Surveys, 2003, 2004, 2005

LESSONS LEARNED

Unlike Middle College High School, which is an institutionalized high school–college collaborative funded with public funds, GEAR UP was a six-year federally funded grant. It no longer exists and serves as a reminder that not all effective programs survive beyond the life of their external funding. However, there was much to learn about creating and implementing partnership by those involved in the process. By the sixth and final program year, the LaGuardia Community College/Queens Urban Partnership GEAR UP had become an integral part of the three targeted high schools. The evaluations of the program indicated that the program learned more each year about how best to reach the cohort, and most importantly, put those lessons in to action to benefit their targeted audience. The following reflects the lesson learned.

1. A Clear Understanding about the Proposed Services and their Implementation

School administrators need to be involved in the planning of the program, particularly activities that would impact their personnel and building during the school day. Specifically, the subject assistant principals were an important group as they were better able to indicate to their teaching staff the benefits of their involvement in the academic offerings of the program and the overall benefits of collaborating with other schools, community organizations, and higher education institutions.

2. Support of Teachers

The support of teachers is crucial as they are the main vehicle through which students are referred to GEAR UP services. While the GEAR UP on-site staff (guidance counselors and social workers) had access to the classroom, teacher buy-in was critical to student participation in the program's activities. More communication with the classroom teacher and GEAR UP onsite staff was needed to better connect students with the appropriate intervention.

3. More Emphasis in the First Year on "Selling GEAR UP" to the Students

The program needed to better publicize the program as a whole rather than separate services. For example, more general assemblies were needed in the middle schools and each year in the high schools. The absence of the home room period at the high school level made it difficult to capture the attention of the entire cohort at one time about the benefits of their participation in GEAR UP resulting in the inability to get to the students who desperately needed the services: students who were not on track to graduate on time.

4. Getting to the "Hold-over Student" Earlier

Program staff tried to identify students among the "hold-over" group who, with some intervention, counseling, and assistance, would have had the possibility of recouping sufficient academic credits to join the cohort. However, program staff needed to work more closely with the counseling staff toward the early identification of students who were underachieving and entering into risky attendance behaviors. Also, program staff needed to provide counseling and mentoring support in coordination with the attendance office, guidance counselors, and others on the school staff, who have the resources to work with this student group.

5. Sharing More Success Stories

Sharing more success stories about GEAR UP's impact on student performance and attitude about college needed to be shared with the school community. The program needed to better publicize its success at each school and at LaGuardia Community College.

6. Working Closely with Support Staff

Counseling and mentoring, key components to the academic engagement of students, were much more intensified during this time. Each member of the cohort was contacted by onsite staff through individual meetings, group sessions, and classroom visits, enabling GEAR UP to have a much clearer sense of the needs of students. The effectiveness of this effort hinged on a support structure provided by the administration at the GEAR UP schools. The onsite teams were part of the guidance department, giving them more access to students, student data, and GEAR UP cohort teachers than an "outside" program normally achieves. They worked closely with the assistant principal of guidance and the college advisor to identify students at risk of failing to graduate, while enhancing the level of college information normally provided to juniors and seniors on track to graduate on time. More students visited the College Office inquiring about the college process in all three high schools than ever before.

7. Engage Community Partners for Support

The "hold-over" student needed much counseling and support services. The GEAR UP partner, Queens Child Guidance Center, was able to work with this group of students but only if they and their parents would allow them access. However, placing an additional social worker and site counselor in the participating schools, allowed GEAR UP to attempt to address the needs of this population at a quicker rate than the schools alone would have been able to do.

CONCLUSION

Grant-funded collaborative programs are successful when they can tailor their services to the needs of the individual students. Overall, the customization of services was an example of the use of assessment data to address the gaps in student performance and make the necessary programmatic adjustment. Left alone, without grant dollars and community partners, these schools would have found it extremely difficult to customize services to students and to allow so many to graduate with members of their cohort. A central figure in identifying the needs of students is the classroom teacher. No longer can a teacher be prepared to teach only subject matter. The classroom teacher and support staff must partake in professional development offerings if they are to better serve the needs of students. The next chapter engages the reader in the experience of staff involved collaborative programs.

KEY TERMS

- Hold-over student
- Student engagement
- Student outcome data
- Assessment

CHAPTER 11

Building Community through Professional Development

INTRODUCTION

Regardless of the educational background of teachers when they enter the profession, they need sustained, ongoing professional development in order to offer students a high-quality education. Teachers must continue to learn new or additional content, study how students learn, analyze issues in teaching, and use new materials and technology. Teachers and administrators must also develop and renew a professional portfolio of their experiences. School leaders cannot assume that new state or district policies will magically reach the classroom and change teacher practice without an effective professional development plan. The community is an important source of information for educators to sharpen their skills while seeking vital knowledge of the very students they teach. Adopting the premise that "it takes a village," educators can use a professional portfolio to reflect on their growth and development while creating effective partnerships for school improvement. This chapter explores two programs' plans for providing professional development opportunities for school personnel.

Educational Leadership Constituent Council (ELCC) Standards

This chapter meets the needs of advanced academic programs in preparation for educational leadership:

> Standard 2.0: Candidates who complete the program are educational leaders who have the knowledge and ability to promote the success of all students by promoting a positive school culture, providing an effective instructional program, applying best practice to student learning, and designing comprehensive professional growth plans for staff.

> Standard 3.0: Candidates who complete the program are educational leaders who have the knowledge and ability to promote the success of all students by managing the organization, operations, and resources in a way that promotes a safe, efficient, and effective learning environment.
>
> (National Policy Board for Education Administration, 2002)

★   ★   ★

Professional development for teachers (i.e., staff development, in-service education, continuing education, teacher training) is the range of formal and informal processes and activities that teachers engage in both inside and outside of the school, in order to improve their teaching knowledge and skills (Jackson & Davis, 2000). Effective professional development is focused, ongoing, and embedded into a teacher's workday (National Staff Development Council, 2010). Teachers need to be reflective practitioners with an implicit knowledge base built through ongoing investigation and analysis, continuous rethinking and reevaluation of their own values and practices (Schön, 1987). Additionally, school leaders need to provide a structure for teacher involvement and learning outside the school building that encourages exchange among the members, which results in new norms of collegiality, a broadened view of leadership, and enhanced teacher perspectives on students' needs (Lieberman & McLaughlin, 1992).

While an organizational structure and a culture of inquiry are essential to effective professional development and student success, teachers need to have the necessary skills, tools, and support.

> Simply trusting that structural and logistical changes will translate into significant improved learning is wishful thinking. Teachers need concrete, continuous professional development to hone their current skills and learn new ones. And they need to be respectfully treated as adult learners who bring skills and experiences to meet the challenge of increasing student achievement.
>
> (The Center for Comprehensive School Reform and Improvement, 2006, p. 4)

Researcher Daniels emphasizes this point:

> Teachers must be helped—not just commanded—to teach in new, different, better ways. The way to make this happen . . . is through sophisticated professional training—the final step in delivering the promise of reform.
>
> (Daniels, 2006)

The learning community model of professional development improves learning opportunities and outcomes for both students and teachers. Teachers who are involved in this process engage in collaborative activities that are directed toward improving their instructional practices (Roberts & Pruitt, 2003). While both Middle College High School and LaGCC/QUP GEAR UP recognized the importance of professional development as central to the goal of increased student retention, graduation from high school as well as preparation for college, their strategies of implementation were somewhat different. Since its commencement, Middle College has emphasized the professional development of teachers while connecting key curricular and organization features to its host institution and to the structure of public education (Houle, 1996). Before the GEAR UP grant, the professional development offerings at six participating schools were too limited and fell far short of what was needed to fulfill the schools' reform agenda. The descriptions below illustrate how Middle College embedded professional development into its organizational structure and GEAR UP's efforts to supplement the shortage of support to the schools' staffs. The following descriptions illustrate these two program efforts to bring the various educational sectors together, along with community agencies, to engage their faculty in professional development opportunities.

BUILDING COMMUNITY THROUGH PROFESSIONAL DEVELOPMENT AT MIDDLE COLLEGE

Middle College was created around the same time as its host institution. The school, emphasizing the "seamless web of education" (Boyer 1991), was developed to address some of the academic problems that the City University of New York faced in dealing with under-prepared students in the onset of the 1969 Open Admissions policy. The location of Middle College on a college campus is not only beneficial to the school's students but to their teachers. Most faculty in other public high schools have no experience with the environment that permeates college faculty relations. Exposure to college faculty and college students benefit school faculty as they get an idea of what the college expects and what high school students need to know. Middle College faculty who teach at LaGuardia have a longitudinal view of the learning process of their students. They can foresee what their high school students can become when they enter college and what steps they must take to prepare them to succeed in college. The school expanded its collaboration with the LaGuardia Community College community by engaging in joint professional development. For example, student cohorts enroll in Algebra and Pre-Calculus courses at the College. These courses are team-taught by Middle College High School and LaGuardia faculty. The school also developed college courses in American Sign Language, Cooperative Education, and Sociology, all taught by college professors. Access to the college also allows Middle College faculty to participate in professional development offerings provided by LaGuardia creating an environment where faculty from both sectors can update their skills and engage in curricular discussions.

The small class size, in most cases 15–20 students, allows for experimentation and creativity in their curriculum and pedagogy and more time with their students. There is greater decision-making in curriculum content and teachers can create courses they wish to teach with administrative approval. In keeping with its tradition of using alternative assessments and methods, while aligning expectations for college courses, the school partners with the New York Performance Standards Consortium. The Consortium, which represents 28 schools across New York State that oppose high stakes testing, adopts the philosophy that "one size does not fit all" and has developed an assessment system that focuses on quality teaching to enhance the education of students. The school engages its faculty and LaGuardia Community College faculty in a partnership with the Quantum Leap Coaching and Training Institute on curriculum development and project-based learning. Other community partners involved in supporting the work of Middle College staff include the Liberty Partnership Program, a New York State funded early dropout prevention program that hires Middle College faculty to teach in the Saturday classes. Additionally, Middle College teachers are involved in the World Savvy organization that provides teacher training on global issues using contemporary art as a tool.

Professional development is ongoing and fully integrated into the school's structure:

> Conversations among teachers around the issues of curriculum, assessment and instruction take place weekly. Regular staff meetings include activities such as reviewing student work and peer assessment of student assignments. These staff development meetings create a culture of collaboration and accountability resulting in higher levels of student performance.
>
> (MCHS Charter Proposal, 1999, p. 16)

In addition to using external experts, the school utilizes its own resources, school staff, to discuss their ongoing work with students. The school is divided into six learning communities or instructional teams, each comprising five teachers and 75 students. The teams meet twice weekly to plan, revise, develop, and implement curriculum and instruction. Team members discuss classroom management strategies, engage in peer visitation and peer evaluations, and model collaborative work for their students. One major responsibility of these instructional teams is the hiring of faculty, a long-time tradition since the inception of the Middle College model. Teams typically interview and hire their team members, and meet at the beginning of the year to help each other develop goals. Periodically, all teams share their experiences with one another to ensure that information on all students is provided and that strategies for school improvement are discussed (MCHS Comprehensive Educational Plan, 2011).

Teachers underscore the benefits of this type of professional development:

> It's very different [to other schools]. We get together as a faculty more than I have seen in any other school. There are different committees that work on different

issues, such as curriculum and school related issues. Right now we're organizing a peer visitation committee. We chose people amongst the faculty we wanted to work with and we visit each other's classes.

(Carter, 2004, p. 80)

In addition to the above, the school provides various supports to all staff. These include:

- Action research projects. Small self-selected groups of teachers engage in research throughout the year to learn about specific ESL methodologies and strategies. Faculty then present their findings and recommendations to the rest of the staff.
- Peer observations. Teachers observe each other and write reflective letters pinpointing new strategies and techniques they have learned.
- Conferences. Faculty attend a variety of external conferences each year in order to keep abreast of new trends in ESL and other content areas.
- DYO formative assessment. Staff participate in ongoing professional development throughout the school year in developing and refining formative assessments for our school (in conjunction with the NY Performance Standards Consortium).
- Middle College National Consortium workshops. The school is a founding member of the Middle College National Consortium. Its staff attends workshops and conferences throughout the year on a variety of issues related to getting students to become college ready.
- New York City Department of Education workshops for preparing guidance counselors and school leaders in transitioning English Language Learner students through high school and beyond.

(Comprehensive Educational Plan, 2011)

Clearly, Middle College creates a richer learning environment for students by placing emphasis on a professional supportive working environment for their staff.

FILLING THE GAPS: BUILDING COMMUNITY THROUGH PROFESSIONAL DEVELOPMENT IN GEAR UP

For the designers of the LaGCC/QUP GEAR professional development was central to the goal of preparing students for high school completion and entry into college. Teachers were provided with a variety of opportunities to enhance the ways in which they support student learning: content area workshops, technology training for classroom use, teacher-mentor training, and Cross-GEAR UP Dialogues (see Appendix L for specifics). Before the introduction of GEAR UP in 1999, the school principals involved in the program had a passing and formal knowledge of one another's schools. The guidance counselors associated with the respective pairs of middle schools and their feeder high schools exchanged information about students in May or June in order to facilitate the transition to high school as much as possible. This certainly is not enough time to prepare the incoming school with information about the students they will receive in September. This lack of information often leads to staff at each level blaming each other for the gaps in student learning.

Toward the end of the GEAR UP grant, there was an improved knowledge of each school's challenges, discussions, and development of approaches. All GEAR UP professional development offerings were designed with one main criterion: all educational sectors, including the college, must be represented and where possible, the other community partners could participate. The program enabled principals more opportunity to meet with one another, exchange strategies, and to understand one another's environment. Also, faculty from the middle school, and high school levels, and, at times, the college level, had significant professional development opportunities to exchange information about the challenges and demands that beset their practice. Similarly, guidance staff in all of the participating schools greatly increased their knowledge of one another's educational context. GEAR UP workshops and teachers training "[was] a terrific opportunity for teachers to get new and innovative training" (Teacher, Capital Assessments, Inc., 2002).

They were no longer blaming one another or wondering about the state of preparation in the sending school. Rather, they were engaged in problem solving, program development, and program implementation discussions: "The best aspect of the professional development sessions was cross pollination with professionals from other schools" (Teacher, Capital Assessments, Inc., 2002).

In a 2004 survey administered to teachers about their involvement in GEAR UP, many expressed satisfaction about the workshop offerings. These teachers came from both the middle school and high school although by that time, the GEAR UP student cohort was in the high school. GEAR UP's professional development offerings preserved the relationship with the original middle schools by continuing to provide services to their teachers. The following are samplings from 35 teachers who responded to the survey:

> The activities actually can be used in the classroom. I understand how to implement them.
>
> (Middle School Teacher, Capital Assessments, Inc., 2004)

> Meeting with colleagues, sharing ideas and problems common to us all. Developing new approaches to our jobs.
>
> (High School Teacher, Capital Assessments, Inc., 2004)

Participation in GEAR UP's professional development was varied, with 35 percent of the teachers participating to a great extent, 47 percent participating to a moderate extent, 14 percent participating to a small extent, and 3 percent reportedly not attending any staff development sessions. Professional development opportunities provided prior to the implementation of GEAR UP in their schools were rated with a mean score of 5.5 on a scale of one to ten, with one being "not at all satisfied" and ten being "extremely satisfied." Using the same scale as above, teachers gave the professional activities offered by GEAR UP an average rating of 8.3. Teachers were clearly much more satisfied with GEAR UP workshops than with their schools' usual offerings (Capital Assessments, Inc., 2004).

REFLECTIVE EXERCISE 11.1

GEAR UP Professional Development Activities

Staff at the participating GEAR UP middle and high schools, higher education institutions, and community partners were involved in the following activities (see appendix for detailed workshop descriptions).

How will you customize these activities to suit the needs of your school?

- **Instructional Strategy Seminars**
  The Instructional Strategy Seminars provided ongoing support and development for the teachers in the three middle and high schools. Seminars were designed to inform classroom practice, model the use of learning communities, active learning, and the development of project-driven, interdisciplinary curricula. They assisted faculty in meeting the English Language Arts and Mathematics Standards and were focused on strengthening oral, reading, and written communication and mathematics. Several faculty from the participating higher education institutions led these workshops, along with representatives from various community-based organizations. Topics included: *Using Improvization and Theater Games in the Classroom; An ESL-Enhanced Look at Mathematics Instruction; Helping Students to Succeed in Science: What Do We Need to Do?*; and *American Culture and the Immigrants Experience: Using Theater Techniques in the Multicultural, Multilingual*.

- **Technology Workshops**
  Workshops were provided to teachers on the use of technology in the classroom: its integration with the new standards, and in effective classroom management. These workshops gave teachers the opportunity to engage in inter-school and cross-sectoral dialogue on pedagogical matters.

- **Cross-GEAR UP Schools Dialogues**
  The Cross-GEAR UP Schools Dialogues convened teachers, guidance counselors, and administrators to focus on issues relating to curricular content, scope, sequence, and pedagogy. Staff across the GEAR UP feeder pattern schools identified the needs of students at each step in the educational spectrum and made recommendations. Teams were organized around one of the following academic disciplines: English Language Arts, Mathematics/ Science, Counseling, and Social Studies.

LESSONS LEARNED

Educational leaders can provide high quality learning opportunities for teachers to have meaningful and continuous conversation about their beliefs, their teaching, and what they have learned about teaching. Furthermore, engaging in an ongoing process leads teachers to identify and carry out practices that result in increased graduation rates, improved college admission rates, and higher academic achievement for their students (Ancess, 2000). The following lessons learned capture the experiences of professional development of teachers involved in collaborative efforts.

1. Linking Professional Development to Classroom Practice

Given the school staff satisfaction with the professional development opportunities offered by GEAR UP and Middle College, the question remains, how useful were these workshops and the extent to which teachers actually used what they learned in the classroom. For example, there was great variability in the extent to which teachers were implementing teaching strategies from their GEAR UP professional development experiences in the classroom. About one in five teachers (22 percent) were not only fully integrating those strategies, but also exploring ways of refining their use of the information. On the other hand, more than half of the teachers (53 percent) were still in the early stages of implementing the instructional strategies, characterized by uneven usage. Nineteen percent of the teachers were somewhat in between the extremes, using instructional strategies routinely or integrating them fully into their classrooms.

2. Sustaining Practice after Funding Ends

As with any grant-funded program, the key question is "Will these activities continue after funding ends?" More importantly "Will the educational sectors and their community partners continue to work together?" Some practices did not require funding but the opportunity for staff from the various sectors to come together to discuss common problems and set into place various programs and policy changes that will improve their schools. For example, the Cross GEAR UP Counseling Dialogues examined in-school suspension, a practice implemented across the middle and high schools, which maintains suspended students within one classroom for a period of days under the watchful eye of a teacher and then sends them back to their respective classrooms. As it currently is implemented, in-house suspension complicates and reinforces the behavior of the student, who is not-on-track, keeps him/her out of the classroom and builds no bridge back to the sending classroom or teacher. The dialogues brought together assistant principals of security, student activities coordinators, and guidance counselors to consider the benefits of this practice, whether in-house suspension could be used more productively and, if so, how. Also, GEAR UP convened faculty and assistant principals together from all of the participating middle and high schools for a discussion on the benefits of integrating English Language Arts skills and content into Social Studies classes. Also, each school described their approaches toward such integration, the benefits they perceive as well as the barriers (GEAR UP Report, 2005). A complete list of professional development offerings provided by GEAR UP is listed in Appendix L.

PORTFOLIO BUILDING 11.1

Involving the Community in Creating a Professional Development Plan for a School

Research clearly shows that a well-trained teacher is the greatest factor in predicting student achievement more than materials, written curriculum, and even class size. Researcher Linda Darling Hammond (1999) has found that improving the expertise of teachers, dollar for dollar, results in far greater gains in student learning than do investments in tests, materials, or programs.

1. Research the professional development offerings a college provides for its faculty.
2. Identify the gaps in high school student learning from the professional development provided by the college to its faculty.
3. When you become a principal of a school, what type of professional development would you provide to your faculty and staff?
4. How will you utilize the skills of college faculty and personnel from community-based organizations in developing your professional development plan?

PORTFOLIO BUILDING 11.2

Creating a Professional Development Program

Develop a plan for staff development around the following areas:

*   Building a literacy program.
*   Working with K–16 teachers in a specific content area.
*   Developing a cohesive plan for high school and college guidance counselors.
*   Using the spoken word as a teaching tool.

1. Why is each area so important?
2. Develop a plan of action for your school.
3. How will students benefit from the professional development activities of your project?
4. How will you sustain the gains made by the professional development efforts?

3. Increased Repertoire of Teaching Strategies with Respect to Reading, Second Language Acquisition, and Writing

Teacher surveys, administered by GEAR UP evaluator Capital Assessments, Inc., indicated that most teachers were supportive of the GEAR UP program and have rated the professional development offerings highly. A substantial number of the teachers indicated that GEAR UP had increased their knowledge of the processes involved in oral communication, reading, and writing, and had given them a number of valuable strategies to test.

4. Sustaining Effective Professional Development Practices

GEAR UP staff felt that, where funding is not a factor, staff and faculty from all of the schools and community partners were able to consider and set into place various programs and policy changes that will improve their schools. The Cross GEAR UP Counseling Dialogues, for example, examined in-school suspension, a practice implemented across all six schools, which maintains suspended students within one classroom for a period of days under the watchful eye of a teacher and then sends them back to their respective classrooms. As it was implemented prior to the GEAR UP program, in-house suspension complicates and reinforces the behavior of the student, who is not-on-track, keeps him/her out of the classroom, and builds no bridge back to the sending classroom or teacher. The Dialogues brought together assistant principals of security, student activities coordinators, and guidance counselors to consider the benefits of this practice, whether in-house suspension could be used more productively and, if so, how. From this exchange, many good ideas emerged and GEAR UP staff was confident that several of them will be tried.

5. Developing a Professional Portfolio

Creating a professional portfolio provides aspiring school leaders and practicing leaders with the opportunity to reflect on their practice. It requires considerable effort, careful planning and much creativity. It demonstrates a teacher's approach to teaching and administrator's approach to leadership and offers a picture of an educator's practice over time (Martin-Kniep, 1999). Researchers Pruitt and Roberts state that collaborative portfolio development:

> helps to diminish the isolation of educators as they share their portfolios, discuss their practice, and exchange ideas about teaching and learning. Teachers often report that their collaborative portfolio experiences give them a greater sense of community.
>
> (Pruitt & Roberts, 2003, p. 162)

While a portfolio is powerful when developed collaboratively with other educators, it is even more so when it embodies community partnerships as an essential tool to effective leadership practice. The following question prepares the school leader to reflect on his or her work using the framework of "it takes a village to raise a child" as a foundation.

Developing a professional portfolio can be useful in assessing a school leader's commitment to creating effective partnerships while assisting him or her to meet the needs of the school building.

PORTFOLIO BUILDING 11.3

Developing Your Professional Portfolio

Begin answering these questions; add to the list as necessary:

1. What is your educational philosophy?
2. How do you define community?
3. Describe your approach to teaching and learning.
4. Describe your approach to leadership.
5. How do you identify student strengths and needs and how do you meet them?
6. How do you document student achievement?
7. Describe results of classroom research you conducted.
8. List the conferences, student groups, or workshops you have led or attended.
9. What work have you done in professional associations on the school, district, community, state, or national level?
10. Do you attend "non-educational related" conferences?
11. What steps have you taken to improve your leadership practice?
12. What impact has professional books, articles, or educational research had on your practice?
13. As a future educational leader, what challenges do you see yourself facing in the school system?
14. What strategies would you implement to address these challenges?
15. List three to five goals and objectives you hope to address as an instructional leader.
16. How can the community assist you in meeting these goals and objectives?

CONCLUSION

To accomplish the goal of helping teachers become lifelong learners, it is necessary for school leaders to develop a culture of inquiry through providing regular exposure to new ideas, reading, discussing, experimenting, getting feedback, and reflecting. School leaders, too, need to constantly reflect on their practice and their beliefs as they move forward to include the community in the transformation of schools. This culture of inquiry can be sustained through collaborating with the community. The following chapter addresses the issue of sustainability of collaborative programs.

KEY TERMS

- Embedded professional development
- External professional development
- Cross-sectoral dialogues
- Reflective practice

CHAPTER 12

Some Concluding Thoughts

Collaborative relationships between schools, colleges, and the community carry with them certain inherent benefits. They blur the institutional boundaries and reinforce a sense of collective responsibility for a community's children. Collaboratives heighten the sense of the educational continuum, pre-kindergarten through college, and, as a result, become a source for innovative and productive institutional problem solving. Children benefit from the added options and resources. School and college faculty benefit from opportunities to focus on common interests, exchange information, sharpen the policy and program agenda, and forge a continuum of support. In the end, schools, colleges, parents, and communities benefit because collaborations facilitate the possibility of:

- reducing the isolation that schools and teachers, in particular, experience
- invigorating the flow of information and resources among community, senior colleges, schools, business, and community sectors
- reducing duplicative educational costs
- creating a flexible educational process that addresses the transitional needs of students
- providing for the continuing education of experienced teachers and drawing upon all resources to prepare new teachers.

Issues of access and student achievement are not housed in any one sector but extend along the educational pipeline and colleges are part of these discussions. One of the underutilized strengths of many higher education institutions in urban school reform is their ability to share resources across educational levels. In fact, many colleges and universities cannot fully carry out their mission without stronger and more sustained collaborations with the school system and the wider community. Institutions coming together for collaborative efforts typically have a passing and formal knowledge of one another. Effective partnerships result in an improved knowledge of each institution's challenges. For example, school principals involved in the programs illustrated in this book have had many occasions to meet with one another, to call one another on the phone, and seek advice and help. Similarly, faculty from the middle school and high school levels have had significant professional development opportunities to exchange information about the challenges and demands that beset them. The result is an increased knowledge of context. They stopped blaming one another or wondering about the state of preparation in the sending school. Community leaders see a clearer role for them in their attempt to work with the schools and colleges. Rather, the partners engage in problem solving, program development, and program implementation discussions, which were much more productive. Participating institutions moved toward a culture of evidence and strategy as opposed to the culture of blame. It must be believed that all stakeholders want to maintain this stance.

Effective partnerships are knowledge-based unions in which partners teach each other, learn from each other and together. The success of school–college–community collaboration demands the academic and administrative partnership between the participating institutions. The more critical issue is that educational institutions often do not nurture and maintain collaborative relationships. Problems often occur when partners in traditional school–college collaborations must work in an area that is not an integral part of their everyday responsibilities. One of the essential features of collaboratives is for both entities to share resources, including human resources. For example, middle and high school students could have college students as mentors or tutors. To be effective, collaboration has to be institutionalized and part of the organizational structure and culture of both entities.

Partnerships focus on mutual benefits. For this to occur, there needs to be personal connections, individual initiatives, and commitment of like-minded individuals. Active involvement of the college administrators is important for practical and symbolic reasons and necessary to maintain the goals of the original plan. However, executive administrators cannot unilaterally create and sustain partnerships or mandate faculty and student involvement. Administrators need to identify faculty leaders who will sustain partnerships and include collaboration as part of their scholarly work. They have access to college faculty and their participation strengthens the idea that collaboration with schools is valued and an important academic goal of the college. College faculty can benefit from knowledge of their future college students, gaps in their learning, and the school curriculum. College administrators must prioritize collaboration with schools as a goal for their faculty. Schools also have to do their part. School leaders need to have a more aggressive outreach to college faculty who could benefit from collaborating with their peers at the school level.

Unlike Middle College High School, which is an institutionalized high school–college collaborative funded with public funds, GEAR UP was a six-year federally funded grant. It no longer exists and serves as a reminder that not all effective programs survive beyond the life of their external funding. However, there was much to learn about creating and implementing partnerships by those involved in the process. By the sixth and final program year, the LaGuardia Community College/Queens Urban Partnership GEAR UP had become an integral part of the three targeted high schools. The evaluations of the program indicated that the program learned more each year about how best to reach the cohort, and most importantly, put those lessons in to action to benefit their targeted audience. As important as leaders are to the effectiveness of partnership programs, so too is the need to actively pursue external funding for collaborative programs. This allows public (and private) funded institutions to be innovative, flexible, and to realize their dreams. The challenge is to institutionalize collaborative programs when external funding ends.

A NEW IDEA: SOMETHING TO THINK ABOUT

The following is an idea for a new community partnership project: *Building the Future by Redesigning the Senior Year in High School*.

The senior year of high school must be redesigned so that it functions as a transition year, a "jumpstart" to college. Such a year envisions a work/community service experience, college courses, the strengthening of academic skills, exposure to and study on the college campus. Another way of facilitating the college transition lies with the nature of the support mechanisms for students and faculty that are available within urban schools. Middle College and LaGuardia have long recognized and provided for the importance of counseling, the needs for students to clarify their personal goals and career goals, the value of experience and interaction with other adults. It will be valuable to extend the experience to mainstream high schools, reaching out to counselors, neighborhood workers, teachers, and other students. This initiative can assist schools to:

- examine how their school supports the affective development of students and develop an action plan that addresses the needs
- provide assistance and information concerning college choice, admissions, and financial aid
- construct theme-based curricula, which would enable students to grasp the future, the demands, the opportunities, the needs, and to come to grips with what they want for themselves.

Building the Future can accent the study of demography, the economy, various careers, the structure of organizations, and skills that will be in demand. Against this backdrop, students might select a career of interest to them, and, via readings, interview, field visits, and internships in the community, analyze the changes that will occur and the preparation they might need.

What do you think?

LaGuardia Community College/ Queens Urban Partnership GEAR UP Activities

SERVICES TO STUDENTS AND PARENTS

Counseling

The GEAR UP site counselors and social workers provided counseling services to groups of students in the three high schools. Site counselors and social workers met with students weekly for academic and social support. Some groups met around a theme, such as leadership, college awareness, and preparation, or as a book club.

Tutoring

In an effort to provide intensive, individualized support to the cohort, our GEAR UP supported a tutoring program. While individual assistance was available, tutors provided homework assistance, led study groups, and prepared students for the city-wide tests. Reading continued to be a major thrust in the tutoring program, as well as mathematics. The program was supervised by teachers at each of the participating schools, along with the LaGuardia tutor trainers who periodically visited each school.

Mentoring

The mentors, many of whom reflected the language and cultural groups resident in each of the school sites, were selected based upon their leadership potential, compassion, and commitment to working with the eighth grade cohort. The Queens Child Guidance Center conducted the Mentor Training Program with a trainer from the Big Brothers Big Sisters of New York City to prepare the mentors for their responsibilities. The training consisted of workshops centered around: Mentor Definition; Relationship Building; Child Development; Critical Skills; Problem Solving; Family Issues; Cultural Competency; and Train the Trainer for Group.

College Admissions Initiative

GEAR UP social workers and site counselors visited classrooms and met with students to provide information and counseling on the college admissions process. Students also met with college mentors after school for assistance with conducting college searches on the internet, guidance in the college selection process, and assistance with completion of college applications and financial aid forms.

College Portfolio

With an increased emphasis on college awareness and preparation for the cohort, students in twelfth grade English classes developed their college portfolios. Students conducted a "Scavenger Hunt" of finding answers to questions on college and career preparation. Some of these questions included:

1. If you wanted to study history in Hawaii, which institution might you attend?
2. Which book gives you a description of possible careers?
3. What training is necessary in order to become an architect? How much does an architect earn on average?
4. What is the nature of work for teachers, librarians, and counselors?
5. If you are planning a career in nursing, where would you obtain scholarship information?

Newtown High School

GEAR UP collaborated with the Saturday Academy at Newtown High School to provide additional classes and support to the senior cohort.

Saturdays at the College Workshop Series

GEAR UP offered a series of Saturday workshops and events centered on various themes, including College Exploration, College Admissions, Financial Aid, SAT Preparation, Leadership, Career Exploration, and Writing the College Essay.

College Now!

This CUNY sponsored program enabled the GEAR UP cohort at Newtown and Flushing high schools to take college credit and non-credit bearing courses at their high schools.

College Connection

A LaGuardia-sponsored program that enabled the GEAR UP cohort to take LaGuardia Community College courses on campus during LaGuardia's Spring I and Spring II semesters.

Mini Seminars

Mini Seminars, led by LaGuardia Community College faculty and other professionals, were offered during the school day at the GEAR UP high schools. These seminars were planned collaboratively with the twelfth grade faculty and the classroom teacher, and were intended to supplement, extend, and enrich classroom curricula, as well as expose the GEAR UP cohort to college faculty, expectations, style, and knowledge of the college environment.

Liberty Partnership Program

GEAR UP collaborated with the Liberty Partnership Program, a high school retention and college preparation program, to offer classes in PSAT/SAT, Regents Review, and Digital Photography, as well as classes to parents of GEAR UP students such as Introduction to Computers and Conversational ESL.

Workshops by the Queens Borough Public Library

Through GEAR UP, the Queens Borough Public Library (QBPL) expanded its outreach and reconstructed the relationship between branch libraries and the classroom. QBPL will continue to offer cultural, educational, and informational workshops for the students and parents of GEAR UP students.

Summer Programs

GEAR UP served the cohort during the summers with enrichment, academic classes, weekly trips, residential experiences, and an Internship program.

SERVICES TO SCHOOL STAFF

Instructional Strategies Seminars

These seminars brought teachers across grades 7–12 together to provide high quality professional development opportunities linked to reading, writing, and mathematics. For example, one seminar examined strategies to encourage student expression and creativity through writing. The seminars, presented in various subject areas by faculty from local colleges as well as other educational professionals, provided an opportunity for teachers to share information and exchange ideas.

Round Table Discussion Groups

These discussion groups, an outgrowth of the Cross GEAR UP School Dialogues, brought together faculty from six middle schools, high schools, and colleges to discuss relevant issues. For example, a social studies group met to compare experiences with language skills development in the social studies classroom. The groups met for three weeks to discuss these types of issues in teaching.

Site Planning Teams

Three Site Planning Teams, which included representatives from the middle schools, their corresponding receiving high school, parents, the Queens Borough Public Library, and GEAR UP staff met monthly to plan and provide feedback about the program. These regular meetings helped GEAR UP know what activities were working well as well as any problem areas that needed to be addressed.

Teaching Matters, Inc. (TMI)

TMI provided online and face-to-face seminars and in-class assistance for teachers engaged in infusing technology into their classrooms.

GEAR UP Coordinating Council

May 3, 2001

12:00–2:30 p.m. in Room C-235

A G E N D A

I. Program Updates

- Student Activities
- Professional Development
- Site Planning Teams
- New Proposal Submission

II. Transition to High School

- High School Bound
- Preliminary Discussions with High School Staff and Administrators
- Site Counselor and Social Worker Preparation for High School Transition

III. Elements of the Ninth Grade Cohort Program

IV. Retreat

- Issues
- Tentative Agenda

First Governance Meeting: Minutes of the Coordinating Council

CONCERNS

- Are we reaching this student population and their parents as much as we need to? Do the students know that they are in GEAR UP? Are they aware of the program's services?

- Does the program know who among the eighth grade cohort needs what services (e.g., English Language Learners; social skills and mentoring; health; tutoring; librarian)? Are those identified as needing particular services receiving them?

- Is the assessment qualitative as well as quantitative? Will an increase or a decrease of scores be attributed to GEAR UP?

- How can the outreach librarians effectively reach parents, tutors, and mentors and identify what students and parents need? For the library this is somewhat difficult since one part of the Library's mandate is anonymity. With regard to the mentors, Queens Child Guidance Center suggested that mentor training was ongoing and coordination with the Library could be broached.

- Student performance on the Regents Examinations constitutes a major concern, particularly with the new Math A, Science, and the Document-Based Questions on the Social Studies Regents.

- There is need for a formal line for dissemination of information to parents.

- Examination re: the nature and kinds of counseling that students receive. How is it provided now? Does it work?

- As students leave the intermediate schools, how will it be possible to keep the intermediate schools engaged in GEAR UP?

- How will this year prepare for the move to high schools next year (e.g. space for the site counselors; transitional meetings between the site counselors and counselors at the high school)?

THE GEAR UP LEGACY: WHAT ASPECTS OF SCHOOL REFORM SHOULD GEAR UP CONCENTRATE UPON?

- Relationship between the schools and the library—strengthen inter-agency program coordination and use of the library's resources.

- Increased knowledge of social agencies and services within the local communities, referral mechanisms, and case management.

- Increased relationships between schools in the "feeder patterns."

- Expanded knowledge and use of instructional strategies that are effective with English Language Learners.

- Increased coordination between the Intermediate, Junior High, and High Schools with respect to the Regents examinations and courses that students will be expected to take in high school.

- Careful scrutiny with respect to GEAR UP successes and thought concerning how to maintain aspects of the program (e.g., peer mentoring) even if it cannot be done precisely as it is now. Look for ways to build on the expertise of the English Language Learner (e.g., English dominant students having difficulty learning Spanish). How can junior high school students be trained to work in a peer mentoring or tutoring capacity within their own schools? How can high school students be trained to work within their high schools?

PARTNERS

- Parents have a perspective. Should they have representation on the Coordinating Council?

- Should there be a college or a high school mentor or tutor on the site team? (Everyone agreed that the team should be kept small.)

- Business partners should not be sought until it is clear what role they are going to play. They have an interest in career awareness.

- What community-based organizations are located in the high schools and intermediate schools? They should be involved in the Coordinating Council.

RECOMMENDATIONS

- District staff should be included on the Cross School Dialogues.

- Queens Borough Public Library should have a table and disseminate information at any events, which parents attend (e.g., Open House).

- With respect to the transition to the ninth grade, GEAR UP should aim for a Perfect Start in order to avert what often happens during the first year of high school: kids get lost, don't get into the right class. In order to change this, a structure for communication has to be established. Records have to be properly exchanged. Math is key. Right now, this transition, in at least the view of a few of the persons at the table, does not work very well.

- Elementary school principals are overwhelmed. They don't see GEAR UP as affecting their schools and so do not want to participate. This should be accepted and their participation not pushed.

NEXT STEPS

The next meeting of the Coordinating Council was set for Tuesday, January 9, for lunch from 12:30–2:30, place to be determined.

APPENDIX D **GEAR UP: Governance Teams Meetings**

(Site Planning Teams and Coordinating Council)

November 2003–June 2004

	November	*December*	*January*	*February*	*March*	*April*	*May*	*June*
	Opening Session	*Monthly Meeting*	*Monthly Meeting*	*Monthly Meeting*	*Monthly Meeting*	*Monthly Meeting*	*Monthly Meeting*	*End of Year Retreat*
Coordinating Council	6th Wyndham Hotel Conference Room 4–7 p.m.		3rd LaGuardia Community College		12th LaGuardia Community College			Wyndham Hotel Conference Room 4–7 p.m.
Team IS 61/ John Bowne HS	6th Wyndham Hotel Conference Room	11th IS 61 2:30–4 p.m.	18th IS 61 2:30–4 p.m.	15th IS 61 2:30–4 p.m.	15th IS 61 2:30–4 p.m.	19th IS 61 2:30–4 p.m.	31st John Bowne 2:30–4 p.m.	Wyndham Hotel Conference Room 4–7 p.m.
Team IS 145/ Newtown HS	6th Wyndham Hotel Conference Room	11th Newtown 3:00–4:30 p.m.	22nd IS 145 3:00–4:30 p.m.	12th Newtown 3:00–4:30 p.m.	12th IS 145 3:00–4:30 p.m.	16th Newtown 3:00–4:30 p.m.	14th IS 145 3:00–4:30 p.m.	Wyndham Hotel Conference Room 4–7 p.m.
Team JHS 189/ Flushing HS	6th Wyndham Hotel Conference Room	8th JHS 189 7:30–9:00 a.m.	19th Flushing 7:30–9:00 a.m.	11th Flushing 7:30–9:00 a.m.	12th JHS 189 7:30–9:00 a.m.	18th Flushing 7:30–9:00 a.m.	19th JHS 189 7:30–9:00 a.m.	Wyndham Hotel Conference Room, 4–7 p.m.

Sample Evaluation Plan Summary Chart

Evaluation Objective	Source of Data/Instrument	Sample/Comparison	Performance Target
A. PROCESS EVALUATION			
1. Student Perceptions: Determine students' perceptions of the helpfulness of in-school, after-school, & Saturday programs.	Student surveys, focus groups, and questionnaires, administered three times during the school year	All students participating in in-school, after-school & Saturday programs	75 percent of student respondents evaluating programs as helpful
2. Teacher Perceptions: Evaluate the effectiveness of professional development offerings.	Teacher surveys and questionnaires, administered after each PD workshop	All teachers participating in professional development	75 percent of teacher respondents evaluating professional development as helpful
3. Student Attendance: Determine the effectiveness of program recruitment & retention for after-school & Saturday programs.	Program Participation/Attendance Logs, examined monthly during the school year	All program log forms	Realistic targets for enrollment/retention will be developed during the first program year
B. OUTCOME EVALUATION			
Objective 1: Increase Academic Performance & Preparation for Postsecondary Education			
4. Reading & Writing Achievement: Evaluate student ELA performance.	a) NYC ELA Test – 7th grades b) NYS ELA Test – 8th grade c) Regents English Exam – 1st grade	a) Program students will be compared with themselves b) Program students will be compared with non-program students from the same school c) Program students will be compared with non-program students from the same school	a) Program students attaining proficiency (Level 3–4) will increase by 10 percent between grades 7 & 8 b) 10 percent more program students will attain proficiency (Level 3–4) than non-program students c) 10 percent more program students will pass the Regents exam than non-program students

Evaluation Objective	Source of Data/Instrument	Sample/Comparison	Performance Target
5. Mathematics Achievement: Evaluate student math performance.	a) NYC Math Test—7th grade b) NYS Math Test—8th grade c) Regents Math A Exam—10th grade d) Course grades from Pre-Algebra & Algebra 1	a) Program students will be compared with themselves b) Program students will be compared with non-program students from the same school c) Program students will be compared with non-program students from the same school d) Program cohorts will be compared over successive years	a) Program students attaining proficiency (Level 3 or above) will increase by 10 percent between grades 7 & 8 b) 10 percent more program students will attain proficiency (Level 3 or above) than non-program students c) 10 percent more program students will pass the Regents exam than non-program students d) Program students who complete Pre-Algebra by end of 7th grade & Algebra 1 by end of 9th grade will increase by 10 percent each year
6. Science & Social Studies Achievement: Evaluate student science & social studies performance.	a) Regents Science Exam—10th grade b) Regents Global Studies Exam—10th grade c) Regents US History & Government Exam—12th grade	a–c) Program students will be compared with non-program students from the same school	a–c) 10 percent more program students will pass the Regents exams than non-program students
7. Academic Rigor: Determine student enrollment in academically challenging courses.	a) School records of enrollment in honors, pre-AP & AP courses	a) Program students will be compared with non-program students from the same school	a) 10 percent more program students will enroll in academically challenging courses than non-program students

Evaluation Objective	Source of Data/Instrument	Sample/Comparison	Performance Target
Objective 2: Increase the Rate of High School Graduation & Participation in Postsecondary Education			
8. High School Graduation: Determine percentage of students who graduate.	a) School records	a) Program students will be compared with non-program students from the same school	a) 15 percent more program students will graduate from high school than non-program students
9. Postsecondary Education: Determine enrollment in postsecondary education.	a) School records	a) Program students will be compared with non-program students from the same school	a) 15 percent more program students will enroll in postsecondary education than non-program students
Objective 3: Increase students' & their families' knowledge of postsecondary education options, preparation, & financing.			
10. Knowledge of Postsecondary Options	a) Annual Student Survey b) Annual Parent Survey	a) Program cohorts will be compared over successive years b) Parents of program cohorts will be compared over successive years	a–b) The following percentages of program students/parents will show familiarity with post-secondary educational options, preparation required & financing: Year 1: 50%; Year 2: 60%; Year 3: 70%; Year 4: 80%; Year 5: 90%; Year 6: 90%
Additional Objectives:			
11. Attendance	a) School records	a) Program students will be compared with non-program students from the same school	a) Program students' average daily attendance will be 15 percent higher than non-program students
12. Grade Promotion	a) School records	a) Program students will be compared with non-program students from the same school	a) Program students' on-time grade promotion will be 15 percent higher than non-program students

Sample College Fair Flyer
(in Spanish and English)

College Fair

No se lo pierda!

QUIEN:
Inscripción es gratuita para todos
los estudiantes de GEAR UP
Padres son bienvenidos!

DONDE:
LaGuardia Community College
31-10 Thomson Avenue
Long Island City, NY 11101
Tel. (718) 482-5033
<u>Poolside Cafeteria, E-building</u>

CUANDO:
Sábado 6 de Diciembre de 2003
9:00 am - 2:30 pm

No pierda la oportunidad de aprender acerca de:
* Ayuda Financiera
* CUNY, SUNY y Universidades Privadas
* Hable con representantes de diversas Universidades
* Obtenga información de varias Universidades
* Programas Especiales de admisión a la Universidad: EOP,
HEOP, SEEK y College Discovery

Para mas información favor de llamar a la oficina de GEAR UP en su escuela

Flushing High School	John Bowne High School	Newtown High School
Guidance Counselor	r, Guidance Counselor	Guidance Counselor
ocial Worker	social Worker	Room 473 718-595-8400 ext. 2440
Room B18 718-888-7500 ext. 618/ 617	Room 347 718-263-1919 ext. 3472/ 3473	

Save the Date!

WHO:
Registration is free and open to
all 11th grade GEAR UP Students.
Parents are welcome!

WHERE:
LaGuardia Community College
31-10 Thomson Avenue
Long Island City, NY 11101
Tel. (718) 482-5033
<u>Poolside Cafeteria, E-building</u>

WHEN:
Saturday, December 6, 2003
9:00 am - 2:30 pm

Don't miss the opportunity to learn about
*Financial Aid
*CUNY, SUNY and Private Colleges and Universities
*Speak to college representatives
*Get informational materials from various colleges
*Special Opportunity Admissions Programs: EOP, HEOP, SEEK
and College Discovery

For more information and registration please contact the GEAR UP Office at your school

Flushing High School	John Bowne High School	Newtown High School
Guidance Counselor	Guidance Counselor	, Guidance Counselor
Social Worker	, Social Worker	Room 473 /18-595-8400 ext. 2440
Room B18 718-888-7500 ext. 618/ 617	Room 347 718-263-1919 ext. 3472/ 3473	

College Admissions Conference Agenda

**LAGUARDIA COMMUNITY COLLEGE
GEAR UP PROGRAM**

College Admissions Conference

**Saturday, October 23, 2004
8:30 a.m.–2:30 p.m.**

A G E N D A

8:30–8:55 a.m.   Arrival and Breakfast

Main Stage Lobby

9:00–9:10 a.m.   Welcome

Main Stage Theater
Dr. Hazel Carter, Director, GEAR UP

Purpose of Program
Principal Investigator, GEAR UP

9:10–10:15 a.m.   Writing the College Essay:

Main Stage Theater
This workshop will teach the fundamental techniques of writing
required essays for selective college admission.

Presenter: College Writing Consultant

10:15–10:20 a.m.   College Admissions Workshops

Presenter: Director of Student Activities, GEAR UP

Please turn over for workshop schedule

10:30–11:30 a.m.   Workshop Session #1 Topic:
Overview of CUNY, SUNY, and Private Colleges
Admissions

City University of New York (CUNY)	State University of New York (SUNY)	Private Colleges & Universities
Room C139	*Room C144*	*Room C148*
Presenter: Counselor/Recruiter CUNY Central Office	Presenter: Counselor SUNY Central Office	Presenters: Director Outreach Programs, Commission on Independent Colleges and Universities
City University of New York (CUNY)	**State University of New York (SUNY)**	**Private Colleges & Universities**
Room C140	*Room C146*	*Room C149*
Presenter: Counselor/Recruiter CUNY Central Office	Presenter: Senior Admissions Advisor SUNY Central Office	Presenters: Director Outreach Programs, Commission on Independent Colleges and Universities

11:40–12:40 p.m.   Workshop Session #2 Topic:
Overview of CUNY, SUNY, and Private Colleges
Admissions

CUNY	SUNY	Private Colleges & Universities
Room C139	*Room C144*	*Room C148*
CUNY	**SUNY**	**Private Colleges & Universities**
Room C140	*Room C146*	*Room C149*

12:40–12:50 p.m.   Break: Light Refreshments Served

11:40–12:40 p.m.   Workshop Session #2 Topic:
Overview of CUNY, SUNY, and Private Colleges
Admissions

CUNY	SUNY	Private Colleges & Universities
Room C139	*Room C144*	*Room C148*
CUNY	**SUNY**	**Private Colleges & Universities**
Room C140	*Room C146*	*Room C149*

2.00–2:30 p.m.   Lunch: (C Building Cafeteria 3rd Floor)

APPENDIX H

College Prep Program

College Coach

COLLEGE COACH TIMELINE

January

- **Student Recruitment:** College Coach Supervisors, in collaboration with College Coaches, will recruit 75 students at each high school from the tenth grade cohort. An additional 15 students (five per College Coach) should be placed on a waiting list. Selection criteria includes: willingness to be an active participant in four sessions that will take place after school; willingness to do homework assignments; willingness to attend college trip; passing grades and good attendance.

- College Coaches provide College Coach Supervisors with final lists of students. Supervisors submit lists to College office via fax to (718)609-2048. Attn: Joe Johnson by January 24.

- College Coach distributes Capital Assessment, Inc., Parent Consent Forms, Parent Letter/Consent Form, and Liability Forms to all students. All forms must be collected prior to the first session. Completed forms must be submitted to the College office following the first session.

- Each College Coach Supervisor will submit dates for all sessions to College office via fax to (718)609-2048. Attn: Joe Johnson by January 24.

February

Pre-campus visit sessions take place. Sessions are to take place after school. Each session will be 1.5 hours.

- A College Staff Member will observe a session with students. A schedule of observations will be sent to College Coach Supervisors.

- Each College Coach Supervisor will submit trip request forms to Superintendent's Office for campus visit. A copy of approval should be submitted to the office Attn: Joe Johnson 2 weeks prior to the college visit.

- College Coach Supervisors and College Coaches make arrangements for chaperones for campus visit.

- College office will forward campus visit agendas to College Coach Supervisors and College Coaches.

March

- College campus visits.

March/April

- Campus visit debriefing session.

A G E N D A

December 16, 2012
4:30 p.m.–7:30 p.m.

1. Welcome/Introduction Remarks

2. College Awareness Workshops: Goals, Objectives, and Strategies

3. Program Logistics: Timelines, Documentation, and other Considerations

4. Where Do We Go from Here? – Issues and Concerns

PARENT CONSENT FORM

Dear Parent:

Your child, _____, has been selected to participate in the College Coach Program. This year COLLEGE PREP PROGRAM is placing a stronger emphasis on college awareness through the development of a college portfolio and the College Coach Program. Faculty serving as College Coaches, will work with students to explore the college admission process, identify the critical issues of choosing a college, visit a college and analyze student needs. High School Teachers, each working with a group of 25 students, will conduct three sessions designed to prepare students for the visit, attend the college visit and meet for one session with students to debrief this experience.

The college visit will involve an entire school day. Students will meet at the high school in the early morning and be transported by bus. They will return to the high school at approximately _____ p.m. and will be expected to return home unaccompanied.

Meetings will take place once a month, after school from _____ p.m. to _____ p.m. Refreshments will be provided. The following are the tentative meeting dates:

_____

_____

We will also visit _____ (*name of college or university*) on _____ (*date*)

Please detach and sign the bottom of this form and complete the attached liability form. Have your child return it to me by _____ (*date*). Please feel free to contact me at _____ (*school phone #*) if you have any questions or concerns. Thank you for your time and cooperation.

(College Coach's Name)

(School)

- -

PLEASE PRINT

I, _____ (*parent's name*), allow my child, _____ (*student's name*), to participate in the College Coach Program. I understand that he/she will participate in 4 sessions that will take place after school and he/she will visit a college campus.

_____   _____

(*Parent's signature*)   (*Date*)

The mission of College Prep Program is to significantly increase the number of low-income students who are prepared to enter and succeed in postsecondary education. One of the goals of the College Prep Program is to support the academic growth of the tenth grade cohort through increased personal attention and instructional support so that they complete high school and are well prepared for college.

This year the introduction of the College Coach Program helped to strengthen our emphasis on college awareness. Faculty serving as College Coaches, will work with students to explore the college process, identify the critical issues of choosing a college, visit a college, and analyze students' needs. These faculty members will meet with a group of 25 students for three sessions to prepare students for a college campus visit. Faculty will attend the college visit with the students and will facilitate one additional session to debrief this experience.

College Coach: Duties and Responsibilities

The College Coach will:

- In collaboration with the College Coach supervisor, recruit 25 tenth grade students.

- Work with a maximum of 25 students, conducting four seminar sessions designed to prepare and to debrief students for a college campus visit.

- Meet with students after school in 1.5 hour sessions to be held at each school.

- Plan the Seminar curriculum and the college campus visit in collaboration with College Prep Program staff and College Coach supervisor.

- Attend the campus visit each semester and meet for one session with students to debrief this experience.

- Be responsible for taking student attendance and forwarding attendance sheets to the Supervisor of the College Coach program at each school.

- Complete monthly logs and document activities as requested by the College Prep Program.

- Report to his/her school's College Coach supervisor.

Participants will receive $36.50/hour for up to 20 hours of work per semester based on attendance.

Supervisor, College Coach Program: Duties and Responsibilities

The purpose of this activity is to expose students to colleges and prepare them for a campus visit that will occur during the semester. The College Coach supervisor will supervise three sessions designed to prepare students for the visit, attend the college, visit and meet with the College Coaches and students to debrief this experience.

Sophomores!

GEAR UP

Gaining Early Awareness and Readiness for Undergraduate Programs

Services Available For 10th Grade Students:

Mentoring

Work with a high school teacher in small groups or individually. Receive continuous support over the academic year to improve your academic performance and clarify your goals.

Counseling

Need someone to talk to? There is a guidance counselor and social worker available to you. *Stop by your GEAR UP office to see your GEAR UP Counselor and Social Worker.*

Groups

Make new friends and find out your peer's opinions. Groups held during your lunch or free period.

College For Teens

Come and enjoy 8 adventurous Saturdays at LaGuardia Community College. Classes offered are Adventures in Literature & the Arts, Culture & Dance and Culture& Theater. Come make new friends! We will provide tuition, transportation and lunch.

College Bound

Participate in College Bound and find out where your education can take you! Plan your future! Work with a College Coach to get information on applying for college! Visit college campuses!

Test Prep Courses

Need some help preparing for tests? Take our test prep courses and get your questions answered by an experienced high school teacher. Watch your grades soar, learn, and have fun while doing it.

Summer Program

Spend your summer on a college campus! Meet new people and take courses in English, Math, Dance and Theater. Exciting trips every week! We provide tuition, transportation, breakfast and lunch.

W.O.R.K. Program

Prepares you for success in the workforce through academic classes and work readiness training and development. Get paid while you learn! (*There are some eligibility requirements that must be met for enrollment into the program.*) The program offers tutoring and use of LaGuardia Community College's computer labs. Eligible students are guaranteed a job with LaGuardia Community College's Summer Youth Employment Program.

Don't be left behind! Come to the GEAR UP office and find out what is happening!

Flushing HS	**Guidance Counselor**	**Social Worker Room B18A 718-888-7500 ext.615/617**
John Bowne HS	**Guidance Counselor**	Social Worker Room 347 718-263-1919 ext. 3471/ 3473
Newtown HS	Guidance Counselor	Social Worker Room 473 718-595-8400 ext. 2440

The College Coaches Supervisor will:

- Identify, recruit, interview, and recommend students to College Prep Program College Coaches.

- Design, in collaboration with College Prep Program staff and participating College Coaches, the campus visit that will occur each semester.

- Coordinate and arrange the logistics of each student seminar session, including the provision of announcements and reminder notices, room arrangements, refreshments, and special needs.

- Observe and monitor the student seminars on a regular basis.

- Attend the campus visit each semester.

- Serve as a liaison to the College Prep Program, meeting periodically with College Prep Program staff, reporting on the program and documenting activities as requested.

- Verify the attendance at student seminars, keeping copies of attendance sheets that each College Coaches will fax to the College Prep Program office.

- Collect College Coach monthly logs.

The College Coach supervisor will receive the per session rate of $36.50/hour for up to 20 hours per semester, based on attendance.

College Readiness

Lesson #1

Topic: College Readiness-Beliefs and Reality

Aim

How do my beliefs about college affect the college exploration process?

Objectives

Students will be able to:

- Identify their current beliefs about college

- Explore feelings related to college

- Analyze current myths about the college selection process

- Evaluate interests, needs, and values related to college selection

Motivation

Ice Breaker: *Worksheet I: Find A Person Who . . .*

Processing Questions

- What feelings did you have when you participated in this activity?
- What did you learn about yourself from this exercise?
- What did you learn about others?
- If you were asked to repeat this exercise, what would you do differently? Why?

Development

Activity I

Direct students to complete the sentences on *Worksheet II*.

Assign each student to partner and ask students to share their answers with one another.

Large Group Discussion Questions

- How did you feel sharing your thoughts and feelings with your partner?
- What did you learn about yourself?
- What did you learn about your partner?
- What new ideas came up for you?
- What surprised you about your answers, feelings, or reactions?
- How can you apply what you learned today to your future college exploration process?

Activity II

Large Group Discussion Questions

- What have you heard about college?
- To what extent do you believe the things you have heard about college?
- What do you expect to get out of college?
- Should everyone go to college? If not, who should go to college? Who should not go to college?
- In what ways do you believe college will be similar to high school? In what ways do you believe college will be different from high school? Explain.

Activity III

Distribute True/False Quiz: *Worksheet III: Myths About College*

- Direct students to complete the quiz.
- Discuss correct answers with the students.
- What facts about college most surprised you? Why?

Homework

Interview a family member or friend who attended college, using the following questions as a guide:

- Describe the college you attended. Include location, size, campus facilities (housing, dining, activity centers, library, athletics and recreation, health, and special student services), special programs or classes, college life (safety, cultural opportunities, diversity, extracurricular activities), and any other information that may be relevant.

- Why did you choose this college?

- What was the best part of the college experience? Why?

Summary

- What have you learned about yourself today?

- In what way(s) is this self-knowledge important to your future college exploration?

- How have your beliefs about college changed as a result of this workshop?

- How can you apply what you have learned today to the college exploration process?

Worksheet I: Find a Person Who . . .

_____	was born in the same month as you.
_____	has a pet.
_____	has three or more siblings in the family.
_____	plans to go to college.
_____	has visited a college campus.
_____	will be the first in his or her immediate family to go to college.
_____	has an older brother, sister, or cousin in college.
_____	speaks another language.
_____	plays an instrument.
_____	belongs to a school club or team.
_____	was born in another country.
_____	works part time.

Worksheet II: Sentence Completion

Thinking about college makes me feel _____

When I imagine myself at college, I see _____

I would be happy at a college if _____

I would be excited with a college that _____

I would be comfortable at a college if _____

I would be angry at college if _____

I would feel proud at college when _____

The people who will probably influence me the most in choosing a college are

_____

_____

Worksheet III: Myths about College

TRUE/FALSE

1. _____   The most important factor in considering candidates for college admissions is the academic transcript.

2. _____   Colleges don't really look at Senior grades.

3. _____   It is not necessary to take math in the Senior year.

4. _____   Science in the Junior and Senior year is a waste of time unless you want to be a doctor.

5. _____   Having a prestigious undergraduate degree will generally guarantee self-fulfillment, admission to graduate school, and an excellent job.

6. _____   Most colleges ask to see your PSAT scores.

7. _____   Students who list many extracurricular activities have a better chance of acceptance to college than students who list fewer involvements with leadership positions.

8. _____   Students should take advantage of every opportunity they have to prepare for the SAT beginning in the junior year.

9. _____   Admissions officers generally place the college interview at the bottom of those factors considered important in the admissions process.

10. _____   Only the rich can afford to attend private colleges.

Bonus: _____   Colleges will only accept students who have an 80+ average.

Worksheet III: Myths about College—*Teacher's Answer Sheet*

TRUE/FALSE

1. T   The most important factor in considering candidates for college admissions is the academic transcript.

2. F   Colleges don't really look at Senior grades.

3. F   It is not necessary to take math in the Senior year.

4. F   Science in the Junior and Senior year is a waste of time unless you want to be a doctor.

5. F   Having a prestigious undergraduate degree will generally guarantee self-fulfillment, admission to graduate school, and an excellent job.

6. F   Most colleges ask to see your PSAT scores.

7. F   Students who list many extracurricular activities have a better chance of acceptance to college than students who list fewer involvements with leadership positions.

8. T   Students should take advantage of every opportunity they have to prepare for the SAT beginning in the junior year.

9. T   Admissions officers generally place the college interview at the bottom of those factors considered important in the admissions process.

10. F   Only the rich can afford to attend private colleges.

Bs F   Colleges will only accept students who have an 80+ average.

Sample Collaborative Program Parent Survey 2012

Directions: This survey is an important part of an independent evaluation of Collaborative Program, and your answers will help to improve and continue the program in your child's school. Please answer all questions as candidly as possible. The information you provide will be treated strictly confidentially and you will not be identified with any response.

Background Information

1. What school does your child(ren) attend?

   ☐ (1) Terry H.S.   ☐ (2) Noland H.S.   ☐ (3) Franklin H.S.

   ☐ (4) Other: _____

2. Which racial/ethnic group do you belong to?

   ☐ (1) African-American   ☐ (4) Hispanic

   ☐ (2) White   ☐ (5) Asian/Pacific Islander

   ☐ (3) Native American   ☐ (6) Other _____

Note: If you have more than one child attending this school, please answer the rest of the survey questions based on your 11th grader.

Collaborative Program Activities

3. Check all of the activities you participated through your child's school or Collaborative Program so far this year.

   ☐ (a) Went to parent/teacher meeting to discuss my child's progress.

   ☐ (b) Had a special meeting with my child's teacher/counselor to discuss how to help him/her do better in school.

   ☐ (c) Attended a workshop or College Preparation and Career Preparation.

☐ (d) Met Collaborative Program staff at Open School Night.

☐ (e) Had telephone contact with Collaborative Program staff.

☐ (f)   Attended Parent Orientation.

☐ (i)   Went to a workshop to learn about how to get help paying for college.

4. Have you talked with your child about attending college?

☐ (1) Yes   ☐ (2) No

5. How much education do **you** want your child to get?

☐ (1) Finish 11th grade   ☐ (4) Two-year college

☐ (2) Graduate high school   ☐ (5) Four-year college

☐ (3) Technical training after high ☐ (6) Graduate school
       school (e.g., welding)

6. What is the main reason your child would not continue his/her education after high school? **Check one**.

☐ (1) Not applicable: My child will continue his/her education.

☐ (2) It costs too much/cannot afford it.

☐ (3) College is too far from home.

☐ (4) He/she needs/wants to work.

☐ (5) His/her grades are not good enough.

☐ (6) He/she is not interested.

☐ (7) He/she has a disability (physical, learning, or emotional).

☐ (8) He/she wants to join the military service.

☐ (9) He/she wants to start a family.

☐ (10) Other (please specify) _____

7. Have you talked with someone about how to apply to a college?

☐ (1) Yes

☐ (2) No

8. Do you feel you have enough information about how your child must prepare for college?

☐ (1) Yes

☐ (2) No

9. As part of your child's participation in GEAR UP, has he/she received a 21st Century Scholar Certificate?

☐ (1) Yes

☐ (2) No (Go to question 14)

☐ (3) Don't know (Go to question 14)

10. This certificate indicates how much financial assistance your child may be eligible to receive from the federal government for college. Do you believe your child will receive this assistance?

☐ (1) Yes   ☐ (2) No

11. Has receiving this certificate changed your child's plans about college?

☐ (1) Yes   ☐ (2) No

12. How much do you think it will cost for your child to attend each of the following types of institutions for one year?

(a) Community college or two-year public institution $_____

(b) Four-year public college or university $_____

(c) Four-year private college or university $_____

13. Have you saved any money for your child's college education?

☐ (1) Yes   ☐ (2) No

14. Have you talked with anyone about any financial assistance that your child may be able to receive for college?

☐ (1) Yes   ☐ (2) No

15. Have you talked with anyone about college entrance requirements?

☐ (1) Yes   ☐ (2) No

16. Are you familiar with the entrance requirements for these schools?

(a) Two-year college   ☐ (1) Yes   ☐ (2) No

(b) Four-year college or university   ☐ (1) Yes   ☐ (2) No

(c) Vocational, trade, or business school ☐ (1) Yes   ☐ (2) No

(d) Other (please describe)   _____

17. Do you think your child would be able to afford to attend a four-year college or university after high school?

☐ (1) Definitely

☐ (2) Probably

☐ (3) Not sure

☐ (4) I doubt it

☐ (5) Definitely not

18. In general, how satisfied are you with the Collaborative Program project?

☐ (1) Very satisfied

☐ (2) Satisfied

☐ (3) Somewhat satisfied

☐ (4) Dissatisfied

☐ (5) I do not know enough to comment. This is my first year of being involved in the Collaborative Program.

THANK YOU FOR TAKING THE TIME TO COMPLETE THIS SURVEY!

Roles and Responsibilities of Staff in a Collaborative Program

PROJECT DIRECTOR

The Project Director reports directly to the Director of School/College Collaborations at the College.

Job Description

Oversees all operations of the Project; assures compliance with all regulations, manages budgets, writes Annual Program Reports; writes required budget revisions and Grant Applications and coordinates services of these projects with the cohort at the participating schools. Chairs the Schools Site Planning Teams. This is a full-time position.

Requirements

M.A.; minimum of five years' management experience; minimum five years' College teaching experience; excellent communication skills; extensive experience in serving under-represented groups; grant writing experience; computer literate in database management and word-processing; ability to work flexible schedule including Saturdays and in the summer.

Duties

1. Recruit, interview, and hire projects staff as necessary.

2. Prepare and manage project budgets, oversee process of payroll, and budget oversight through supervision of the Senior Administrative Assistant and coordination with the College Grants office.

3. Coordinate services between GEAR UP and other programs outlined in the project plan of operation.

4. Serve as liaison to all participating intermediate/junior high and high school principals.

5. Prepare all required government reports and grant proposals.

6. Supervise the office assuring that all project activities take place and run smoothly.

7. Meet regularly with the Site Planning Teams.

8. Evaluate success of academic year and summer project activities to determine which, if any, require modifications.

9. Oversee maintenance of computer database on all project participants to ensure compliance and progress of project participants.

10. Write all required reports and any required budget revisions.

11. Oversee all steps in the project evaluation process.

12. Disseminate knowledge of project in professional and scholarly arenas as well as to target area business and community agencies.

13. Disseminate knowledge of project to college and school community.

14. Evaluate effectiveness and performance of all project staff.

15. Interpret and disseminate legislation and directives as they pertain to project personnel.

16. Maintain frequent contact with the College Director of School/College Collaborations reporting on all project activities.

ASSISTANT DIRECTOR

The Project Assistant Director reports directly to the Director of Program.

Job Description

Coordinates services of the Program in the academic year including the Saturday and summer programs. This is a full-time position.

Requirements

M.A. Human Resource Management, Education, or related area; experience coordinating academic services for disadvantaged youth; management experience; excellent communication skills; computer literate in database management; ability to work flexible schedule, including Saturdays and throughout the four-week intensive summer program.

Duties

1. Together with the Activities Director, the Assistant Director will plan, implement, and assess student programs.

2. Supervise all after-school and in-school student activities at each site.

3. Work with the Activities Director to coordinate the Saturdays at the College program.

4. Assume primary responsibilities for supervising, recruiting, and assessing the peer tutoring and peer mentoring programs.

5. Assume primary responsibilities for developing and implementing a parent program for students.

6. Supervise the activities staff.

7. During the academic year, make frequent visits to target schools for consultation with onsite staff and school personnel.

8. Create/enhance student and parent communication vehicles such as newsletters.

9. Assist Director in writing Annual Program Report, and grant proposals.

10. Evaluate success of academic year and summer project activities to determine which, if any, require modifications.

11. Disseminate knowledge of project in professional and scholarly arenas as well as to target area business and community agencies.

12. Disseminate knowledge of project to college and school community.

13. Contact person for Princess Borough Public Library and Kings Child Guidance Center.

STUDENT ACTIVITIES DIRECTOR

The Student Activities Director reports to the Director of the Program.

Job Description

Coordinates services to students of the Program in the academic year, including Saturday and summer programs. This is a part-time position: 3 days, 25 hour-week.

Requirements

M.A. Human Resource Management, Education, or related area; experience coordinating academic services for disadvantaged youth; management experience; excellent communication skills; computer literate in database management; ability to work a flexible schedule, including Saturdays and throughout the four-week intensive summer program.

Duties

1. Develop, schedule, and coordinate student activities during the academic year and the summer.

2. Visit target schools weekly, observing scheduled activities, meeting with site counselors, social workers, teachers, and administrators for planning and feedback as needed.

3. Supervise all after-school and in-school student activities at each site.

4. Assist Director in writing Annual Program Report and grant proposals.

5. Assume primary responsibilities for implementing the Saturday program at the College program.

6. Attend meetings, reporting on student activities.

7. Assist in the development and implementation of the summer program.

8. Work with data collection clerk in assembling and maintaining participant database.

9. Day-to-day management and liaison with the schools.

PROGRAM COORDINATOR FOR STUDENT ACTIVITIES/BUDGET

The Program Coordinator will report directly to the Director of the Program.

Job Description

Full-time, general administrative, assistance for the Director, the Assistant Director, and the Activities Director.

Requirements

A.A. Degree, B.A. preferred in Business Administration, Finance or related area; excellent communication skills; computer literate in database management; ability to work flexible schedule.

Duties

1. Coordinate and schedule student activities meetings at the college and the schools.

2. Arrange transportation for students in the College for Teens, Mentoring and College Coach programs, and any other visits.

3. Order refreshments and supplies for the student activities program and process payments.

4. In consultation with the Director and the Senior Program Coordinator, oversee the student activities budget and provide monthly updates to the Director.

5. Distribute and process pay packets to student activities personnel involved.

6. Collect attendance records and timesheets and transmit payroll information to the payroll clerk.

7. Assist the Student Activities Director in the planning and implementation of the Summer Program.

8. Liaise with the College Grants Development Office and the Research Foundation in all matters relating to the budget.

9. Maintain the Site Planning Team calendar; distribute meeting reminder notices to team members; and prepare meeting materials.

10. Work with the Director on special projects.

SENIOR PROGRAM COORDINATOR/PROFESSIONAL DEVELOPMENT

The Senior Program Coordinator will report directly to the Director of the Program.

Job Description

Full-time, general administrative, assistance to the Director, Assistant Director, and Activities Coordinator.

Requirements

A.A. Degree, B.A. preferred and/or extensive knowledge of all of Microsoft Professional Office, Emailing, Internet. Excellent mathematics, writing, communication, and telephone skills as well as good interpersonal skills, ability to work independently and initiate necessary clerical procedures on his/her own schedule; ability to work flexible schedule.

Duties

1. Assist the Director and Assistant Director on projects.

2. Order and maintain supplies, process purchase orders, and request payment of bills related to Professional Development and other vendors.

3. Liaise with the College Office in regards to payment requests related to Professional Development and other areas as well.

4. Assist in preparing locations for project workshops and other activities and functions, including booking and overseeing professional development, on-site and internal staff and subcontractors meetings, ordering refreshments and supplies needed.

5. Do word-processing and provide other assistance for other project personnel, approved by the Program Director.

6. Maintain Director and Professional Development calendars.

7. Assist/manage the office with daily needs including writing own correspondence related to daily tasks, meetings, purchases, etc.

8. Oversee the office in the absence of directors.

PROGRAM STUDENT ACTIVITIES ASSISTANT

The Program Student Activities Assistant reports directly to the Senior Activities Coordinator.

Job Description

Full-time, general administrative responsibilities, assistance to the Coordinator of Student Activities.

Requirements

A.A. Degree, B.A. preferred in Business Administration and/or extensive knowledge of Microsoft Professional Office, Emailing, Internet. Excellent communication and telephone skills as well as good interpersonal skills, ability to work independently and initiate necessary clerical procedures on his/her own schedule; ability to work flexible schedule.

Duties

1. Assist the Senior Activities Coordinator on student activities projects.

2. Order and maintain supplies, process purchase orders related to student activities.

3. Design and produce project brochures/flyers and other documents related to student activities.

4. Liaise with the High Schools/on-site staff on student activities matters.

5. Collect attendance records and transmit information to the data collector personnel.

6. Assist the Senior Activities Coordinator in the planning and implementation of the Summer Program.

7. Work with the Director and Assistant Director on special projects.

8. Do word processing and provide other assistance for other project personnel, approved by the Program Director and the Student Activities Coordinator.

9. Maintain the student activities calendar.

10. Help answer incoming calls related to student activities.

11. Maintain files/records related to student activities.

12. Assist with planning and coordination of materials for all student activities and related meetings.

13. Maintain project databases, as well as create new databases as needed.

RECEPTIONIST

The receptionist reports to the Senior Program Coordinator, Activities Coordinator, Director, and Assistant Director.

Job Description

Full-time. General clerical, typing, database entry, assistance for the Coordinator and Activities Coordinator.

Requirements

High School Diploma or GED, excellent word processing and database entry skills. Excellent math and telephone skills. Good interpersonal skills. Ability to initiate necessary clerical procedures on his/her own.

Duties

1. General typing.

2. Answer the Office (main number) telephone calls.

3. Disseminate reports, memos, and other project materials.

4. Help keep and maintain project hardcopy and database files.

5. Order and maintain supplies from the College Stockroom Supplies.

6. Prepare parking requests for project participants.

7. Prepare project publicity packets; materials for meetings.

8. Assist Senior Program Coordinator with office daily needs.

9. Assist Director and Assistant Director on special projects.

10. Assist Senior Activities Coordinator on projects including the Summer Program.

11. Maintain Payment Requests database.

12. Do word-processing and provide other assistance for other project personnel, approved by the Program Director and the Student Activities Coordinator.

13. Help answer incoming calls related to student activities.

14. Assist in maintaining files/records related to student activities.

DATA COLLECTOR/ANALYST

The Data Collector/Analyst reports directly to the Director and the Assistant Director.

Job Description

Part-time. General data collection and documentation.

Requirements

A.A. Degree, B.A. preferred. Ability to work independently and initiate necessary data requests from the schools; ability to work a flexible schedule.

Duties

1. Contact school liaisons for information necessary for data collection.

2. Make blank activity logs available for service providers as needed.

3. Thoroughly examine the received paper-based data logs content for any anomalies prior to being inputted in the computerized in-house database.

4. Notify the Program Director and Director of Student Activities of any anomalies found in the paper-based data collected.

5. Accurate input of records in the respective database forms by provider, high school, nature of service provided, mode of service, and contact date.

6. Constantly add new participants to the student and provider database tables.

7. Run daily backup of in-house database.

8. Generate queries and reports that provide information about: recruitment, monitoring of attendance, program activities update reports, student performance, and contacts.

9. Update database tables, forms, queries, reports, data types, fields, labels, and values, to accommodate changes and implementation of new services provided.

10. Analyze and manipulate in-house database records to fulfill Annual Performance Report guidelines.

PAYROLL CLERK

The Payroll Clerk reports directly to the Program Director.

Job Description

Part-time, payroll general administrative responsibilities, assistance to the office personnel on payroll/hiring matters.

Requirements

A.A. Degree, B.A. preferred in Business Administration and/or extensive knowledge of Microsoft Professional Office, Emailing, Internet. Excellent writing and mathematics skills as well as communication, telephone, and interpersonal skills; ability to work independently and initiate necessary clerical procedures on his/her own schedule; ability to work flexible schedule.

Duties

1. Prepare employment appointment and termination forms for project personnel.

2. Oversee collection of timesheets for project personnel.

3. Administer all payroll requests submitted to the Grants Administration Office.

4. Maintain payroll files for project personnel.

5. Remain in regular contact with the Director, Assistant Director of Student Activities, Professional Development and Governance informing them of any situation that may cause delays in payment, stipends, and other related problems.

6. Remain in regular contact with the Grant's Development Office and the Research Foundation to resolve any issues in a timely manner.

7. Process paperwork in a timely manner reducing the potential for unnecessary delays in salary.

SITE-COUNSELOR

Full-time. The roles and responsibilities of the Site Counselor include working closely with the school staff/providing and overseeing services to the cohort. In this capacity, he/she:

1. Accepts referrals from teachers for students related to a range of academic, personal, and social issues.

2. Meets periodically with the school counselor and social worker to determine appropriate actions on referrals and to delegate responsibility for the referral to the appropriate person.

3. Reports to team and referring teacher decisions related to referrals on Activity Log.

4. Participates in regular Guidance team meetings.

5. Assists the school counseling staff "in the crunch times", e.g., student admissions in September and February and summer school registration.

6. Keeps Assistant Principal, Guidance, and all school staff advised of all activities.

7. Participates in school-wide committees and activities.

8. Works closely with the Assistant Principal for Guidance and all school coordinators (e.g., attendance, cutting, lateness).

9. Assists in Annual Review.

10. Recruits students and teachers for activities.

11. Visits student cohort in order to provide whole class group guidance.

12. Conducts small-group counseling sessions.

13. Interviews students who are failing their classes, referring them to appropriate school and community resources.

14. Makes parental contacts by phone and mail.

15. Plans parent workshops, paying particular attention to providing students and parents with information on the benefits of and preparation for a college education, the college admission process, and financial aid.

16. Confers individually with students and parents.

17. Provides crisis counseling.

18. Conducts orientation programs for students, parents, and staff.

19. Interviews all students leaving high school for any reason prior to graduation.

20. Documents services on activity logs as per.

21. Referrals to programs in school.

22. Supervises the site coordinator.

SOCIAL WORKER

Full-time, serve as Social Worker in the program based at the school site. He/she will conduct social skills groups; help identify at-risk youth; provide individual group and/or family counseling for youngsters; and conduct parent education workshops.

Requirements

Master's degree in Social Work and ability to communicate in at least one language other than English, which is used by students in a school.

Duties

1. Conduct adolescent groups around social skills development and peer relationships.

2. Conduct parent's education workshops that are culturally sensitive and language specific.

3. Assess the needs of at-risk youth.

4. Provide crisis intervention, short-term counseling, parental guidance, and family therapy for adolescents, as needed.

5. Refer youngsters and families to other social services, as needed.

6. Attend all Site Planning Team and work together with other school personnel to effectively support youth in the cohort.

7. Complete administrative tasks related to the above duties.

8. Report to Clinical Administrator and school's Assistant Principal for Guidance.

9. Provide crisis and mediation services, as needed.

10. Recruit teachers and students for activities in collaboration with Site Counselor.

11. Plan parent workshops, paying particular attention to providing students and parents with information on the benefits of and preparation for a college education, the college admission process, and financial aid.

12. Participates in school-wide committees and activities.

13. Conduct small group sessions.

14. Other duties as assigned.

15. Supervise and oversee peer mentoring.

16. Individual counseling and advising students who are failing classes.

Collaborative Program Budget (Year 1)

COLLABORATIVE PROGRAM
2011-2012

$1,692,800

	Salary	Fringe	Subtotal
Personnel			
Project Director	$ 86,822	$ 30,127	$ 116,949
Assistant Director	$ 75,245	$ 26,110	$ 101,355
Student Activities Director	$ 70,195	$ 24,358	$ 94,552
Senior Project Coordinator/Professional Development	$ 48,200	$ 16,629	$ 64,829
Program Coordinator Student Activities/Budget	$ 48,200	$ 16,629	$ 64,829
Program Assistant/Data Entry	$ 34,533	$ 11,914	$ 46,447
Administrative Assistant	$ 26,925	$ 8,885	$ 35,810
Total @ 34.5%	$ 390,120	$ 134,652	$ 524,771
Released Time			
Director for School/College Collaboration 25% of $92,272	$ 23,068	$ 6,459	$ 29,527
Grant Research Associate 10% of $74,979	$ 7,498	$ 2,099	$ 9,597
Tutor Trainer $1,143/contact hrs x 3 contact hrs x 2 semester	$ 6,858	$ 1,920	$ 8,778
Professional Development Facilitator $1,143/contact hrs x 3 contact hrs x 2 semester	$ 6,858	$ 1,920	$ 8,778
Mini Seminar Faculty $1,143/contact hr x 2 contact hrs x 2 sems x 3 faculty	$ 13,716	$ 3,840	$ 17,556
Total @ 28%	$ 57,998	$ 16,239	$ 74,237
LaGuardia Office Staff Budget Assistant (10hrs/wk x 52.2wks x $18/hr)	$ 9,396	$ 940	$ 10,336
Student Activities **API -Tutors** **Training** 16 Tutors x 12 wks x 2 semester x 1 hrs/wk x $10 (plus 10 hrs x $10 x 16 Tutors for Training)	$ 5,440	$ 544	$ 5,984

Instruction 16 Tutors x 4 hrs x 12 wks x $10 hrs x 2 semester (2 Eng & 2 math)	$ 15,360	$ 1,536	$ 16,896
Mini Seminar **College Faculty** 2 Classes x 2 semester x 4 school x 15 hrs x 53.60	$ 12,864	$ 1,286	$ 14,150
School Faculty Planning 2 Classes x 2 semester x 4 school x 3 hrs x $36.50	$ 1,752	$ 175	$ 1,927
Summer Program 4 Teachers/Counselor x 35 hrs x 4 wks x 36.50	$ 20,440	$ 2044	$ 22,484
Cross Age Tutoring **Supervisor** 1 Class x 4 schools x 2 semester x 15 hrs x $36.50	$ 4,380		$ 4,380
Welcome Academy **Instructional** 45 hrs x 53.60 x 1 semester x 1 classes x 4 school	$ 9,648		$ 9,648
Teacher 45 x 36.50 x 1 hr x 1 class x 4 school	$ 6,570		$ 6,570
Planning 1 faculty x 2 class x 4 school x 15 hrs x 36.50 x 1 semester	$ 4,380		$ 4,380
1 faculty x 1 class x 4 school x 15 x 53.60	$ 3,216		$ 3,216
Coordinator-Planned monthly meeting 19 hrs x 20 wks x $25	$ 9,000	$ 900	$ 9,900
Book Club (QBPL Budget)			
Young Authors Workshop (See QBPL Contract)			
Saturday Enrichment Series 2 Classes x 4 wks x 4 hrs x 2 faculty x 2 semester x $53.60	$ 6,861	$ 686	$ 7,547
2 Chaperone for 6 hrs x $10 x 4 wks x 2 semester	$ 960		$ 960
Peer Mentoring from QCGC Budget			
Group & Individual Counseling (See Dept. of Ed. Contract)			
Parent Workshops (See QCGC Contract)			
Professional Development **ISS** 2 Seminar x 9 hrs x 21 participant x $36.50/hr x 2 semester	$ 27,594		$ 27,594
ISS Facilitator 4 Faculty x 15 hrs x $53.60	$ 3,216		$ 3,216
Roundtables 2 sessions x 2 hrs x 2 semester x $36.50 x 14 participant (Meeting @ schools)	$ 4,088		$ 4,088
QEC Roundtables Facilitator (LaGuardia Realease Time) 3 Session x 3 hrs x 2 Teacher x 2 semester x 53.60			
Total @ 10%	**$ 145,165**	**$ 8,111**	**$ 153,276**

2- Fringe Benefits Summary	Salary	Fringe	Total
Full Time: 34.7%	$ 390,120	$ 134,652	$ 524,771
Release Time: 28%	$ 57,998	$ 16,239	$ 74,237
Part Time: 10%	$ 145,165	$ 8,111	$ 153,276
Total Personnel & Fringe Benefits	**$ 593,283**	**$ 159,002**	**$ 752,284**

Travel			
Transportation			
16 Buses @ $325 (Saturday Programs)	$ 5,200		$ 5,200
2 Buses per wk x 4 wks x 2 semester x $325 (Saturday Program)			
Summer Program			
6 Buses x $925	$ 5,500		$ 5,500
Conferences			
Conferences	$ 9,000		$ 9,000
Trips	$ 2,500		$ 2,500
Refreshment			
James-Regis Hotel	$ 8,000		$ 8,000
Local Travel	$ 1,500		$ 1,500
	$ 31,700		**$ 31,700**
Materials & Supplies			
Materials (Office Supplies)	$ 4,000		$ 4,000
Materials (Saturday Program)	$ 2,200		$ 2,200
Materials	$ 2,500		$ 2,500
Meals & Meetings	$ 6,000		$ 6,000
Refreshment (2 Parent Workshops)	$ 1,327		$ 1,327
Refreshment			
8 months @ $100 (Tutors)	$ 800		$ 800
Refreshment			
4 wks @ $6 per student x 80 students x 2 semester (Saturday Program)	$ 3,840		$ 3,840
Summer Program Meals			
100 student x $6 per student x 4 days per wk x 4 wks (lunch only)	$ 9,600		$ 9,600
	$ 30,267		**$ 30,267**
Contracts			
Department of Education			
4 Counselors	$ 288,325		$ 288,325
Kings Child Guidance Counselor			
4 Social Workers & Mentoring Program	$ 290,000		$ 290,000
ITT Evaluators	$ 65,000		$ 65,000
Princess Borough Public Library	$ 58,800		$ 58,800
	$ 702,125		**$ 702,125**
Other			
Mailing	$ 13,000		$ 13,000
Telephone	$ 9,000		$ 9,000
Photocopying	$ 13,000		$ 13,000
Supplies (College Stationary)	$ 6,000		$ 6,000
	$ 41,000		**$ 41,000**
Subtotal	**$1,398,375**	**$ 159,002**	**$1,557,376**
Indirect Cost	**$ 135,424**		**$ 135,424**
Grand Total	**$1,533,799**	**$ 159,002**	**$1,692,800**

Expected Grant is $1,692,800
Total Budget $1,692,800

LaGCC/QUP Gear Up Professional Development Offerings 1999–2005

INSTRUCTIONAL STRATEGIES SEMINARS

1. You Don't Have to Speak the Language: Monolingual Teachers and Multilingual Students

A hands-on workshop that focuses on reading, writing, and process techniques, which will help students develop their language proficiency. In addition, the workshop examines graphic organizers, collaborative groupings, and theme based projects. Participants have the opportunity to explore how their content-specific curriculum may be developed for use with heterogeneous groups of English Language Learners. (Offered twice.)

2. Reading Process and Strategies for the Multi-Cultural Students

The seminars explore the significant challenges English Language Learners (ELL) face in learning English. Highlighted is their unfamiliarity of the culture, interference of the native language, and limited knowledge of English. The seminar also demonstrates effective methods in teaching ELL readers by employing knowledge, strategies, and processes gained from students' native language in their second language reading. (Offered three times.)

3. Creating a Proficient Writer Using Multi-Cultural Literature

How do you effectively engage students in the writing process? How do you infuse writing across the curriculum? Participants examine how to use multicultural literature in historical and social contexts; how to help students organize an essay and how to infuse research techniques onto various disciplines. (Offered twice.)

4. Solid Shapes, Usable Space and Architectural Structures: Mathematics Applications for the Classrooms

This seminar is concerned with practical applications of key concepts in mathematics, which students must master, e.g., arithmetic functions, fractions, scales measurements, area, ratio, and volume. Participants are engaged in hands-on activities, which develop mathematical thinking, the processing of information, and a heightened awareness of the use of mathematics in architecture and other aspects of everyday life.

5. American Culture and the Immigrants Experiences: Using Theater Techniques in the Multicultural-Multilingual Classroom

Participants learn the techniques for creating, monitoring, and developing curriculum related improvizations. They also learn how to analyze and incorporate intercultural non-verbal behavior into the classroom; create short plays and skits based on text, student histories, and literary subjects; and improvization. Participants experience short performances by theater artists and attended a play on Broadway. (Offered year 1 and 2.)

6. Collaborative Working Groups to Improve Student Learning

How can teachers work together to improve students learning and understanding? The seminar explores various ways of promoting professional growth and showing the link to student learning. As a group, teachers examine student-learning goals and help each other think about better teaching practices. Participants also review their curriculum and samples of students work.

7. Teaching English Language Learners in Multicultural Contexts

This seminar explores the significant challenges that English Language Learners face because of limited knowledge of English, unfamiliarity with American culture, and interference from the native language. Participants learn how to help ESL students integrate listening, speaking, reading, and writing skills while learning contents in multicultural contexts.

8. Using Improvisation in the Multicultural and Multilingual Classroom

Defining what is an improvization, how to create and structure one for the classroom, and how it can be used for curriculum-based activities. Focusing on communication issues shared by the participants in the classroom. Understanding how theater skills are useful for the classroom for improved self-esteem, confidence, and such hard skills as pronunciation, fluidity of speech, verbalization of ideas, improving grammar, group activities. Stress how seemingly "fun" activities can be applied to "serious" topics and how to adapt an improvization for your particular classroom needs. Participants will learn how to use improvizations by: participating in the improvizations (Session 1), Creating own improvizations for the sessions (Session 2), Critiquing and developing improvizations for the sessions (Session 2), Creating at least one good improvization for use in the classroom (Session 3).

9. Helping Students to Succeed in Science: What Do We Need to Do?

Eighth grade GEAR UP students take an examination in Science in June and the Regents examinations in high schools as well. What skills do these examinations require? What are the new science standards and how are they manifested in the new Science curriculum? How can science be taught so that all students can understand? This Instructional Strategies Seminar focuses on these questions, and in particular, practical classroom activities, which engage students in doing research and using the scientific method; inquiry and the national science standards and problem-solving and ways to make it happen in the classroom.

10. Using Improvization and Theater Games in the Classroom

Participants will design specific theater games and improvization for their own classes. Using the other members of the workshop as surrogate students, every participant will have the opportunity to plan, implement, and receive feedback on exercises he/she has adapted from those taught in the first sessions. The emphasis will be on the process of learning HOW to do an improvization. Participants should come to each session with an idea for an improvization or theater game that they would like to use in their own classroom. (Offered year 1 and 2.)

11. Language Skills for Content Learning

This workshop series help teachers develop strategies for teaching course content by drawing on students' basic communication strategies so essential to success. Rooted in collaborative learning principles that teachers can apply in any curricular area, the workshops address issues such as developing successful writing strategies to enhance content learning; strategies for helping students read successfully in discipline based courses; and strategies for drawing on students' speaking and listening skills as a means of access to content. Teachers will produce usable assignments for class instruction and will benefit from peer review for all instructional activities produced in the workshop.

12. Language Skills for Content Learning: Focus on Writing

These workshops will help teachers teach course content by drawing on students' basic communication strategies. Rooted in collaborative learning principles, the workshops focus on developing classroom strategies to help students with writing and understanding content materials. Among a variety of approaches to content learning and critical thinking, we will explore ways of dealing with vocabulary across the curriculum; useful steps to guide students' successful writing in discipline-based courses; and effective techniques for using course textbooks to full advantage. Teachers will produce usable assignments for class instruction and will benefit from peer review for instructional activities produced in the workshop.

13. Language Skills for Content Learning: Focus on Reading

These workshops will help teachers teach course content by drawing on students' basic communication strategies. Rooted in collaborative learning principles, the workshops focus on developing classroom strategies to help students with reading and under-standing content materials. Among a variety of approaches to content learning and critical thinking, we will explore ways of dealing with vocabulary across the curriculum; useful steps to guide students' successful reading in discipline-based courses; and effective techniques for using course textbooks to full advantage. Teachers will produce useable assignments for class instruction and will benefit from peer review for all instructional activities produced in the workshops.

14. "Active Learning and Social Studies"

This course will present various strategies for engaging students actively in social studies. The course employs role-playing and debating based on research from multiple sources, including the U.S. Constitution, past Supreme Court cases, and historical excerpts. The emphasis will be on active inquiry and engagement. Team-work and competition are stressed to promote the kind of interactions that adolescents are drawn to. Literacy issues inherent in reading, writing, speaking, and listening will be addressed throughout. The sessions will be conducted by enacting the activities ourselves so that all participants can experience the curriculum. Work with primary source documents and content relevant to the Regents will be included.

15. "Math in the Mirror, Seeing Yourself as a Math Learner"

Math in the Mirror is a workshop that will empower you to see beyond the way you think or have thought about mathematics. We will investigate mathematical topics through problem solving, group work, and sharing. During the three sessions, we will be taking on the role of mathematicians figuring out the relationships and patterns, which are the basis for the rules and formulas that govern mathematics. These workshops will include work with manipulatives that can be used in the classroom. The goal of Math in the Mirror is to reflect on the way you understand, learn, and think about mathematics. These workshops are open to all math teachers as well as middle school and high school teachers who would like to experience math in a unique way.

16. Using Improvization and Theater Games in the Classroom (Upgraded)

In this workshop you will learn the basic rules and principals of how to adapt theater games and improvizations to your particular classroom needs. Participants will be able to apply and adapt some of the exercises during the course of the workshop. Emphasis will be on: how to adapt the exercise to the particular classroom; how to use exercises to explore multicultural issues and problems; how to adapt exercises to explore and enhance curricula; how to adapt exercises for classroom group dynamics; how to use exercises for self-esteem work; how to have fun in the classroom in a different work format. (Year 4.)

17. Can Our Approach to Teaching Make a Difference?

This workshop series will focus on the development of academic language skills and learner strategies through content-based instruction. The workshop will be geared to content teachers (particularly English, History, and Science) and teachers of ESL and academically under-prepared readers and writers. There will be three sessions: each session will be devoted to a particular phase of the lesson.

Session One: The Pre-Reading Phase

Participants will experience the importance of background knowledge in reading, and create a list of learner strategies. Results of a Reading Survey administered to a group of High School students, and student writing samples will illustrate the role of the teacher in eliciting and/or providing background knowledge, diagnosing and responding to learner difficulties, and fostering learner development. Current thinking about the Reading and Writing Processes, Task-Based Grammar Learning, integration of the four language skills, and the Zone of Proximal Development will underlie the discussion. Time and materials will be provided for hands-on group projects appropriate for the Pre-Reading Phase.

Session Two: The While-Reading Phase

Techniques for training learners to be more active, more strategic, more aware of their own learning process, and more effective readers and writers, will be demonstrated. Writing to Learn will be discussed. Participants will work in groups to design scaffolded materials for the While-Reading Phase, share ideas, and receive feedback.

Session Three: The Post-Reading Phase

What languages follow-up activities can be designed to assess content understanding and retention, language development and strategy use? Extension activities will be modeled and then developed by participants working in groups. Activities will be shared; feedback and discussion will follow.

18. Urban Word NYC

Urban Word NYC is a community committed to reciprocal teaching and learning. It promotes critical literacy and positive social dialogue across boundaries of age, race, class, gender, culture, and sexuality.

Through a series of GEAR UP sponsored workshops, teachers will explore:

- brief history of oral poetry, spoken work, rap/hip hop forms
- *Urban Word* methodology and student-centered pedagogy
- in-class (low-risk) writing and performing exercises
- strategies to encourage student expression and creativity through writing
- simulation of youth open mic/teen slam—with *Urban Word* youth poets—and strategies to incorporate this in the classroom
- discussions around hip hop/spoken word
- team-teaching, and creative teaching-journals.

19. "An ESL-Enhanced Look at Mathematics Instruction"

ESL Workshop

This workshop series for teachers of mathematics will try to raise awareness of the culture and language-based difficulties students must cope with in doing word problems, particularly on the eighth grade and the Math A Regents Exams. Connections will be made between certain linguistic structures and vocabulary, and a core of high-frequency types of math problems and operations. Strategies for teachers and learners, such as translating word problems into symbolic representations (and vice versa), will be explored. Going beyond testing, the workshops will also address teaching practice: the increased use of reading and writing in the math classroom, contextualization through an inquiry-based approach, and enrichment in view of providing students with opportunities to deal with concepts on a higher plane.

Teaching Matters, Inc. (TMI)

After-school workshop #1: Introduction to Program
    Tuesday, March 2, 2004
    (4–7 p.m.)

Online class #1: Introduction to Student Publishing
    Wednesday, March 17
    (7:00 p.m.–8:30 p.m.)

Online class #2: Setting Learning Expectations by Designing Rubrics
    Wednesday, March 31
    (7:00 p.m.–8:30 p.m.)

After-school workshop #2: TrackStar: Creating web-guided lessons
    Tuesday, April 20
    (4–7 p.m.)

Online class #3: Creating a Plagiarism-Free Learning Environment
    Wednesday, May 5
    (7:00 p.m.–8:30 p.m.)

Continuation of Year V

Online class #4: Managing Technology in the Classroom
    Wednesday, May 12
    (7:00 p.m.–8:30 p.m.)

After-school workshop #3: Preparing for the Looking At Student Work online session
    Tuesday, May 25
    (4–7 p.m.)

Online classes #5 and #6: Teacher Presentations and discussion about "best practices" in writing and technology.

Cross-GEAR UP Schools Dialogues

The Cross-GEAR UP Schools Dialogues have been established to work with two questions: how well are students in particular academic disciplines being prepared from one year to the next so that they can meet rigorous academic standards? Two, from one educational level to the next (i.e., from intermediate to high school and high school to college), how well are students being prepared to make the transition? Where are the gaps? What needs to be done? What needs to be reshaped? Our hope is that within and across feeder patterns, participants will identify student needs, make specific recommendations and curricular suggestions that will improve the academic preparation of students.

The Dialogues will bring faculty and administrators from grades 7–14, representing all six GEAR UP schools, the School Districts, the Queens High Schools division, LaGuardia Community College, and the Queens Borough Public Library together within four teams: the English Language Arts/Social Studies, Mathematics, Science, and Counseling. This year, three teams will begin: English Language Art/Social Studies, Mathematics, and Counseling.

Faculty and administrators who indicate their willingness to participate should:

- have taught in one of these two curricular areas for a minimum of three years
- possess a record of good attendance
- be interested in participating in discussions concerning the professional literature, pedagogy, and curricular practice and be willing to do independent research, where this is applicable
- have good interpersonal skills
- be willing to attend four to five meetings of their curricular team, dates and locations to be announced. These meetings will occur after school hours between the hours of 4:30–7:30 p.m.

Year VI

September 1, 2004–August 31, 2005

Using Improvization and Theater Games

In this workshop you will learn the basic rules and principles of theater games and improvization for the classroom by participating in theater exercises and discussions. In addition, the workshop will help you create specific curriculum-based improvizations to apply directly to your classroom.

Emphasis will be on:

- How to adapt the exercises to the particular classroom.
- How to use exercises to explore multicultural issues and problems.
- How to adapt exercises to explore and enhance curricula.
- How to adapt exercises for classroom group dynamics.
- How to use for self-esteem work.
- How to have fun in the classroom in a different work format.

Middle Schools Initiative (MSI)

Twenty teachers and the principal at IS 145 participated in the MSI program provided by GEAR UP.

On-Site Training

Participation teachers will receive training from TMI's Professional Developers in their classrooms. Our Professional Developers will assist in the implementation of customized work geared toward Exit Projects in the middle schools and Social Studies/Literacy in the high schools.

Online/Face-to-Face Workshop

Teachers will participate in an initial face-to-face meeting to review the scope of the year's work and to begin training on @School Anytime, TMI's online service (www.atschool.org). Through @School Anytime, teachers will have the opportunity to participate in a G-credit course from their homes. The course includes four face-to-face sessions (delivered at a convenient location in Queens) and a choice of 12 out of 13 live online sessions. In addition, teachers will be able to collaborate during online "office hours" available on @School Anytime on topics relevant to the group.

Administrator Training

TMI will provide training for principals and/or assistant principals through its Principals 2000 Program. Participants will be introduced to a host of school and technology-related issues that are pertinent to today's school leaders. The training cohort is scheduled to begin this winter and continue throughout the year. For a fuller description, see the sheet titled "Technology Leadership Institute for Principals."

Teaching Matters, Inc., Professional Development

The program consists of two modules

Module one prepares teachers of any level and subject area to learn how to use technology in their classroom. Topics include specific skills teachers will have to learn to use technology, basic classroom management with limited computers, and instructional strategies that can be applied in a number of technology-based activities. Module one will run from January to February.

Module two, building on the skills learned in module one, provides teachers with in classroom support from a Teacher Matters' Professional Developer. Teachers from each school will have the choice of selecting between a session on "Technology-based student research projects" or "Student Publishing in the Classroom and on the Web." Participation in module one is required for any teacher interested in module two.

Bibliography

Adelman, C. (2006). The toolbox revisited: Paths to degree completion from high school through college. Washington, D.C.: U.S. Department of Education.

Alliance for Excellent Education (2006). Saving futures, saving dollars: The impact of education on crime reduction and earnings. Washington, D.C.: Author.

Ancess, J. (2000). The reciprocal influence of teacher learning, teaching practice, school restructuring, and student learning outcomes. *Teachers College Record*, 102(3).

Armour-Thomas, E., Clay, C., Domanico, R., Bruno, K. & Allen, B. (1989). An outlier study of elementary and middle schools in New York City: Final report. New York: New York City Board of Education.

Asche, J. A. (1993). Finish for the future: America's communities respond. Alexandria, VA: National Association of Partners in Education.

Barone, C., Aguirre-Deandreis, A. I. & Trickett, E. J. (1991). Mean-ends problem-solving skills, lifestress, and social support as mediators of adjustment in the normative transition to high school. *American Journal of Community Psychology*, 19(2), 207–225.

Barton, P. (2005, February). One-third of a nation: Rising dropout rates and declining opportunities. Princeton, NJ: Educational Testing Service.

Belcher, D. C. & Hatley, R. V. (1994). A dropout prediction model that highlights middle level variables. *Research in Middle Level Education Quarterly*, 18(1), 67–78.

Berla, N., Henderson, A. T. & Kerewsky, W. (1989). The middle school years: A parent's handbook. Columbia, MD: National Committee for Citizens in Education.

Bickel, W. E., Bond, L. & LeMahieu, P. (1986). Students at risk of not completing high school. Pittsburgh, PA: Pittsburgh Foundation.

Blum, R. (2005). School connectedness: Improving the lives of students. Baltimore, MA: Johns Hopkins Bloomberg School of Public Health.

Bogdan, R. & Biklen, S. (1992). *Qualitative Research for Education*. Boston, MA: Allyn and Bacon.

Boyer, E. (1991). *Ready to Learn: A Mandate for the Nation*. Princeton, NJ: Princeton University Press.

Brint, S. & Karabel, J. (1989). *The Diverted Dream: Community Colleges and the Promise of Educational Opportunity in America, 1900–1985*. New York: Oxford University Press.

Bry, B. H. & George, F. E. (1980). The preventive effects of early intervention on the attendance and grades of urban adolescents. *Professional Psychology*, 11(2), 252–260.

Capital Assessments, Inc. (2002). LaGuardia Community College/Queens Urban Partnership GEAR UP Final Evaluation Report 2001–2002. Unpublished Report.

Capital Assessments, Inc. (2004). LaGuardia Community College/Queens Urban Partnership GEAR UP Final Evaluation Report 2003–2004. Unpublished Report.

Capital Assessments, Inc. (2005). LaGuardia Community College/Queens Urban Partnership GEAR UP Final Evaluation Report 2004–2005. Unpublished Report.

Capital Assessments, Inc. (2006). LaGuardia Community College/Queens Urban Partnership GEAR UP Final Evaluation Report 2005–2006. Unpublished Report.

Cardenas, J. A., Montecel, M. R., Supik, J. D. & Harris, R. J. (1992). The Coca-Cola Valued Youth Program: Dropout prevention strategies for at-risk students. *Texas Researcher*, 3, 111–113.

Carnegie Commission on Higher Education. (1973). *Continuity and Discontinuity: Higher Education and the Schools*. New York: McGraw-Hill.

Carnegie Council on Adolescent Development. (1989). Turning points: Preparing American youth for the 21st century. New York: Carnegie Corporation.

Carnegie Foundation. (1986). An imperiled generation: Saving our urban schools. Princeton, NJ: Carnegie Foundation.

Carter, H. (2004). A case study of middle college high school, 1972–2003: An effort to improve the persistence of at risk students in high school and to facilitate their access to college. UMI: 3124943.

Carter, H. (2011). The power of the site: Support for professionalism in a school-college.

The Center for Comprehensive School Reform and Improvement, (2006). Redefining professional development: Characteristics of effective professional development. Newsletter, February. Available: www.centerforcsri.org.

Center for Urban Ethnography. (1990). An evaluation of the City University of New York and New York Board of Education collaborative programs, IV. Middle College High School. New York: MCA.

Cognato, C. A. (1999, October). The effects of transition activities on adolescent self-perception and academic achievement during the progression from eighth to ninth grade. Paper presented at the annual meeting of the National Middle School Association, Orlando, FL.

Cohen, A. & Brawer, F. (1989). *The American Community College*. San Francisco, CA: Jossey-Bass.

Collaborative Program. *Urban Education*, 46(3), 371–389. Thousand Oaks, CA: Sage Publications.

Comer, J. P., Haynes, N. M., Joyner, E. T. & Ben-Avie, M. (1996). *Rallying the Whole Village: The Comer Process for Reforming Education*. New York: Teachers College Press.

Community School District 25 (1997). Correspondence, New York.

Cooney, S. & Bottoms, G. Middle grades to high school: Mending a weak link. Research brief. Atlanta, GA: Southern Regional Education Board, 2002. Retrieved August 26, 2002, from www.sreb.org/programs/hstw/publications/briefs/MiddleGradestoHS.asp.

Cotton, K. (1991). School-community collaboration to improve the quality of life for urban youth and their families. School improvement research series. Retrieved November 28, 2011, from http://educationnorthwest.org/webfm_send/504.

Creswell, J. (1998). *Qualitative Inquiry and Research Design: Choosing among Five Traditions*. Thousand Oaks, CA: Sage Publications.

Creswell, J. (2008). *Educational Research. Planning, Conducting, and Evaluating Quantitative and Qualitative Research*. Upper Saddle River, NJ: Pearson Prentice Hall.

Cullen, C. (1991). Membership and engagement at Middle College High School. *Urban Education*, 26(1) (April).

Cullen, C. & Moed, M. (Ed.). (1988). *Serving High-Risk Adolescents* (Vol. 63). San Francisco, CA: Jossey Bass.

Daly, W. (Ed.). (1985). *College-School Collaborations: Appraising the Major Approaches*. San Francisco, CA: Jossey-Bass.

Daniels, H. (2006). The missing link in school reform: Professional development. Presentation before the U.S. Senate Labor and Human Resources Committee Subcommittee on Education, Arts and Humanities (n.d.) (testimony of Harvey A. Daniels). Retrieved February 27, 2006, from www.ncrel.org/mands/docs/7–10.htm.

Daresh, J. C. (2004). Mentoring school leaders: Professional promise or predictable problems? *Educational Administration Quarterly*, 40(4), 495–517.

Darling-Hammond, L. (1990). Teacher quality and equality. Access to knowledge: An agenda for our schools. College Entrance Examination Board.

Darling-Hammond, L. (1999). Teacher quality and student achievement: A review of state policy evidence. University of Washington: Center for the Study of Teaching and Policy. Retrieved July 30, 2001, from www.ctpweb.org.

Darling-Hammond, L., LaPointe, M., Meyerson, D., Orr, M. T. & Cohen, C. (2007). Preparing school leaders for a changing world: Lessons from exemplary leadership development programs. Stanford, CA: Stanford Educational Leadership Institute.

De La Paz, S. & Graham, S. (1997). Strategy instruction in planning: Effects on the writing performance and behavior of students with learning disabilities. *Exceptional Children*, 63, 167–181.

De La Paz, S. & Graham, S. (2002). Explicitly teaching strategies, skills, and knowledge: Writing instruction in middle school classrooms. *Journal of Educational Psychology*, 92(4) (December).

Druva, C. A. & Anderson, R. D. (1983). Science teacher characteristics by teacher behavior and by student outcome: A meta-analysis of research. *Journal of Research in Science Teaching*, 20(5), 467–479.

Dryfoos, J. G. (1990). *Adolescents at Risk: Prevalence and Prevention*. New York: Oxford University Press.

Eccles, J. S., Lord, S. & Midgley, C. (1991). What are we doing to early adolescents? The impact of educational contexts on early adolescents. *American Journal of Education*, 99(4), 521–542.

Editorial Projects in Education, Diplomas Count 2011: Beyond High School, Before Baccalaureate, special issue, *Education Week*, 30(34).

Epstein, J. L. (2001). *School, Family, and Community Partnerships: Preparing Educators and Improving Schools*. Boulder, CO: Westview Press.

Epstein, J. L. et al. (2002). *School, Family and Community Partnerships*. California: Corwin Press.

Felner, R. D., Ginter, M. & Primavera, J. (1982). Primary prevention during school transitions: Social support and environmental structure. *American Journal of Community Psychology*, 10(3), 277–290.

Frey, B. B., Lohmeier, J. H., Lee, S. W. & Tollefson, N. (2006). Measuring collaboration among grant partners. *American Journal of Evaluation*, 27(3), 383–392.

Fullan, M. G. (1994). Coordinating top-down and bottom up strategies for education reform. In R. Anson (Ed.), *Systemic Reform: Perspective on Personalizing Education* (pp. 7–23). Washington, D.C.: Department of Education, Office of Educational Research & Improvement.

Fullan, M. G. & Hargreaves, A. (1991). What's worth fighting for: Working together for your school. Toronto, Ontario Public School Teachers Federation.

Gay, L. R., Mills, G. E. & Airasian, P. (2009). *Educational Research: Competencies for Analysis and Applications (9th edn)*. Upper Saddle River, NJ: Pearson.

GEAR UP (1999). Proposal for funding from the United State Department of Education. LaGuardia Community College.

GEAR UP (2001). Annual performance report. LaGuardia Community College.

GEAR UP (2002). Third year evaluation report. LaGuardia Community College.

GEAR UP (2003a). Evaluation report. LaGuardia Community College.

GEAR UP (2003b). Cross dialogues school counseling internal report (2003). LaGuardia Community College.

GEAR UP (2005). Annual performance report. LaGuardia Community College.

GEAR UP (2005). Internal document. LaGuardia Community College.

Geiger, L. G. (1970). *Voluntary Accreditation: A History of the North Central Association*, 1945–1970. Menasha, WI: North Central Association of Colleges and Secondary Schools.

Glaser, B. G. & Strauss, A. L. (1967). *The Discovery of Grounded Theory: Strategies for Qualitative Research*. New York: Aldine De Gruyter.

Goldberg, M. F. (September 1990). Portrait of James P. Comer. *Educational Leadership*, 48(1), 40–42.

Gomez, M., Bissel, J., Danziger, L. & Casselman, R. (1990). *To Advance Learning: A Handbook on Developing K–12 Postsecondary Partnerships*. Lanham, MA: University Press of America.

Government Accounting Office. (1994). Hispanics' schooling. Risk factors for dropping out and barriers to resuming education. Washington, D.C.

Greenberg, A. & Moed, M. (n.d.). Middle college high school: Community college and high school partnerships: An approach to the high school dropout problem. New York: LaGuardia Community College.

Gregory, L., et al. (1989). An evaluation of the City University of New York/New York City Board of Education Collaborative Programs. New York: Public Private Ventures.

Hawk, P., Coble, C. & Swanson, M. (1985). Certification: Does it matter? *Journal of Teacher Education*, 36, 13–15.

Hemphill, Clara. (2010). Yet another reorganization of New York City's public schools. The New School Milano Center for New York City Affairs, January 22.

Henderson, A. & Mapp, K. (2002). *A New Wave of Evidence: The Impact of School, Family, and Community Connections on Student Achievement*. Austin, TX: Southwest Educational Development Laboratory, National Center for Family & Community Connections with Schools.

Hertzog, C. J., Morgan, P. L., Diamond, P. A. & Walker, M. J. (1996). Transition to high school: A look at student perceptions. *Becoming*, 7(2), 6–8.

Hertzog, C. J. & Morgan, P. L. (1999). Transition: A process not an event. Reston, VA: National Association of Secondary School Principals.

Hispanic Dropout Project. (1994). Hispanic dropout project. Washington, D.C.: United States Department of Education.

Hodgkinson, H. (1994). *Bringing Tomorrow into Focus: Demographic Insights into the Future*. Washington, D.C.: Center for Demographic Policy, Institute for Educational Leadership.

Horn, L. & West, J. (1992). *National Education Longitudinal Study of 1988: A Profile of Parents of Eighth Graders*. Washington, D.C.: U.S. Government Printing Office.

Houle, C. O. (1996). *The Design of Education* (2nd edn). San Francisco, CA: Jossey-Bass.

Hunt, G. (2003). *The Modern Middle School*. Springfield, IL: Charles C. Thomas.

Jackson, A. & Davis, G. (2000). *Turning Points 2000: Educating Adolescents in the 21st Century*. New York: Teachers College Press.

Justiz, M., Wilson, R., & Bjork, L. (1994). *Minorities in Higher Education*. Phoenix, AZ: Oryx Press.

Kaufman, P. & Alt, M. N. (2001). *Dropout Rates in the United States: 2000*. Washington, D.C.: NCES, U.S. Department of Education.

Kidder, E. B. (2005, January/February). Students weigh in on ways to raise achievement. *Harvard Education Letter*, 21 (1). Retrieved June 9, 2007, from Harvard Principals' Center website: http://subscriber.edletter.org.

Klem, A. M. & Connell, J. P. (2004). Relationships matter: Linking teacher support to student engagement and achievement. *Journal of School Health*, 74(7), 262–273.

Lee, C. D. (2004). Literacy in the academic disciplines and the needs of adolescents struggling readers. *Voices in Urban Education*, 3, Winter/Spring.

LGCC. (1973). Middle college plan. New York: LaGuardia Community College, City University of New York.

Levine, A. (2005). Educating school leaders. New York: The Education School Project.

Levine, D. U. & Lezotte, L. W. (1990). Unusually effective schools: A review and analysis of research and practice. Madison, WI: National Center for Effective Schools Research and Development.

Lieberman, A. & McLaughlin, M. W. (1992). Networks for educational change: Powerful and problematic. *Phi Delta Kappan*, 73(9), 673–677.

Lieberman, A., Saxl, E. R. & Miles, M. B. (1988). Teacher leadership: Ideology and practice. In A. Lieberman (Ed.), *Building a Professional Culture in Schools* (pp. 129–147). New York: Teachers College Press.

Lieberman, J. E. (1986a). Combining high school: LaGuardia's middle college high school. *New directions for teaching and learning*, 24 (December).

Lieberman, J. E. (1986b). Middle college: A ten year study. New York: LaGuardia Community College.

Lieberman, J. E. (1989). Turning losers into winners: Integrating structural change. The College Board Review (Fall), 19.

Lundquist, S. & Nixon, J. (1998). The partnership paradigm: Collaboration and the community college. In D. McGrath (Ed.), *Creating and Benefiting from Institutional Collaboration: Models for Success* (Vol. 103). San Francisco, CA: Jossey Bass.

McAdoo, M. (1999). Studies in transition: How to help adolescents navigate the path to and from middle school. *Middle Ground*, 2(3), 21–23.

Maccoby, E. & Maccoby, N. (1954). The interview as a tool of social science. In G. Lindzey (Ed.), *Handbook of Social Psychology*. Cambridge, MA: Addison-Wesley.

MacIver, D. J. (1990). Meeting the needs of young adolescents: Advisory groups, interdisciplinary teaching teams, and school transition programs. *Phi Delta Kappan*, 71(6), 458–464.

McLeod, B. (1996). *Educating Students from Diverse Linguistic and Cultural Backgrounds* (Santa Cruz, Calif.: The Bilingual Research Center, Internet posting.

Maeroff, G. I. (1987). Schools and colleges: Partnerships in excellence. Princeton, NJ: The Carnegie Foundation for the Advancement of Teaching.

Martin-Kneip, G. (1999). *Capturing the Wisdom of Practice: Professional Portfolios for Educators*. Alexandra, VA: Association for Supervision and Curriculum Development.

Maute, J. K. (1991). Transition concerns of eighth-grade students in six Illinois schools as they prepare for high school. Unpublished doctoral dissertation, National Louis University, Evanston, IL.

MCHS. (1999). Middle college high school charter proposal. New York: LaGuardia Community College.

Merriam, S. (1998). *Qualitative Research and Case Study Applications in Education*. San Francisco, CA: Jossey Bass.

The MetLife Survey of the American teacher: Teachers, parents and the economy (2012) (New York: Metropolitan Life Insurance Company, March).

Mizell, M. H. (1992). The achieving middle school: Remarks made at Clark Day Conference, November 5. San Antonio, TX.

Mizelle, N. B. (1995). Transition from middle school into high school: The student perspective. Paper presented at the annual meeting of the American Educational Research Association, San Francisco, CA.

Mortenson, T. (1999). High school dropouts. *Postsecondary Education Opportunity*, 90 (July 1998).

Morse, A. B., Anderson, A. R., Christenson, S. & Lehr, C. A. (2004). Promoting school completion. *Principal Leadership Magazine*, 4, 9–13.

National Center for Charitable Statistics (2007) Foundation Center.

National Center for Educational Statistics (2005). The NAEP reading assessment sample. Retrieved September 9, 2005, from http://nces.ed.gov/nationsreportcard/reading/sample design.asp.

National Center for Educational Alliances (n.d.). New York.

National Educational Association (1983). Report of the Committee on Secondary School Studies (commonly known as The Committee of Ten Report). Washington, D.C.: Government Printing Office.

National Policy Board for Education Administration (2002). *Standards for Advanced Programs in Educational Leadership*. Austin, TX: University of Texas at Austin.

National Staff Development Council. (1997). Filling a crack in the middle: The need for staff development in the middle grades. Dallas, TX: National Staff Development Council.

National Staff Development Council. (2010). NSDC's definition of professional development website. Retrieved March 17, 2010, from http://nsdc.org/standfor/definition.cfm.

National Task Force on Minority High Achievement. (1999). Reaching the top: A report of the national task force on minority achievement. New York: The College Board.

Newman, B. M., Lohman, B. J., Newman, P. R., Myers, M. C. & Smith, V. L. (2000). Experiences of urban youth navigating the transition to ninth grade. *Youth & Society*, 31, 387–416.

New York City Department of Education (2006). Annual school report 2005–2006. New York: Middle College High School.

New York City Department of Education. (2007a). Annual school report, 2006–2007. New York: Middle College High School.

New York City Department of Education. (2007b). Quality review report, 2006–2007. New York

New York City Department of Education. (2008a). Annual school report, 2007–2008. New York

New York City Department of Education. (2008b). Quality review report, 2007–2008. New York

New York City Department of Education. (2009a). Annual school report, 2008–2009. New York

New York City Department of Education. (2009b). Learning environment survey report, 2008–2009. New York.

New York City Department of Education. (2006). Annual school report, 2005–2006. New York: Middle College High School.

New York City Department of Education. (2007). Annual school report, 2006–2007. New York: Middle College High School.

New York City Department of Education. (2008). Annual school report, 2007–2008. New York: Middle College High School.

New York City Department of Education. (2009). Annual school report, 2008–2009. New York: Middle College High School.

New York City Department of Education. (2011). MCHS Comprehensive Educational Plan. New York: Middle College High School.

Noam, G. G. (2004). The four Cs of Alter School Programming: A new case method for a new field. Afterschool Matters occasional papers series. New York, NY: Robert Bowne Foundation.

No Child Left Behind Act of 2001, Pub. L. No. 107–110, Sect. 9101(32), 115 Stat. 1425 (2002). Retrieved September 15, 2006, from www.ed.gov/policy/elsec/leg/esea02/pg107.html#sec9101.

Oates, J., Flores, R. & Weishew, N. (1998). Achieving student success in inner-city schools is possible. *Research in Middle Level Education Quarterly*, 21(3), 51–62.

Peck, N., Law, A. & Mills, R. C. (1987). Dropout prevention: What we have learned. Educational Resources Information Center/Counseling and Personnel Services Clearinghouse, ED 279 989.

Perdue, N., Manzeske, D. & Estell, D. (2009). Early predictors of school engagement: Exploring the role of peer relationships. *Psychology in the Schools*, 46(10), 1084–1097.

Peterson, K. (1994). Building collaborative cultures: Seeking ways to reshape urban schools. NCREL.

Phelan, P., Yu, H. C. & Davidson, A. L. (1994). Navigating the psychosocial pressures of adolescence: The voices and experiences of high school youth. *American Educational Research Journal*, 31(2), 415–447.

President's Commission on Higher Education. (1947). *Higher Education for American Democracy* (Vol. 1–6). New York: Harper & Brothers.

Queens Urban Partnership (1993). Proposal to the Ford Foundation for Implementation of the Queens Urban Partnership, New York.

Queens Urban Partnership (1998). Internal report. New York.

Queens Urban Partnership (1996). Internal evaluation report. New York.

Ramirez-Smith, C. (1995). Stopping the cycle of failure: The Comer model. *Educational Leadership*, 52(5), 14–19.

Rebora, A. (2008). Empowering teachers. *Teacher Magazine*. Maryland: Editorial Projects in Education, Education Week: Teachers PD Sourcebook, 1(02), 30, 32–330.

Roberts, S. M. & Pruitt, E. Z. (2003). *Schools as Professional Learning Communities: Collaborative Activities and Strategies for Professional Development*. Thousand Oaks, CA: Corwin Press.

Rothman, R. (2004). Adolescent literacy. *Harvard Education Letter*, 20(5), September/October.

Rutherford, B., Anderson, B. & Bilig, S. (1997). *Parent and Community Involvement in Education: Studies of Education Reform*. Washington, D.C.: U.S. Department of Education.

Ryan, J. (2003). Educational administrators' perceptions of racism in diverse school contexts. *Race, Ethnicity and Education*, 6(2), 145–164.

Schneider, M. & Yin, L. (2011). The high cost of low graduation rates: How much does dropping out of college really cost? Washington, D.C.: American Institutes for Research.

Schön, D. (1987). *Educating the Reflective Practitioner: Toward a New Design for Teaching and Learning in the Professions*. San Francisco, CA: Jossey-Bass.

Selltiz, C., Jahoda, M., Deutsch, M. & Cook, S. (1959). *Research Methods in Social Relations*. New York: Holt, Rinehart & Winston.

Silberman, C. E. (1970). *Crisis in the Classroom.* New York: Random House.

Southern Regional Education Board (2010). The three essentials: improving schools requires district vision, district and state support, and principal leadership, August, p. iii. New York: Wallace Foundation.

Smink, J. (1990). What really works? *National Dropout Prevention Newsletter*, 3/2.

Smylie, M. A. (1988). The enhancement function of staff development: Organizational and psychological antecedents to individual teacher change. *American Educational Research Journal*, 25(1), 1–30.

Stage, F. K. & Rushin, P. W. (1993). A combined model of student predisposition to college and persistence in college. *Journal of College Student Development*, 34(3), 276–281.

Southern Regional Education Board (2007). The district leadership challenge. New York: Wallace Foundation.

Terry, P.M. (1999–2000). Empowering teachers as leaders. *National Forum of Teacher Education Journal*, 10E, 3.

U.S. Department of Education, Office of Innovation and Improvement (2004). Innovations in education: Innovative pathways to school leadership, Washington, D.C.

Vernes, G. & Krop, R. (1999). Projected Social Context for Education of Children: 1990–2015. New York: National Task Force on Minority High Achievement, The College Board.

Waschak, M. R. and Kingsley, G. (2006). Alternative approaches to evaluating STEM education partnerships: A review of evaluation methods and application of an interorganizational model, Georgia Institute of Technology National Science Foundation sponsored Research, Evaluation, and Technical Assistance (RETA) project (NSF 02–061 Award #: 0231904): April 24.

Wechsler, H. (2001). *Access to Success in the Urban High School: The Middle College Movement*. New York: Faculty College Press.

Wells, M. C. (1996). *Literacies Lost: When Students Move from a Progressive Middle School to a Traditional High School*. New York: Teachers College Press.

Yazzie-Mintz, E. (2010). Charting the path from engagement to achievement: A report on the 2009 High School Survey of Student Engagement. Bloomington, IN: Center for Evaluation & Education Policy.

Index